A
LITERARY
HISTORY
OF
GERMANY

A LITERARY HISTORY OF GERMANY

General Editors: KENNETH J. NORTHCOTT
Professor of German, University of Chicago
R. T. LLEWELLYN
*Lecturer in German, University of Cambridge and
Fellow of Christ's College*

FROM THE BEGINNINGS UNTIL THE LATER THIRTEENTH CENTURY
by PETER JOHNSON
*Lecturer in German, University of Cambridge and Fellow of
Pembroke College*

THE LATE MIDDLE AGES TO FISCHART, 1250–1600
by KENNETH J. NORTHCOTT

THE GERMAN BAROQUE
by R. T. LLEWELLYN

FROM BAROQUE TO STORM AND STRESS, 1720–1775
by FRIEDHELM RADANDT
Professor of German, Lake Forest College, Illinois

WEIMAR CLASSICISM
by T. J. REED
*Lecturer in German, University of Oxford and Fellow of
St John's College*

THE ROMANTIC MOVEMENT
by ALAN MENHENNET
Professor of German, University of Newcastle upon Tyne

THE NINETEENTH CENTURY, 1830–1890
by G. WALLIS FIELD
Professor of German, University of Toronto

THE TWENTIETH CENTURY, 1890–1945
by RAYMOND FURNESS
Lecturer in German, University of Manchester

A LITERARY HISTORY OF GERMANY

THE NINETEENTH CENTURY
1830-1890

A LITERARY
HISTORY OF GERMANY

The Nineteenth Century
1830–1890

G. WALLIS FIELD
Professor of German, University of Toronto

LONDON & TONBRIDGE
ERNEST BENN LIMITED

BARNES & NOBLE BOOKS
NEW YORK

First published 1975 by Ernest Benn Limited
25 New Street Square, Fleet Street, London, EC4A 3JA
& Sovereign Way, Tonbridge, Kent, TN9, 1RW
and Harper & Row Publishers Inc.
Barnes & Noble Import Division
10 East 53rd Street, New York 10022

Distributed in Canada by
The General Publishing Company Limited, Toronto

© G. Wallis Field 1975

Printed in Great Britain

ISBN 0 510–32308–1

Paperback 0 510–32318–9

ISBN 06 492077–1 (U.S.A.)

FOREWORD BY THE GENERAL EDITORS

A Literary History of Germany is designed to give a rounded, but personal, survey of German literature from its beginnings to the present day. By 'personal' we mean that each of the eight volumes has been written by an individual and that these individuals have made certain personal judgements in the selection of the works which they have chosen to treat. From the outset it was not our intention to produce a series of volumes which would serve as catalogues of German literary output. The intention was rather to try to capture the spirit and literary genius of a given period through a selection of typical and outstanding texts and by the extensive use of quotation as a means of introducing the general English-speaking literary public to German literature. The present work is the result of collaboration between scholars on both sides of the Atlantic, of whom everyone has received his academic training, at least in its advanced form, outside Germany; it is our hope that the series will provide a different perspective on what is important for the non-German student of German literature, not merely the specialist in German, but students of other literatures who wish to find out what was happening in German literature at a given time, and for the intelligent layman who seeks *entrée* into the literature and the background to that literature.

One practical note may be added here. Those readers who are concerned with maintaining an up-to-date bibliographical knowledge of German literature are recommended to consult: Paul Raabe, *Einführung in die Bücherkunde zur deutschen Literaturwissenschaft*, 6th edition, Stuttgart, 1969 for details of bibliographical aids.

The genesis of the work which was originally designed to consist of four volumes, goes back many years to the interest of the late Professor Norman in the project, which still owes much to his original conception.

K.J.N.

R.T.L.

ACKNOWLEDGEMENTS

A LARGE PART of the work on this volume was done in Oxford in the spring and summer of 1971. I should like to record here my thanks to the University of Toronto for a travel grant which made possible my stay in Oxford. To Mr T. J. Reed of St John's College and Mr D. Shorthouse, Treasurer of Oriel College, I am grateful for arranging accommodation, and to Mr Giles Barber, Librarian of the Taylor Institution, for unrestricted use of library resources. The final form of the manuscript owes much to the felicitous suggestions of Dr R. T. Llewellyn, Christ's College, Cambridge, and Professor Kenneth J. Northcott, University of Chicago. Last, but not least, Mr Robert L. Roseberry, Toronto, had many useful suggestions on reading the typescript which was completed in July 1972, except for certain additions made in the autumn of 1973.

Toronto   G. W. FIELD
January 1974

CONTENTS

ABBREVIATIONS

dtv	Deutsche Taschenbuch Verlag
DVLG	*Deutsche Vierteljahrsschrift für Literatur und Geistesgeschichte*
ÉG	*Études Germaniques*
GLL	*German Life and Letters*
GQ	*German Quarterly*
GR	*Germanic Review*
KFLQ	*Kentucky Foreign Language Quarterly*
MLN	*Modern Language Notes*
MLR	*Modern Language Review*
PMLA	*Publications of the Modern Language Association of America*
TWAS	Twayne World Authors Series

Chapter 1

HISTORICAL BACKGROUND—
THE AGE OF METTERNICH 1815–48

1. THE NINETEENTH CENTURY:
GENERAL CHARACTERISTICS

FROM THE PERSPECTIVE of the late twentieth century, its predecessor seems to be the last to present an orderly appearance, the last era to be marked by clearly prevailing trends, movements, or schools, in thought, in economic and social development, and in literature. The latter can be neatly packaged in the successive stages: Romanticism, *Epigonentum, Biedermeier*, Regionalism, Poetic Realism, Symbolism, Impressionism, Naturalism. Great names represent most of these schools. Poetic Realism is typified in the giants Stifter, Keller, Storm. But one cannot pin this school-label so easily upon Raabe or Fontane whose genius is no less. Even the typical three show disparities resulting from Stifter's Austrian tradition, Keller's Swiss nationality, and Storm's limitation to his north German region.

When one stands back and looks at the century as a whole, it becomes apparent that the age may be even more conspicuous for the 'outsiders' (*die Unzeitgemäßen* of Nietzsche) than for the 'schools' and their typical representatives. Thus in philosophy, while Hegel and the *Althegelianer* held sway in the overall current of German Idealism basically optimistic, Schopenhauer created his anti-Hegelian structure of pessimistic Idealism which was destined to become fashionable and influential in the latter half of the century. The prevailing tendencies of Idealism in mid-century were countered by the different materialisms of Marx and Feuerbach. Nietzsche fits into no preconceived pattern of philosophy or of literature. Heine (venerated by Nietzsche), Büchner, Grabbe, and the late Raabe are all idiosyncratic geniuses bound to no school. Except for Heine, they were in various degrees isolated or unappreciated in their times. We may wonder whether the exceptional 'outsiders' are not the most significant figures of the nineteenth century. In fact the regularity and serenity on the surface concealed subterranean ferments and counter-currents.

Little can be said here of painting, sculpture, architecture, and music. German painting in the nineteenth century resembles litera-

ture in its conflicting currents which arise partly from the twin ancestors, Classicism and Romanticism, and partly from the ever more
rapid changes in the cultural and social environment and the widening gulf between the artistic consciousness and public awareness.
Terms common to literature and the graphic arts – Romanticism,
Classicism, *Biedermeier*, Realism, Impressionism – have related but
often indirect significance and sequence. Perhaps the greatest artist of
the century was Caspar David Friedrich (1774–1840), who together
with Philipp Otto Runge (1777–1810) may be considered to represent
Romanticism – transcendental or religious yearning, symbolic and
emotionally charged landscapes in which isolated human figures
seem to seek release and oneness, e.g., 'Mondaufgang am Meer' and
'Mönch am Meer'. Roughly parallel with literary trends and with
the rise of the middle class, *Biedermeier* and Realism in painting
began to dominate in the 1830s. Adolf von Menzel (1815–1905),
Ludwig Richter (1803–34), Moritz von Schwind (1804–71), Karl
Spitzweg (1808–85), and later Hans Thoma (1839–1924) were among
those painters who catered to the sober and realistic taste of the
Biedermeier-age. But genius in art soars above the limitations of
schools and epochs. The French Realist Corot is said to have completed two versions of many paintings, one for the plain taste of the
public, and one for himself and his inner vision. Adolf von Menzel,
for example, developed an Impressionistic vision comparable to
the French, while the Swiss Arnold Böcklin (1827–1901) went his
individual way combining aspects of Realism with Romanticism and
Idealism (e.g., 'Toteninsel'). Against the Realistic and *Biedermeier*
currents of the age, Anselm Feuerbach (1829–80) and his followers
aspired to an Idealistic Italianate Classicism which is strikingly
evident in Feuerbach's depiction of Iphigenie 'das Land der Griechen
mit der Seele suchend' (in Goethe's words). Hans von Marees (1837–
1887) and Julius Schnorr von Carolsfeld (1794–1872) belong among
those who sought form and inspiration in Italy. Yet the latter is also
noted for *Biedermeier*-like religious pictures, while von Marees later
developed an almost Impressionistic style. Andreas Achenbach (1815–
1890), a graduate of the Düsseldorf academy, painted storm-tossed
seascapes and realistic landscapes of his native Lower Rhineland,
while his brother Oswald (1827–1905), who became an instructor in
the famous Düsseldorf academy, sought his inspiration and subject-
matter in his Italian sojourns. Anselm Feuerbach declared: 'Was ich
geworden bin, habe ich zunächst den modernen Franzosen von
achtundvierzig (Courbet und Couture), dem alten und jungen Italien
und mir selbst zu verdanken'. The statement illustrates the eclectic
combination of Realism from France and Classicism and Idealism
from ancient and modern Italy, while the third factor stresses the
individuality of the artistic genius, for the nineteenth century saw an

ever widening abyss between the strivings of the artist and the public taste. The Austrian Moritz von Schwind, who spent most of his creative life in Munich, the major art centre of the German world, had a foot in both the Romantic and *Biedermeier* schools. The latter is reflected in such works as 'Hochzeitsreise'. Hans Thoma and Wilhelm Leibl (1844–1900) are remembered today more for their Realistic-*Biedermeier* portrayals of the social and natural environment than for their 'Historical-Idealism'. The French Impressionists had relatively little impact on German art in the Wilhelmian era and it was only with Expressionism at the beginning of the twentieth century that German painting enjoyed a renaissance in such masters as Barlach, Kirchner, Kandinsky, Kokoschka, and Paul Klee.

Architecture alone never achieved anything beyond imitative epigonal representation: the simultaneous hodge-podge of neo-Byzantine, neo-Romantic, neo-Classic, neo-Gothic, neo-Renaissance, neo-Baroque, and even neo-Rococo corresponded to no new distinctive spiritual content of the age, but served merely as decorative façades. The achievements of music from Beethoven to Brahms represent, on the other hand, a spiritual manifestation of the first magnitude.

II. REVOLUTION AND REACTION

Napoleon in the English-speaking world stands for militarism and tyranny. The image he left in Germany is complex and ambivalent. While the Congress of Vienna could – temporarily – restore the Bourbons and reactionary *émigrés* in France, there was in Germany no possibility of undoing the work of Napoleon in sweeping away a host of principalities, large and small (including all of the ecclesiastical states), which had lingered on in the already moribund Holy Roman Empire. The Rhineland and Westphalia and other parts of Germany (such as occupied Hanover, the other realm of George III) under the French Empire had enjoyed the benefits of the French Revolution brought by Napoleon. Thus to many Germans – including Heine – Napoleon represented the liberator rather than the oppressor. This, of course, was not true of Prussia or Austria, and it was mainly in Prussia that national-patriotic reaction in the middle class culminated in the enthusiasm of the War of Liberation which drove Napoleon out of Germany in 1813.

The German Confederation (*Bund*) of 1815 accepted the reduction from over 300 (not including nearly 2,000 *reichsunmittelbar* feudal domains and free towns) to thirty-nine constituent states. This reduction had resulted from Napoleon's annexation of the Rhineland and his secularization of ecclesiastical states and 'mediatization' of free towns, in order to compensate dispossessed princes. Newly born nationalist aspirations for a united Germany were thwarted in Vienna by dynastic rivalries and the diplomacy of Talleyrand and Metternich, who both desired a divided Germany, the one for French, the other for Habsburg interests. The loose confederation of 1815 was just as ineffective an instrument as the Holy Roman Empire had been since the Peace of Westphalia in 1648. It resembled a conclave of diplomatic delegates of member-sovereigns rather than a legislative assembly and it had to have a generally impossible two-thirds margin of approval in order to act. In fact unanimity was required for changing 'fundamental laws, organic institutions, individual rights, or matters of religion'.

The *Bund* served to conceal or postpone the basic question of supremacy in Germany for a generation. But the allocation of spoils contained clues to future destiny. Austria, the traditional arbiter of Germany, was enlarged by Lombardy and Venetia, Dalmatia on the Adriatic, and retention of Polish Galicia. The Habsburg dynasty thus added to its already high proportion of non-German subjects (Magyars, Czechs, Slovaks, Slovenes) by adding Italians, Croatians, and Poles. The polyglot multinational character of Austria created problems which were increasingly to preoccupy her rulers and diminish their power and authority within Germany. Prussia, which had previously possessed only sparse and separated islets of territory on the Rhine, emerged with a large homogeneous Rhineland province, which, however, was still separated from Brandenburg by the intervening states of Hanover and Hesse-Cassel. This was a highly developed, populous region, containing the as yet undeveloped iron and coal which was to create in the Ruhr a much greater base of heavy industry than the potential which Prussia had already acquired in Silesia in 1740. In addition more than a third of the kingdom of Saxony contiguous to Brandenburg was ceded to Prussia (to punish the king of Saxony for having been Napoleon's most faithful German ally – or the slowest to shift sides). Only in the east did Prussia gain or regain lands largely Polish: West Prussia and Posen. While Austria had expanded in non-German areas, Prussia was strengthened almost entirely in Germany. Prussia, too, had potential problems: the new Rhenish and Westphalian subjects of the Hohenzollerns were almost solidly Roman Catholic – as were the Poles on the eastern border. No longer did the principle of Augsburg (1555) – *cujus regio, ejus religio* – give religious conformity to the state. The Rhinelanders had different traditions, temperament, and social structure. The middle class was more numerous and more prosperous and had been favourably impressed by the reforms of the Revolution bestowed upon them by Napoleon. Even agriculture, still the economic base of society, did not have the semi-feudal character which existed in East Prussia,

West Prussia, and Brandenburg, even after the freeing of serfs in
1807. Only the genius – or guile – of Bismarck finally juggled the
diverse elements of Prussia. Using the principle of *divide et impera*,
he combined temporarily conservative agrarian Junkers of Brandenburg and East and West Prussia with the liberal-nationalists – and
later the industrialists and capitalists – of the Rhineland – and alterna-
tively combated and used the Catholic Centre party.

The problems of the Hohenzollerns, however, were minimal compared with those of the Habsburgs. The primacy of the latter was so
deeply engrained that Frederick William III and even his unstable
successor (after 1840), Frederick William IV, acknowledged Austrian
leadership. Moreover, the rulers of both states – in common with
other German princes large and small – had the common interest of
holding in check the forces of nationalism and liberalism. Metternich
even advised the German princes against granting constitutions; and
he played upon their fear of revolutionary change to get the slow-
moving Federal Diet to pass repressive measures (Carlsbad Decrees,
1819) against student demonstrators who were, in the main, harmless
– although the murder of Kotzebue by the deranged student Karl
Sand could be considered sufficient provocation.

The tranquil surface-calm (reflected in *Biedermeier* and epigonal
literature), known in history as the 'quiet years', concealed the seething subterranean revolutionary currents which are not truly reflected
in the absurd and futile political gestures in the Rhineland and the
Palatinate after the July Revolution (1830) in Paris: the Hambach
Festival (1832) or the attempt of fifty students in Frankfurt in 1834
to proclaim the republic (they were dispersed by the Town Guard).
The true reflection of the continuing revolution is better mirrored in
drastic writers, such as Büchner and Grabbe, in Börne and in writers
of the school known as *Das junge Deutschland*, in the political poets
Herwegh and Freiligrath, and even in Heine with all his ambiguities.

The age of Metternich was full of diverse tensions and polarities
just beneath the surface. There was also a generation-gap. Older
members of the middle class were surfeited with turbulence and
wanted peace and bourgeois material comfort at any price. Others,
younger, found the post-Napoleonic age unheroic and boring.

As far as political action is concerned, Metternich was unduly
alarmed. Most German rulers disregarded his advice and followed
the example of Grand Duke Karl August of Weimar in granting
constitutions. (Prussia held out until 1848, as did Austria as long as
Metternich prevailed.) The political energies of the people were
diverted from the larger liberal-national problems – which the people
were powerless to solve, as shown in 1848–49 – towards preoccupation with, and participation in, local government. Particularism
– *Kleinstaaterei* – helped to keep alive the basically conservative

dynastic system under Metternich's watchful eye. According to A. J. P. Taylor, 'The German princes without real existence, became the patrons of a constitutional liberalism which was also without roots or popular support: strange alliance of two artificial entities, brought together by a common helplessness'.[1] This is, at least in part, an overstatement. Roots and popular support were much stronger in Bavaria and Württemberg, for example, than in Hesse-Cassel or Detmold-Lippe. Taylor's argument, moreover, presupposes the presence of a mass, literate, intelligent populace willing consciously a uniform liberal nation-state. It is doubtful whether such a population has yet existed; but it certainly was not present in 1815 – or in 1848.

III. *Bürgertum*

The age of Metternich was the apogee of *Bürgertum*. The burgher class had made enormous strides in the late Middle Ages and had been subject to economic reverses with the shifting patterns of trade after the discovery of the New World and the maritime route to Asia. The religious disputes and wars had dealt heavy blows in the sixteenth and seventeenth centuries. But through the eighteenth century, as Bruford shows,[2] the burghers had steadily increased in numbers, wealth, and influence. The great advances in science and technology, in literature and learning, in material improvements of life had placed the burgher squarely on centre stage. The returned aristocrats at the court of Louis XVIII and Charles X were ghosts of the past, destined to be swept into oblivion by the most obvious middle-class institution of the century: the citizen-king Louis Philippe who, with his umbrella, made a show of being one of his Parisian bourgeois subjects. It was so much the age of middle-class, middle-rich, middle-of-the-road trends, that aristocrats like Count Platen or Lenau, who had become impoverished, hovered in a vacuum between aristocratic and proletarian worlds and clung to poetry as a last desperate effort to give meaning to their lives.

The age of large-scale industry and capital lay in the future. The rate of social and economic change was slow, although it accelerated at a growing pace with the beginning of major railways in the early 1840s. The urban proportion of the population changed only fractionally from the 25 per cent in 1815. Economic pressure contributed to a swelling wave of emigration to America in the 1840s.

The dominant burgher class between 1830 and 1850 tended to be narrow in outlook and hence to be content with politics and administration in the virtually independent principalities. The typical burgher was practical and although many wished and worked for a modern nation-state, given the divisive factions in Metternich's system, there was nothing practical to do except to take more and more power in the minor principalities. Prussia and Austria withheld this outlet and hence it is not surprising that the revolutions in 1848 were focused in Berlin and Vienna.

IV. THE *Zollverein*

From the beginning in 1815, the network of internal tariff boundaries was regarded as preposterous and provision was made in the federal constitution for a customs union. The weakness of the federal authority was nowhere more apparent than in its failure to provide this essential service to commerce. The real reasons for failure lay in the Austro-Prussian rivalry. Prussia, however, was slow to take advantage of this economic weapon and reacted only to competitive tariff unions (Bavaria-Württemberg, Middle German) founded in 1828. Prussia then created the *Zollverein* and drew to it most of the middle and south German states by 1834. Ten years later most of Germany was in the *Zollverein* – except Austria. Later, between 1850 and 1863, the Austrian government made successive attempts to enlarge the customs union to include all Habsburg territories – the *großdeutsch* solution – and the last and most nearly successful effort was only foiled by Bismarck's forbidding King William to attend the meeting convened by Francis Joseph in Frankfurt. Without Prussia the other states could not accept the Austrian proposals. It is possible to overemphasize the importance of the *Zollverein* in bringing about German unity, but there is no doubt that it played a part and that it foreshadowed the nature of the eventual union: a gift to the rest of Germany at the hands of Prussia.

V. PHILOSOPHICAL CURRENTS

For a Marxist the philosophical or religious underpinnings of a social order have little relevance, since *die große Magenfrage* determines the course of events. Not only do armies march on their stomachs, but whole civilizations or epochs, in this view. But no nation has attached so much importance to philosophical foundations – *Geistesgeschichte* – and in considering Germany we would do well to concede some importance to the moving spirits of the times.

The basic tendency of the age was utilitarian, materialistic, and yet, especially in the first half of the century, many sought in philosophical systems what religion had conferred in other times: meaning and justification of existence.

The system of Georg Friedrich Wilhelm Hegel (1770–1831) exerted the widest influence, not so much directly, because its difficult and esoteric exegesis was a matter for academicians, but indirectly, as the established philosophy was preached from Berlin first by the master and then by his conservative successors, the *Althegelianer*. The philosophy seemed to give an idealistic basis for accepting the materialistic present. Hegel was one of the last philosophers to erect a complete metaphysical system and in this very fact shows himself to be in the mainstream of German Idealism, building on Kant and Fichte. Hegelianism is sometimes called Absolute Idealism (a term even more fitting for Fichte). The essence of matter is absolute *Geist* which alone possesses reality. Absolute *Geist* or reason expresses itself in nature, i.e., in the physical world which it conjures up and which it confronts in the dialectical process. Thesis summons into being antithesis and from their clash a synthesis is born which in turn becomes a thesis in unending procession.

In ethics and politics Hegel's system tended to glorify the existing Prussian state and absolute obedience to it: 'alles Wirkliche ist vernünftig, alles Vernünftige ist wirklich'. Hegel declared that the Absolute Idea, the Divine Will, reaches its highest freedom in the state; thus the state undergoes an apotheosis and exercises supreme right over the individual whose highest duty is to be a cog in the wheel of state to which he sacrifices himself. The state manifests itself in world history, in which successive peoples hold sway and yield to others.

So much in Hegel seems to glorify the Prussian state, it is only fair to add that he was born in Stuttgart where his father was an official in the service of the duke of Württemberg and that he attended the Tübinger Stift where his closest friends were the poet Hölderlin and the precocious philosopher Schelling, and finally that most of his life was spent outside of Prussia: only in 1818 at the age of forty-six did he accept the chair in Berlin. Moreover, Hegel's ethics insisted on the social context (in conformity with the primacy of the state), and therefore relative validity. In other words a good deal of Hegel's thought has a modern and reasonable cast.

Philosophies often filter down to exert influence in a later age. Hegel was influential in his own age. He seemed to give philosophical justification for Frederick William's refusal to give Prussia a constitution. But Hegelian doctrines are peculiarly ambivalent: on the one hand he glorified the *status quo* as exemplified in the existing Prussian state; on the other hand dynamic process and change are inseparable from his thinking.

In the generation following Hegel's death, the disparate tendencies of his philosophy led to two schools: the 'old Hegelians' and the 'young Hegelians'. The latter fastened upon the radical process of change. Essentially, Karl Marx was a 'young Hegelian' who transposed the Hegelian dialectic into a basically economic and materialistic matrix, although the idealist element is discernible in the doctrine of the communist millennium.

Although Schopenhauer's *magnum opus* was published in 1819, it had virtually no effect until the second edition of 1844 with an added second volume. Schopenhauer's influence belongs to the post-Metternich era (see below, pp. 81ff.).

The Idealism with which the century began is reflected in the famous line of Schiller's *Wallenstein* (1799): 'Es ist der Geist, der sich den Körper schafft'. A quarter of a century later Goethe's Baccalaureus in *Faust II* parodies Fichte's Idealism:

> Erfahrungswesen! Schaum und Dust!
> Und mit dem Geist nicht ebenbürtig.
>
> ﹖ . .
> Ich aber frei, wie mir's im Geiste spricht,
> Verfolge froh mein innerliches Licht. (ll. 6758 ff.)

By the 1850s, materialism had found its exponent not only in Marx but in Feuerbach whose famous dictum, 'Der Mensch ist, was er ißt', is the polar opposite of the previous quotations. Feuerbach soon had followers, including Ludwig Büchner (brother of the dramatist) and Gottfried Keller. The materialism of the age is evident also in David Friedrich Strauß's *Das Leben Jesu* (1835) which caused an upheaval in theological and religious circles because it treated the gospels as myths and applied the principles of historicism to the biography of Christ. Oddly enough the resulting portrait of Christ is sympathetic and compelling. Even devout believers (including Annette von Droste-Hülshoff) found solace as well as malaise in it.

The various utopian socialist doctrines in the 1830s, especially Saint-Simonism which through Heine influenced many Germans, may be regarded as attempts to combine basic utilitarian materialistic trends with idealistic values. In 1832 Heine hailed Saint-Simonism as the Hegelian synthesis of the warring Nazarene and Hellene antitheses which he felt in himself and in European society.

NOTES

1. A. J. P. Taylor, *The Course of German History*, London, 1946, 55.
2. W. H. Bruford, *Germany in the Eighteenth Century: The Social Background of the Literary Revival*, Cambridge, 1935.

Chapter 2

DRAMA IN THE NINETEENTH CENTURY

I. GRILLPARZER

Franz Grillparzer (1791–1872) towers above the epigones in the age overshadowed by Goethe. Born in Vienna where he spent his whole life apart from extensive travels in Italy, Greece, England, and Germany, Grillparzer was a solitary figure both in private and public life. The influence of the Classical age of Weimar – especially of Schiller – is readily discernible, both in style and content. The age of Romanticism had also left its mark on Grillparzer's brooding *Innerlichkeit* and his obsession with the subjective problem of life and art. His first play, *Die Ahnfrau* (1817), was a fate tragedy with many Romantic 'Gothic' aspects. A later and better example of his Romantic predilections is *Der Traum ein Leben* (1834).

Grillparzer inherited personality problems (his father died at an early age and his mother and a brother committed suicide) and he experienced the siege and occupation of Vienna by Napoleon in 1809. He remained a staunch supporter of the Habsburgs and of Metternich. The unstable family background and the shattering tremors imparted to even the most ancient institutions, such as the Holy Roman Empire, and the sweeping-away of a host of dynasties by the Revolution and the Napoleonic whirlwind, these factors must have reinforced a probably innate conservatism and bred a gloomy foreboding which vents itself in prophetic passages in many of his plays. With some reason Grillparzer considered the fall of Metternich in the Revolution of 1848 as ominous for the future of the Habsburg Empire, with the growing revolutionary and centrifugal strivings of its heterogeneous nationalities.

Grillparzer has not always received the recognition deserved by his genius, owing to the tendency of German literary historians in the Wilhelmian Empire to give only grudging acknowledgement to Austrian and sometimes even to Swiss writers. The often repeated charge that Grillparzer suffered from the rigid Austrian censorship under Metternich is a twisted oversimplification. In fact, the first of his Habsburg historical plays, *König Ottokars Glück und Ende* (1825), glorified Rudolf, the founder of the Habsburg dynasty, at the expense of his defeated antagonist King Ottokar of Bohemia. The work was, therefore, held up by the censor, not because it defamed the dynasty but because it was feared that it would have awkward repercussions in Prague where the burgeoning Czech nationalism venerated the memory of Ottokar, symbol of Czech glory and independence.

Grillparzer's contribution to the lyric is decidedly secondary, but in narrative prose he composed two *Novellen*: *Das Kloster bei Sendomir* and *Der arme Spielmann*. The latter was probably written at the end of the 1830s but published only in 1849. It is a masterpiece in this genre which reached an apogee in the middle of the century. The theme of the contrast between life and art is here treated with a fascinating blend of sentimentalism and irony. It is as if Grillparzer saw in the figure of the street musician a potential caricature of himself. Awkward and helpless in the problems of life, Jacob the fiddler is transported to ecstasy via his 'art' which to other ears is excruciating. In the end he sacrifices his life in an act of selfless heroism in which there is an ironic note, for after saving lives, he re-enters the flood waters to rescue his landlord's account books. While the beggar-musician stands for any artist, Grillparzer in this work reveals the profound influence of music and his own musicality which he shared with his mother, with the Fröhlich sisters – and indeed with his fellow Viennese. One of his increasingly rare public acts was his oration at Beethoven's funeral.

His long life was devoted almost exclusively to the drama, in which he continued the tradition of blank verse established by Lessing, Schiller, and Goethe (except for *Der Traum ein Leben* which uses 'Spanish trochees' which recur briefly in the opening pages of *Die Jüdin von Toledo*). His second play, *Sappho* (1818), reportedly written in white heat within three weeks, was an immediate and permanent success. Greek and modern elements form an odd but convincing amalgam in this work which is carried on the wave of the writer's passionate involvement with the theme which Grillparzer himself defined, saying that if *Die Ahnfrau* dealt with d'Alembert's *malheur d'être*, *Sappho* was intended to portray the contrast between art and life, *le malheur d'être poète*.

Grillparzer's tragedy of the Greek poetess sails perilously close to Scylla and Charybdis. A distinguished German actress trained in the realistic modern mode declared (to me) that she simply could not recite Sappho's speeches with their hyperbole and epigrammatic generalizations. Grillparzer is capable, on occasion, of surpassing Schiller in what Nietzsche referred to as 'glänzende knochenlose Allgemeinheiten', but if one can enter or re-enter the idealized milieu and accept the elevated poetic diction, one can still be carried away by the vivid intensity and beauty of this compressed version not only of the legendary Sappho but of the modern poet, isolated and torn between the claims of life and of art:

Wen Götter sich zum Eigentum erlesen,
Geselle sich zu Erdenbürgern nicht;
Der Menschen und der Überirdschen Los,
Es mischt sich nimmer in demselben Becher.
Von beiden Welten *eine* mußt du wählen,
Hast du gewählt, dann ist kein Rücktritt mehr.

(950–4)

The second peril in Grillparzer's portrayal of Sappho is inherent in the situation of an older woman in love with a mere callow youth – a theme which lends itself all too easily to the comic. Luckily Grillparzer was well served by the actress Sophie Schröder, who played the role in the first production. But this remains a potential pitfall which has misled some interpreters, for one's sympathies are naturally evoked for the young lovers, Melitta and Phaon, who seem destined for each other by all the criteria of romantic love. Grillparzer gave to Rhamnes in the fifth act an important role in the halting of this tendency and in directing our centre of interest back to the tragic heroine, Sappho. When Phaon declares it is not her poetic fame that he questions, Rhamnes interrupts:

Du magst es nicht? Ei doch! Als ob du's könntest!
Hoch an den Sternen hat sie ihren Namen
Mit diamantnen Lettern angeschrieben,
Und mit den Sternen nur wird er verlöschen!
In fernen Zeiten, unter fremden Menschen,
. . .
Wird Sapphos Lied noch von den Lippen tönen.

(1835–42)

The denouement of this play is cleverly motivated. Sappho's pursuit of the fleeing lovers was morally wrong and she atones for this with the sacrifice of her life, leaping into the sea from the rocky promontory. But the fate of Sappho is not entirely tragic. Her death has some affinity with that of Schiller's Maria Stuart. It is a virtual apotheosis justifying art and the existence of the artist. Renunciation of life is one side of the picture, but the young Grillparzer eagerly seizes upon the greatness and the compensations offered by art. It is almost an anticipation of the ending of *Tonio Kröger*.

Three years later Grillparzer published his trilogy, *Das goldene Vlies* (1821), which remains one of the great modern re-creations of Medea. The cycle of Greek themes ended in 1831 with *Des Meeres und der Liebe Wellen*, a moving re-evocation of the story of the young lovers, Hero and Leander. The light in the window of the young priestess, Hero, is extinguished by her suspicious uncle, the priest. Leander, swimming the Hellespont at night to the rendezvous with his beloved, without the guiding beacon is swept away by the currents and his body is found by Hero on the rocky shore next morning. It seems unlikely that Grillparzer could work any of his subjective views on life and art into the simple story of these naïve young lovers. Yet he does so in two ways, for it is patent that the sequestered and sublime life of the spirit fostered by the priestly vocation stands for the pole of art, while the physical passion which impinges on Hero in the person of Leander represents 'life'. Secondly, Grillparzer waxes eloquent in the wonderful dialogue at the beginning of Act III in which the virtues of *Sammlung* are praised by Hero's uncle:

> Sammlung? Mein Kind, sprach das der Zufall bloß?
> Wie, oder fühltest du des Wortes Inhalt,
> Das du gesprochen, Wonne meinem Ohr?
> Du hast genannt den mächt'gen Weltenhebel,
> Der alles Große tausendfach erhöht
> Und selbst das Kleine näher rückt den Sternen.
> Des Helden Tat, des Sängers heilig Lied,
> Des Sehers Schaun, der Gottheit Spur und Walten,
> Die Sammlung hat's getan und hat's erkannt,
> Und die Zerstreuung nur verkennt's und spottet.
> Spricht's so in dir? Dann, Kind, Glück auf!
> Dann wirst du wandeln hier, ein selig Wesen,
> Des Staubes Wünsche weichen scheu zurück;
>
> (946–58)

Sammlung is a word rich in meaning. 'Concentration' conveys only a fraction of its total associations in this context. That these lines come from the depths of Grillparzer's soul is evident from the poem 'An die Sammlung' (1835) in which he expresses the complex of ideas with specific reference to his own lot as a creative artist. On another occasion he uses the phrase 'Konzentration aller Kräfte' and it was to preserve this detachment that he shrank from involvements in life, whether of a minor practical nature (as ironized in *Der arme Spielmann*) or the graver step of matrimony. His 'engagement' to the gifted and musical Käthe Fröhlich, his 'ewige Braut', lasted from 1820 to his death half a century later. After the Revolution of 1848 and after the death of their parents, the Fröhlich sisters took in Grillparzer as a boarder and waited upon him with great devotion. Käthe was left the whole of Grillparzer's not inconsiderable fortune and she devoted all of it to charitable purposes until her death in 1879.

Meanwhile Grillparzer had published a second historical drama, glorifying the selfless devotion to the Habsburgs of Bancbanus in *Ein treuer Diener seines Herrn* (1828). After his dream-play, *Der Traum ein Leben* (1834), which is based on Calderón and which has affinity with the Viennese popular stage tradition, Grillparzer produced his only comedy, *Weh dem, der lügt* (1838). Although this has become one of Grillparzer's enduring contributions to the repertoire, in Vienna it met with a poor reception at the first performances. This apparent failure was one of many factors which induced the sensitive and neurotic poet to seclude himself still further. He resolved to publish no more plays and at his death three completed dramas were discovered in his desk. One of these, *Ein Bruderzwist in Habsburg*, focuses on a particularly critical phase of the dynasty: the growth of Protestantism in Bohemia and Hungary which not only trapped the gentle, conciliatory Emperor Rudolf between bitter rival factions but led him to become a sacrificial victim of his own brothers' quest for power. Rudolf's supremacy is gradually stripped away and on his death Ferdinand becomes king of Bohemia and is determined to suppress the Protestants ruthlessly. The final action in the play is the defenestration in Prague which opened the Thirty Years' War.

The remaining two plays in the *Nachlaß* are very different. *Libussa* takes for its starting-point legendary, fairy-tale motifs surrounding the foundation of the kingdom of Bohemia. The most interesting element in this *Lesedrama* – for, with its fourteen changes of scene and numerous monologues, it has not been acted successfully on the stage – is the perspective of human history and the author's gloomy prophecies for the future:

> Das Edle schwindet von der weiten Erde,
> Das Hohe sieht vom Niedern sich verdrängt,
> Und Freiheit wird sich nennen die Gemeinheit,
> Als Gleichheit brüsten sich der dunkle Neid.
> (2384–7)

Even the rise to brief power of modern Germany – 'das blaugeaugte Volk voll roher Kraft' (2413) – is foreseen, to be followed by an egalitarian society of the masses – anticipating Ortega y Gasset. Grillparzer seemed to be passionately convinced of these prophetic insights as he put these words into Libussa's mouth:

> Ich aber rede Wahrheit, Wahrheit, nur verhüllt
> In Gleichnis und in selbstgeschaffnes Bild.
> (2444–5)

Man is basically good, but in modern times is diverted from beneficial actions by the clamour and confusion of modern cities and the diverse demands upon his attention:

> Der Mensch ist gut, er hat nur viel zu schaffen,
> Und wie er einzeln dies und das besorgt,
> Entgeht ihm der Zusammenhang des Ganzen.
> Des Herzens Stimme schweigt, in dem Getöse
> Des lauten Tags unhörbar übertäubt,
>
> ? . .
>
> Doch an die Grenzen seiner Macht gelangt
>
> ? . .
>
> Wird er die Leere fühlen seines Innern.
> (2461–74)

The dichotomy of art and life is also a major motif, for the prophetess Libussa clearly stands for the artist and she is drawn, with tragic results, into the *vita activa*, while her sisters cling to the *vita contemplativa*.

Die Jüdin von Toledo is based upon a quasi-legendary episode in the life of Alfonso VIII of Castile (born 1155, reigned 1170–1214), material which had been twice used by Lope de Vega (in the epic *Jerusalén conquistada* and in the comedy *Las paces de los reyes y judía de Toledo*) and by Vicente de la Huerta in *Raquel* (1778) and by Jacques Cazotte in his *nouvelle, Rachel ou la belle juive* (1789). Grillparzer uses the milieu and motifs in his own modern way so that the original superstitions and prejudices become symbolic of deep-seated aspects of the unconscious, and this is conspicuous in his psychology of sex. There is also some affinity with Dostoyevsky's theme 'through sin to sainthood'. Surprising in Grillparzer is his depiction of the searing thrust of the libido which overwhelms the married but sexually naïve young king, who, with dramatic irony, near the beginning, points to the denouement:

> Besiegter Fehl ist all des Menschen Tugend,
> Und wo kein Kampf, da ist auch keine Macht.
>
> (174–5)

The title of the play misled earlier critics, for the role of Rachel and her tragic end are subsidiary to the central figure of Alfonso, who succumbs to libidinous forces and finally, through contact with death, triumphs over them to return to his duties to family and nation. In exploring the relationship between Eros and Thanatos, Grillparzer penetrates an area which was to be explored more deeply by Freud a generation later.

Grillparzer's portrayal of the Jews in this work is complex. Isaak embodies all the worst attributes of his race. Rachel seems to be simply amoral, a creature of instinctive sexuality. Esther, her half-sister, emerges as a commanding figure of strength and dignity, defending her cringing father and yet denouncing his irrepressible lust for money, so that in her final lines, which end the play, she stands above Christians and Jews. The despicable Isaak, earlier in the play, had defended his avarice with words which again strike the prophetic note and point to a future in which money will be the sole basis of power:

> Geld, Freund, ist aller Dinge Hintergrund.
>
> . . .
>
> Die Zeit wird kommen, Freund, wo jeder Mensch
> Ein Wechselbrief, gestellt auf kurze Sicht.
>
> (837–43)

As the political power of Austria within Germany and within

Europe waned, the contributions of Austrian writers to German literature grew in numbers and in significance, until in the twentieth century the dismembered and shrunken remnant of the Habsburg dominions produced Rilke, Kafka, Werfel, Hofmannsthal, Broch, and Musil – to name only the half-dozen best-known names of a growing host. Grillparzer is probably the greatest Austrian writer of his century, and in his attitudes and in his themes he foreshadowed the problematic existential situation of our century. Yet he did so within the framework of the noble classic form with glorification of sublime ideals and moral virtue. Even in his diction he bridges eighteenth-century Classicism and twentieth-century Naturalism, employing occasional colloquial interjections in his otherwise elevated style, in order to bring out vivid points of characterization or plot.

II. HEBBEL

Friedrich Hebbel (1813–63) occupies a place second only to Grillparzer in the drama of the middle years of the century. In Wilhelmian Germany he was ranked higher and partly as a consequence of the reaction against things Prussian and north German, his reputation since the Second World War has declined, but with the revival of interest in Ibsen, Hebbel too, in many ways a precursor of Ibsen, seems assured a significant place in the history of dramatic literature.

Hebbel is, in many respects, the polar counterpart of Grillparzer. Born and raised in soul-searing poverty under paternal austerity and hostility in the northernmost outpost of the German-speaking world, Hebbel was technically a Danish subject, since the king of Denmark was duke of Schleswig-Holstein. Unlike Storm, Hebbel seems to have been little moved by the patriotic nationalistic ferment and he applied for and received a travelling scholarship from King Christian VIII in Copenhagen. This enabled him to live – or subsist – in Paris, Heidelberg, and Munich, and during these years he continued the succession of remarkable dramas.

His father having died, Hebbel at fourteen entered the employ of the local magistrate Mohr, for whom he cherished a lifelong animosity. But he was indebted at least to Mohr's library, without which he could hardly have become the autodidact writer of ideas.

His literary efforts began early and were first centred on poetry and the *Novelle*. His lyric output was considerable and quite clearly outranks that of Grillparzer. But only a few poems soar above the Romantic models under whose influence he began or the 'pale cast of thought' which marks his later writing. His narrative prose likewise falls short of greatness, partly because of his predilection for drastic situations and problems which are ill-suited to this most realistic of genres. *Die Kuh* (1849), the last and reputedly best of his stories, exhibits the virtues and defects of his *Novellen*.

His escape from Ditmarschen in Holstein to Hamburg in 1835 marks the beginning of his tempestuous career torn between conflicting allegiances. Elise Lensing bore him two sons in Hamburg, but his unsettled life assumed a degree of stability only with his marriage to Christine Enghaus, a leading actress in Vienna, in 1846. Although he now took up residence in the Imperial capital, he and his wife travelled frequently, partly because Laube, director of the Burgtheater in Vienna, was ill-disposed towards him and his work. Hebbel therefore saw most of his late plays premiered in other cities, often with his wife taking the leading role as guest-artist.

The whole of Hebbel's dramatic work stands or falls according to the reader's willingness to concede the primacy of ideas – in this instance primarily Hegelian. This does not mean that Hebbel's plays are deficient in character-portrayal, any more than Schiller's. Indeed Hebbel was always deeply concerned with all aspects of motivation of character. But not infrequently one or other of his characters skates perilously close to the absurd, unless the reader sees through to the underlying ideas represented. His first play, *Judith* (1840), exemplifies all the faults and virtues of his later tragedies. Not only is Judith's opponent, Holofernes, a monster ('Schade, daß ich alles, was ich achte, vernichten muß' [end of Act I]), but the action and motivation of Judith are problematical. The 'universal idea' that the play is supposed to reveal is the clash between oriental despotism and Judaism, between the senseless bloody tyranny of power and the claims of the individual, between the old order which regards women as chattels and the world of female liberation and equality. This drastically condensed summary of the idea content illustrates the multiple planes on which Hebbel's thought moved: the turning-points and crises in history and prehistory reflect contemporary situations, in this case (unconsciously?) anticipating the feminine revolution in the nineteenth and twentieth centuries. The complexity of Hebbel's drama does not end here. Contrary to his apocryphal sources, Hebbel has deliberately made his Judith a complicated figure, a virgin-widow, whose longing for sexual fulfilment becomes focused on Holofernes, the only man whom she might have loved and whose head she severs after he has violated her.

Is Judith a divinely appointed and driven instrument to save God's Chosen People? Is she seeking relief from sexual frustration? Does she kill Holofernes to save her people or because he ruthlessly uses her as a mere chattel? All of these problematic elements are present and it is their mixture in varying degrees which gives the distinctive flavour of a typical tragedy of Hebbel. The ending of this play is particularly moving and revealing of the heroine's problematic situation. Instead of sharing in her compatriots' triumph, Judith, depressed and dejected, demands only one reward of the city of Bethulia: the promise to kill her, should she become pregnant with Holofernes's child.

The following year saw the completion of his second tragedy *Genoveva* (surpassing Maler Müller's and Tieck's dramatizations of this material) and his first comedy, *Der Diamant*. Of Hebbel's comedies, it may be said that they are all failures and uncomic. Perhaps his north German dourness made him incapable of the comic vein, despite his attempts to combine fairy-tale and modern elements in a mixture which, in other hands, might have anticipated the black comedy or theatre of the absurd of our day. His failure to break through in comedy is all the more remarkable when one considers how frequently his tragedies walk the tightrope between seriousness and satire. This was soon perceived by the witty Viennese Nestroy, whose parodistic take-off *Judith und Holofernes* is hilariously funny, whereas Hebbel's 'comedy' *Der Diamant* 'lacks wit and all the characters sound as though they were expounding Hebbel's philosophy from a lecture platform'.[1] It has in fact been suggested that Hebbel's language was too stiff, even where, as in *Der Diamant*, certain motifs are potentially comic. We are reminded not only of the tenaciously serious purposes behind his writing and the grinding poverty and dourness of his north German upbringing, but also of the fact that High German was for Hebbel an acquired 'second' language. Could Joseph Conrad have been a comic writer in English?

Hebbel's third tragedy, his universally acknowledged masterpiece, *Maria Magdalene*, was conceived in Munich, begun in Copenhagen, and completed in Paris in 1843. The symbolic title indicates that here as elsewhere in Hebbel the underlying idea is present, but the plot and characters are not twisted or distorted in order to externalize the concept. The narrow outlook of the master carpenter Anton and his milieu must have been intimate to Hebbel in his boyhood. He reproduced this outlook with maximum psychological realism. The prose, which up to now Hebbel had used for his dramas, finds its most appropriate realistic tones, although Hebbel stopped short of dialect which was to be developed later by Naturalism.

The play has been regarded as the culmination of the *bürgerliches Trauerspiel*, as a worthy successor to Lessing's *Emilia Galotti* and Schiller's *Kabale und Liebe*. Klara is a tragic Maria Magdalena-figure whose goodness and purity of motives lead to her death because they are misunderstood by her father. There is more than a generation-gap involved here, however, for it is clearly implied that the narrow, petty-bourgeois world is *passé*. The famous last lines of the play, spoken by Meister Anton as the body of his daughter is carried in, imply this change in the world order: 'Ich verstehe die

Welt nicht mehr!' But in this situation the philosophical context is completely consistent with the plot and personages.

In the 'Vorwort' to *Maria Magdalene* and *Mein Wort über das Drama* (from which the following quotations are taken), Hebbel presented explicitly his dramatic theories and showed how closely related they are to the philosophic currents of the age. In at least one respect, however, Hebbel's theories strike a new and modern note, namely in the existential nature of guilt: 'Diese Schuld ist eine uranfängliche, von dem Begriff des Menschen nicht zu trennende und kaum in sein Bewußtsein fallende; sie ist mit dem Leben selbst gesetzt'.

The attempt to impose a strict Hegelian matrix of thesis, antithesis, and synthesis upon Hebbel would do violence to his artistic integrity, and in any event Hebbel proclaimed that art was far higher and truer than philosophy. But the clash of different world views, the tragic demise of the protagonists, and the dawn or implied dawn of a new age have obvious affinities with Hegel's thought. In Hebbel's words:

> Das Höchste, was es [das Drama] erreicht, ist die Satisfaktion, die es der Idee durch den Untergang des ihr durch sein Handeln oder durch sein Dasein selbst widerstrebenden Individuums verschafft, eine Satisfaktion, die bald unvollständig ist, indem das Individuum trotzig und in sich verbissen untergeht und dadurch im voraus verkündigt, daß es an einem anderen Punkt im Weltall abermals kämpfend hervortreten wird, bald völlständig, indem das Individuum im Untergang selbst eine geläuterte Anschauung seines Verhältnisses zum Ganzen gewinnt und in Frieden abtritt.

In the case of Meister Anton, Hebbel leaves us in some doubt. Although he declares he no longer understands the world, the stage direction leaves Anton alone, lost in deep thought.

With one exception (*Agnes Bernauer*) the later tragedies of Hebbel are written in blank verse which tends to enhance the ideational content and at the same time to forge a link with classical form. Ignoring the intervening unsuccessful comedies, we come to *Herodes und Mariamne* (1848) in which Hebbel's mastery of blank verse is perhaps not surprising in one who schooled himself as a poet in all metres.

The epoch of the vassalage of the Jewish kings to Rome, the upheavals occasioned by the power conflict between Octavian and Antony, and above all the birth of Christ, all this appealed to Hebbel for obvious reasons. Yet the motivation of Herod, and especially the repetition of the circumstances under which Mariamne is to be killed if Herod succumbs, is relatively unsuccessful, especially to a modern reader or audience. Hebbel was concerned once again with representing the metaphysical dualism, the conflict between the

Whole and the part. Herod represents a form of the Idea in which the individual is of no account, whereas Mariamne and Soemus stand for the sanctity of the individual. They are crushed by Herod, but they go down defiant, signifying that what they represent will emerge once more. Thus the advent of the Three Kings was intended to give meaningful expression to the emergence of the Idea in the form of Christianity. At the first performances the intention of the scene of the Three Kings was quite misunderstood, giving rise to hilarity – yet another indication of the narrow margin that separates some of Hebbel's work from satire.

In *Agnes Bernauer* (1851) Hebbel returned to prose and created one of his most successful stage-plays based on a medieval episode involving the love match and marriage of Agnes and Albrecht, heir to the duchy of München-Bayern. His father, Duke Ernst, disowns his son, transferring succession to his sickly nephew. When the nephew dies and there is no successor, Ernst uses a court decree which has Agnes declared guilty of witchcraft and her marriage invalid. During her husband's temporary absence, Agnes is seized and, refusing to renounce her marriage, is drowned. In the ensuing civil war Albrecht conquers his father and takes him captive, only to have the crushing truth brought home to him that, in spite of the justice of his cause, he has run counter to the spirit of the times to such an extent that he has brought his country to the brink of ruin. Among Hebbel's tragic victims, Albrecht represents one who 'obtains a clarified view of his relation to the Whole'.

If *Maria Magdalene* is the masterpiece of the earlier prose plays, *Gyges und sein Ring* (1854) is certainly the finest of the verse dramas. In his free treatment of the legendary sources Hebbel has brought together the oriental Queen Rhodope and King Kandaules of Lydia, an enlightened progressive monarch whose favourite is the young Greek Gyges. Rhodope, adherent of backward Eastern customs, will not show herself unveiled before any man not her husband. Kandaules, forward-looking as he is, possesses the human but un-enlightened trait that he wants to show off what he *possesses* in his queen. He persuades Gyges to use the magic ring which makes its wearer invisible in order to be present in the royal bedchamber. Gyges half betrays his presence by an involuntary half-audible sigh and by voluntarily turning the ring, making himself for a second visible.

Rhodope suspects and soon finds out all. In her eyes Kandaules is guilty of having betrayed her basely. Two men cannot live who have seen her naked. Gyges is faced with the necessity of killing his friend King Kandaules and then marrying the widowed Queen Rhodope. Returning victorious from the duel – for Kandaules's will to defend himself is lamed by his consciousness of guilt – Gyges is married to

the queen who then commits suicide at the altar. Kandaules represents the tragic victim who understands and parts in peace, achieving
reconciliation with the Whole or the Idea.

> Mir ist, als dürft' ich in die tiefste Ferne
> Der Zeit hinunterschaun, ich seh' den Kampf
> Der jungen Götter mit den greisen alten:
>
> .   .   .
>
> Ich weiß gewiß, die Zeit wird einmal kommen,
> Wo alles denkt wie ich; was steckt denn auch
> In Schleiern, Kronen oder rost'gen Schwertern,
> Das ewig wäre? Doch die müde Welt
> Ist über diesen Dingen eingeschlafen,
> Die sie in ihrem letzten Kampf errang,
> Und hält sie fest. Wer sie ihr nehmen will,
> Der weckt sie auf.
>
> (1785–1818)

Obviously Hebbel is obsessed with the relationship of the sexes and
in some form or other this motif appears in all his tragedies and is
undoubtedly related to his personal situation. Beneath the mythical
elements of the magic ring and the metaphysical aspects of the
evolving Idea, *Gyges und sein Ring* contains fascinating glimpses of
sexuality and male–female relationships.

Hebbel turned next to the *Nibelungenlied*, contending with such
diverse rivals as Wagner (1853) and Geibel (1858). Hebbel's dramatic
trilogy, consisting of a prelude followed by *Siegfrieds Tod* and
Kriemhilds Rache, was written between 1856 and 1860. One wonders
whether Hebbel was drawn to the material immediately after *Gyges
und sein Ring* owing to the similarity of the sexual situation and the
'Tarnkappe' which enabled Siegfried to subdue Brunhild, Günther's
wife, who nevertheless suspects what has happened and exacts
vengeance on Siegfried. The Burgtheater presented both parts successfully before Hebbel's death, but with Wagner's competition in
the opera repertoire, Hebbel's dramatized version of the medieval
epic has not held a permanent place on the stage.

Hebbel's last, fatal illness (1863) overcame him before he had been
able to complete his *Demetrius* (begun 1857). Thus the fate of
Schiller was repeated. In the problem of identity facing Demetrius
we can see the fascination of this theme for Hebbel's enquiring mind.
Enough was completed to suggest his *Demetrius* might have become
his greatest play.

Of Hebbel's achievement Sten G. Flygt has observed that he contributed at least two things to German drama: revelation of the
motives of his characters more penetrating and analytical than had
ever been attempted, and a conception of historical determinism.
The analytical exposition links Hebbel with Ibsen, but philosophically

and aesthetically the two are far apart, for Ibsen was an activist reformer, while Hebbel sees art – especially drama – revealing to the individual an understanding of his relationship to the Whole, of his mysterious separation from and revolt against it, and of his inevitable tragic reconciliation with it. Certainly Hebbel held and developed the most grandiose conception of tragedy in an age which was becoming increasingly less attuned to tragedy in life or in art.

III. BÜCHNER AND GRABBE: THE REBELS

If Grillparzer and Hebbel were each, in different ways, the representative dramatists of the nineteenth century, we have now to consider two rebels against the Establishment whose genius was almost totally unrecognized in their lifetime. Both have been glorified in the twentieth century, but not in the same degree, for Büchner has attracted far more attention than Grabbe.

Both died at an early age, but Büchner's life was spectacularly brief: born in the same year as Hebbel (1813), Büchner died at twenty-three of typhus in his first semester of teaching in the Faculty of Medicine in Zürich. At this date (1837) Hebbel had not yet produced a single play.

Short as Büchner's mature and creative life was, at least two phases may be discerned. He first entered the lists as an idealistic polemicist with a pamphlet designed to incite a revolution in his native Hesse-Darmstadt, whose grand-duke, Ludwig II, was one of the less liberal German princes of the time. Since he was obliged to accept the collaboration of a Lutheran liberal minister, it is not certain how much of *Der hessische Landbote* came from Büchner's pen, but scholars are generally agreed that the first draft was far more revolutionary and was entirely Büchner's. The function of Pastor Weidig seems to have been simply to expunge or tone down the more violent sections.

When Büchner wrote this proto-communist manifesto at twenty-one, Karl Marx was only sixteen and more than a decade removed from the composition of the Communist Manifesto. Of course Büchner built on the French Revolution which provided the motto: 'Friede den Hütten! Krieg den Palästen!' And he used the language of Luther's Bible effectively: 'Das Leben der Reichen ist ein langer Sonntag: sie wohnen in schönen Häusern, sie tragen zierliche Kleider, sie haben feiste Gesichter und reden eine eigne Sprache; das Volk aber liegt vor ihnen wie Dünger auf dem Acker'. But his approach is fundamentally that of the Marxist revolutionary preaching the class struggle and the inevitable victory of the proletariat. Pastor Weidig, on the other hand, was inclined to advocate bourgeois liberal reforms.

The pamphlet was confiscated before distribution was complete. Nevertheless, the Hessian peasants who did receive copies paid no attention and meekly handed them in to the authorities. The liberal Weidig was imprisoned for two years, while the revolutionary Büchner escaped to France, where he immediately began work on his only completed serious drama, *Dantons Tod*.

There are many reasons for the enormous appeal of this play – and of the remaining works of Büchner, especially *Woyzeck* – to cynical, disillusioned Westerners after two World Wars, living with a constant threat of nuclear annihilation.

At twenty-one Büchner was a disillusioned, cynical refugee. His Danton declares: 'Wir haben nicht die Revolution, sondern die Revolution hat uns gemacht' (Act II). There is no free will; human beings are puppets whose actions are determined by the materialistic forces of the universe. The individual consciousness experiences in this world only existential isolation, as described by Camille's dream in which the icy stars descend from heaven and cut him off from any meaningful association. In his existential despair, Camille exclaims: 'Schlafen, Verdauen, Kinder machen – das treiben alle: die übrigen Dinge sind nur Variationen aus verschiedenen Tonarten über das nämliche Thema' (Act IV).

It is easy to appreciate the appeal of the French Revolution and the figures of Danton and Robespierre to Büchner fleeing from the abortive attempt to incite and guide a revolution in Hesse. He has lost his earlier proto-Marxist faith in the proletariat. Lacroix declares: 'Das Volk ist ein Minotaurus, der wöchentlich seine Leichen haben muß, wenn er sie nicht auffressen soll' (Act I).

Yet if *Dantons Tod* consisted only in negative materialistic verdicts of man's role in the universe, it would lack its enormous appeal. In fact there is an underlying tension which questions everything. Danton declares that man is a mistake, but he goes on to raise questions about human actions: 'Was ist das, was in uns lügt, stiehlt und mordet?' (Act II) What is wrong with human nature? Why was man not created in a more perfect form and why must evil remain an integral part of his psychological make-up? With these rhetorical questions, Danton has had his glimpse into the abyss, the 'Abgrund' of human personality. In the fragmentary drama *Woyzeck*, Büchner was to express the issue in a memorable phrase: 'Jeder Mensch is ein Abgrund; es schwindelt einem, wenn man hinabsieht'.

Another undercurrent in the drama is the guilt of which Danton is conscious and this provides yet another tension between the dominant mood of materialism, despair, and nihilism. As the noose closes inexorably around his own neck, Danton is ever conscious of his responsibility for the September massacres.

In the confrontation with the cold paragon of virtue, Robespierre,

Danton unmasks his opponent's façade of incorruptibility. Robespierre with his self-imposed chastity, his lack of debts, and his proper dress represents a 'Lebenslüge' which only conceals his natural, real personality, the animal nature – conceals this not only from others but from himself as well: 'Ist denn nichts in dir, was dir nicht manchmal ganz leise, heimlich sagte: du lügst?' (Act I, last scene) What really disconcerts Robespierre is Danton's attack on his virtue: 'Keine Tugend! Die Tugend ein Absatz meiner Schuhe!... Warum kann ich den Gedanken nicht loswerden?' (ibid.) Unwittingly he is forced to realize the truth, that he has used virtue as a step in his rise to power. More than half a century before Freud, Büchner leads the cold incorruptible Robespierre to glimpse the boiling id beneath the rationally controlled mind:

> Gedanken, Wünsche, kaum geahnt, wirr und gestaltlos, die scheu sich vor des Tages Licht verkrochen, empfangen jetzt Form und Gewand und stehlen sich in das stille Haus des Traums. Sie öffnen die Türen, sie sehen aus den Fenstern, sie werden halbwegs Fleisch, die Glieder strecken sich im Schlaf, die Lippen murmeln. – Und ist nicht unser Wachen ein hellerer Traum? (ibid.)

Danton's rent in the curtain which conceals from Robespierre the abyss within himself provides the prime psychological motivation for Robespierre's action against Danton: 'Ja, ja! Die Republik! Er muß weg' (ibid.). But the first act leaves Robespierre conscious of his isolation: 'Mein Camille! – Sie gehen alle von mir – es ist alles wüst und leer – ich bin allein'.

Büchner's language in this play anticipates the Naturalism which was to come into its own half a century later. But it is not only crude and direct, it also assumes seductive coloration, as in the passage above in which Robespierre slips into libidinous dream fantasies. Over the whole play there hovers a sexually explosive atmosphere which shocked Büchner's contemporaries. Danton makes explicit reference: 'Ich wittre was in der Atmosphäre; es ist als brüte die Sonne Unzucht aus' (Act II). Open sexual allusions and descriptions have a double function. In scenes of the common people, vulgar obscenities provide an element of comic relief. On the other hand, the more serious, pessimistic nihilism of the drama is also revealed in this way: 'Auf der Gasse waren Hunde, eine Dogge und ein Bologneser Schosshündlein, die quälten sich.... Die Mücken treiben's... auf den Händen; das macht Gedanken' (Act I). Sexuality represents a desperate attempt to transcend physical limitation and isolation to become one with the object of desire. Submerged in erotic love, Danton forgets his predicament, but recalled into the conscious world of political dangers and human cruelty, Danton realizes that sex is only a temporary release from *Sein* into *Schein*. Eros is, in fact, closely related with Thanatos.

Even in the prostitute Marion's recital of her history to Danton, the sexual theme reinforces the basic materialism and nihilism. Having been introduced to sex, Marion declares: '. . . ich wurde wie ein Meer, was alles verschlang und sich tiefer und tiefer wühlte. Es war für mich nur ein Gegensatz da, alle Männer verschmolzen in *einem* Leib. Meine Natur war einmal so, wer kann da drüber hinaus?' (Act I)

Several grotesque sacrilegious parallels are drawn between sex and religion. Prostitutes are referred to as nuns of the revelation through the flesh, intercourse as the blessing, and abstinence as fasting. Marion declares it makes no difference in what one takes one's pleasure: 'an Leibern, Christusbildern, Blumen oder Kinderspielsachen; es ist das nämliche Gefühl; wer am meisten genießst, betet am meisten' (Act I).

In this remarkable work, which is both a rebellious attack on the author's age and an uncanny anticipation of what lay hidden in the future, one of the remarkable motifs is that of boredom, *ennui*, *Langeweile*. Bourgeois, middle-class society is destined to become extinct through this particular *mal de siècle*. Büchner, in a letter to Gutzkow, prophesied the demise of *Bürgertum* through boredom:

> Zu was soll ein Ding wie diese [abgelebte moderne Gesellschaft] zwischen Himmel und Erde herumlaufen? Das ganze Leben derselben besteht nur in Versuchen, sich die entsetzlichste Langeweile zu vertreiben. Sie mag aussterben, das ist das einzig Neue, was sie noch erleben kann.[2]

Why then did Danton (and Büchner himself) become engaged in revolutionary efforts? Danton answers: '[Es] war mir zuletzt langweilig. Immer im nämlichen Rock herumlaufen und die nämlichen Falten zu ziehen. Das ist erbärmlich' (Act II, sc. i). Boredom is associated with the basic nihilism, for life is naught but a gradual death, since we start to die at birth.

This sense of boredom in a static social and political system frozen by Metternich Büchner shares with Grabbe and of course also with the *Das junge Deutschland* revolutionaries or would-be revolutionaries. But the genius of Büchner and Grabbe set them apart from the 'political poets' of their generation.

In *Woyzeck* Büchner turned away from the figures (hollow though they were in his eyes) of the pageant of history, and drew the stark tragedy of simple proletarians. The language and imagery reflect the crude rawness of nature without embellishment and in the second half of the twentieth century, productions of *Woyzeck* played some part in liberating the theatre from tabus which previous generations had imposed to prevent obscenity and preserve good taste. In Büchner's age it was *outré* and considered unplayable with its kaleidoscopic succession of short scenes. Precisely this aspect appealed

to the Expressionists who succeeded the Naturalists in their rediscovery and appreciation of Büchner.

At first it may seem strange that the pessimistic nihilism which is
so strong in *Dantons Tod*, *Woyzeck*, and the *Novelle*, *Lenz* can give
way to a charming comedy in *Leonce und Lena*. But humour is not
lacking anywhere in Büchner's writing. Often it is a black or grotesque
humour, the desperate escape from pessimism and despair. Vibrant
with puns and conceits, *Leonce und Lena* approaches in its wit and
charm its Shakespearian models which also inspired Büchner's
Romantic predecessors. But many echoes of the bitter humour of
Dantons Tod can be detected in the light comedy which is also a
work which treats the theme of boredom. The boredom of Büchner
or of Kierkegaard cannot be dispelled by diversion, for it is a macro-
cosmic reflection of the 'fatalism of history', of man's inability to
control his own destiny. Thus Büchner reminds us of the grotesque
humour of Dürrenmatt, Ionesco, Beckett, Grass, or Albee. Büchner's
dramas cannot be dismissed simply as a new experiment in 'realism',
nor can their intellectual content be summarized merely as another
example of nineteenth-century atheism and disillusionment, the
problematic existence of his characters transcends both the historical
period portrayed in his works and the age in which they were written.
Büchner is a rebel not only against Metternich and bourgeois social
and political values, he is the timeless rebel belonging to all ages.
Hebbel's Meister Anton is a tragic victim of a changing social order
which he no longer understands. But always implicit in Hebbel is the
Idea, the Whole, the Hegelian meaningful pattern. This is a far cry
from Büchner, who saw no meaning in a materialistic universe.

Christian Dietrich Grabbe (1801–36) represents an even more
serious case of rebelliousness than Büchner's. Although Grabbe was
the only child of proletarian parents – Büchner came from a middle-
class background – his criticism is aimed primarily not at political or
social institutions. His attack is rather upon life itself – or at least
upon those who claim any virtue or goodness or higher purpose in
life. It has been suggested that his early decline and death resulted
from syphilis. In the nature of things there can be no final proof of
this assertion, but there can be no doubt that his calamitous marriage
(to a woman ten years his senior), his flight from her, and his alcoholic
excesses ruined his health.

His first drama, *Herzog Theodor von Gothland*, has been dismissed by some critics as a product of juvenile hyperbole, written
mainly while he was still a pupil in the Gymnasium of his hated
Detmold, *Residenzstadt* of the principality of Lippe. It would be a
mistake to dismiss this first work cursorily, for it was revised before it
was finally published in 1827 and it contains almost all the typical
qualities of Grabbe's writing: the revelation of a meaningless world

of monstrous violence and evil. As the drama opens, the world seems
serene to Theodor, who rejoices in a happy marriage which has
brought him a son and heir, but he finds even more satisfaction in
the fraternal trinity formed by himself and his two brothers. At the
beginning of the play the harmony is abruptly broken by news of the
sudden death of one brother. The negro leader of the pagan Finns
fans suspicion and plants the accusation of fratricide against the
third brother, who is then killed by Gothland who goes over to the
Finns fighting against the Christian Swedes.

The demolishing of all faith, all ideals, all humanity in the hero
Gothland is accomplished against the background of battles, mutila-
tions, treacheries in the struggle between Swedes and Finns. If it
were a drama by Hebbel, one would be led to attempt to discern the
new emerging Christian Idea in the Swedes ultimately overcoming
the pagan Finns representative of an older stage of the Idea. But this
would be totally wrong, for Grabbe's radical pessimism far exceeds
even Büchner's. Grabbe rejects everything: 'beten ist betteln':

> Es ist kein Gott . . . ewig ist nur der Staub . . . was auf
> Nem Menschenkopf die Läuse sind, das sind
> Die Menschen auf der Erde . . . Des Menschen Dasein hat kein Zweck.
>
> (IV, i)

Berdoa in his blackness seems to symbolize the devil or – if there is
nothing beyond the material world – the universality of evil. Under
Berdoa's influence Gothland declares:

> Ja Gott
> Ist boshaft und Verzweiflung ist
> Der wahre Gottesdienst.
>
> (III, i)

The language of this play – if one overlooks adolescent excesses –
is remarkable testimony to Grabbe's poetic genius. Written in verse
– predominantly iambic blank verse – the drama is driven impetu-
ously forward by a heaping of violence upon violence. Grabbe conveys the hectic pace and the extremes of emotion and violence by
frequent lapses or changes of metre, short broken lines, extended
passages of interlocking rhymes in various combinations. Moreover,
the poetic form is no barrier to Grabbe when it comes to naturalistic
touches, such as defecation. Berdoa tells Gustav, Gothland's son,
whom he seduces to depravity and lust, that the beloved he worships
is a mere creature subject to materialistic animal necessities like
himself:

> Hat sie auf ihrem Kopf viel Haare,
> Was du so rühmst, so hat sie sicher auch
> Viel Ungeziefer drauf, und ihre Nas
> Ist schleimig, wie die Nasen andrer Leute!
> Sie trinkt und ißt so gut als du
> Und so wie du gibt sie's auch wieder von sich!
>
> (III, i)

Gothland's belief in an evil creation turns into nihilism. Gothland asks what distinguishes the hero from the murderer. Arboga replies:

> Die Anzahl der Erschlagenen:
> Wer wen'ge totschlägt, ist ein Mörder,
> Wer viele totschlägt, ist ein Held.
> (IV, i)

Three times he asserts that life was created merely in order that it may be destroyed: 'Weil es verderben soll, ist das Erschaffene erschaffen!' This reminds us of Goethe's Mephisto: 'Alles was entsteht ist wert, daß es zugrunde geht'. But an abyss separates Grabbe's world from Goethe's. Mephisto is countered and thwarted by the Lord in Heaven – 'es irrt der Mensch, solang er strebt' – and by Faust's insatiable striving. In fact Gothland ends in almost nihilistic boredom, a quality shared with Büchner. He dies in boredom, hoping only that if Hell exists, it will provide a novel experience.

No theatre has ever dared to stage this intolerably long play of over five thousand lines which begin at screaming-pitch and never relax. Tieck appreciated the elements of genius in the work and wrote to Grabbe warning him against his nihilistic destructive tendencies and also against his fantastic unrealistic inclinations. For the monstrous actions of the inhuman protagonists are reinforced by thunderclaps and comets – the paraphernalia of the Romantics and of the fate-tragedies. Grabbe uses such devices, but his genius carves his own unique path. The Naturalists saw their doctrines prefigured in Grabbe's works. In an attempt to convey the formlessness of reality, Grabbe wrote formless plays. Sentences are left unfinished, incoherent exclamations are poured forth, scenes change rapidly to give an impression of the many sides of reality. The Naturalists understood this desire to compose according to nature, rather than formal rules. They admired Grabbe's later historical dramas because he seemed not to select his material but to reproduce a slice of history.

Grabbe's second play, *Scherz, Satire, Ironie und tiefere Bedeutung*, was published in the same year as *Gothland* (1827). Unlike the latter it has enjoyed a number of successful productions, first under Expressionist auspices and more recently as part of the current of black or grotesque comedy. Underneath it presents the same chaotic world as *Gothland*: there is no guiding principle, the world is mad and only ignorant, insensitive people are happy. The relief of intoxication is the only solace for sorrow, for reality is ugly, hopeless, and evil. In 1946 Eric Bentley described the work as a 'gem of fantastic comedy' and since then two English translations have appeared. Although some of the satire on the subject of then fashionable playwrights and poets such as Houwald and Hell has lost its point, the jokes (*Scherze*), especially on the devil, much of the irony, and even some of the more general satire still appeal. Consider the poet, Rattengift, who has plenty of rhymes but no ideas:

Ach, die Gedanken! Reime sind da, aber die Gedanken, die Gedanken! Da sitze ich, trinke Kaffee, kaue Federn, schreibe hin, streiche aus und kann keinen Gedanken finden, keinen Gedanken! – Ha, wie ergreife ich's nun? – Halt, halt! Was geht mir da für eine Idee auf? – Herrlich! Göttlich! Eben über den Gedanken, daß ich keinen Gedanken finden kann, will ich ein Sonett machen, und wahrhaftig dieser Gedanke über die Gedankenlosigkeit ist der genialste Gedanke, der mir nur einfallen konnte! Ich mache gleichsam eben darüber, daß ich nicht zu dichten vermag, ein Gedicht! Wie pikant! Wie originell! (*Er läuft vor den Spiegel.*) Auf Ehre, ich sehe doch recht genial aus! (*Er setzt sich an einen Tisch.*) Nun will ich anfangen! (*Er schreibt.*)

Sonett

Ich saß an meinem Tisch und kaute Federn,
So wie –

Ja, was in aller Welt sitzt nun so, daß es aussieht wie ich, wenn ich Federn kaue? Wo bekomme ich hier ein schickliches Bild her? Ich will ans Fenster springen und sehen, ob ich draußen nichts Ähnliches erblicke! (*Er macht das Fenster auf und sieht ins Freie.*) Dort sitzt ein Junge und kackt – Ne, so sieht es nicht aus! – Aber drüben auf der Steinbank sitzt ein alter Bettler und beißt auf ein Stück hartes Brot – Nein, das wäre zu trivial, zu gewöhnlich! ... Hm, Hm! Fällt mir denn nichts ein? Ich will doch einmal alles aufzählen, was kaut. Eine Katze kaut, ein Iltis kaut, ein Löwe – Halt! Ein Löwe! – Was kauet ein Löwe? Er kauet entweder ein Schaf, oder einen Ochsen, oder eine Ziege, oder ein Pferd – Halt! Ein Pferd! – Was dem Pferde die Mähne ist, das ist einer Feder die Fahne, also sehen sich beide ziemlich ähnlich – (*jauchzend*) Triumph, da ist ja das Bild! Kühn, neu, calderonisch!

Ich saß an meinem Tisch und kaute Federn,
So wie ... der Löwe, eh' der Morgen grauet,
Am Pferde, seiner schnellen Feder, kauet –

... Ich erschrecke vor meiner eignen poetischen Kraft! ... Das Pferd eine Löwenfeder! Und nun das Beiwort 'schnell'! Wie treffend! ... O ich muß noch einmal vor den Spiegel laufen! (*Sich darin betrachtend.*) Bei Gott, ein höchst geniales Gesicht! Zwar ist die Nase etwas kolossal, doch das gehört dazu! *Ex ungue leonem*, an der Nase das Genie! (II, i)

The sonnet's progress is halted by the devil who tells Rattengift that he has read his poems. The latter's fear turns into fawning flattery and he urges the devil to compose, whereupon the devil declares that he has already produced several works, such as the French Revolution, 'ein Trauerspiel in vierzehn Jahren, mit einem Prolog von Ludwig XV und Chören von Emigranten'. But it was badly received because the critics 'guillotined it'. These passages illustrate Grabbe's grotesque imagination, effervescent wit, and also the naturalistic coarseness which scandalized his contemporaries.

These two 'shockers' having been published by his friend Kettem-beil in 1827, Grabbe tossed off *Nannette und Maria* in the same year. Grabbe himself placed no value on the piece and viewed it as bait to attract the sentimental public and to strengthen his demands that his plays be performed. He wrote to Kettembeil in September 1827: 'Die liebe Nannette; ich gebrauche sie als eine Hure, sie zieht die Narren an'.

Grabbe's next play was the only one performed in his lifetime: *Don Juan und Faust* (written 1827–28, published 1829). For Grabbe both protagonists are 'great' because they are active: it is far better to be creative criminally than to stagnate. Grabbe's Faust teaches the pessimistic message that ideals are meant to be destroyed. His Don Juan is symbolic of man ruled by materialism and the search for sensual pleasure. There is also considerable social criticism, much of it centred on Don Octavio, the embodiment of bourgeois convention.

Grabbe's remaining dramas deal with history and have therefore often evoked comparison with the plays of Hebbel. With his acute analytical mind, Hebbel in his diary (1846) perceived the difference: 'Ist der Abstand zwischen uns beiden [Hebbel und Grabbe] doch grenzenlos und nicht einmal in den Elementen die geringste Ver-wandtschaft'.[3] Hebbel went on to complain that Grabbe attached too much importance to the reality of history and ignored its 'idea'. From this he concluded that Grabbe's works are 'empty'.

Grabbe presents historical action in the setting of everyday reality, embracing a period of time and a vast space. The action is formless, without unifying idea, with no beginning, no development, no end. Grabbe tried to reflect this in rapid changes of scene, short abrupt incidents, in a kaleidoscopic naturalistic 'slice of life'. His plays appealed not only to the Naturalists and the Expressionists, but perhaps even more to the post-1945 generation.

Marius und Sulla was begun in 1823. Although never completed, the full prose sketches of the final acts leave us in no doubt of Grabbe's intentions. The appearance of Raumer's *Geschichte der Hohenstaufen und ihrer Zeit* between 1823 and 1825 diverted Grabbe's attention from Sulla and he proudly announced his plan to write 'six to eight' dramas on the Hohenstaufen. Only two were completed: *Kaiser Friedrich Barbarossa* (1829) and *Heinrich VI* (1830). A major theme is the friendship and tragic conflict between Herzog Heinrich der Löwe and Barbarossa. The one represents the North, the Germanic, whereas Barbarossa is drawn further and further to the South in his conflict with the papacy and in the exten-sion of his empire. Heinrich VI, son of Barbarossa, is completely amoral, a hypocrite who employs 'infidels' in his army and devotes himself solely to his personal ambitions – only to succumb to a heart attack while looking over his dominions from the summit of Mount

Etna. Nothing could emphasize more the underlying nihilistic message that all is vanity. Heinrich exclaims as he dies:

> So unerwartet, schmählich hinzusterben –
> O wär ich lieber nimmermehr geboren!

Like Alexander the Great in Grabbe's sketch for another play, the hero possessed the world but is left with nothing.

Grabbe's three remaining completed dramas were written in prose, although his vacillation between prose and verse is evident from the fact that much of *Hannibal* was written in verse before he changed to prose on the advice of Immermann. Published in 1835, *Hannibal* was first performed in Munich on 20 December 1918. Behind the figure of Hannibal is Grabbe himself: the genius unsupported by his own people.

Die Hermannsschlacht Grabbe completed on his death-bed, without being able to revise it. Where Kleist's play presented the intrigue, Grabbe attempted to project the battle itself. The Roman Varus is the most admirable character, while Hermann is another of Grabbe's immoral 'strong men' prepared to use any means.

In some ways the most influential of Grabbe's plays, *Napoleon oder die hundert Tage* was published in 1831, played in much-altered form in Vienna in 1869 and as Grabbe wrote it in Frankfurt in 1895. The appeal to the Naturalists of the 1890s is clear: Grabbe in this work was not interested in individuals but in the vast panorama of historical reality. The first act is an acknowledged masterpiece of its kind: the aristocracy is degenerate and dreams of rebuilding the old regime; the Bourbon king is worshipped by people who are ghosts of bygone times. Paris is a motley world where people live and die aimlessly, but it is the people of Paris who play the leading role. As the veteran of the Imperial guard tells us, it was they who made the Revolution and without the Revolution there could not have been a Napoleon. When there is no firm hand to guide them, they are easy prey to exploiters of their violent, animal nature, like Jouve – or like Robespierre and Danton in Büchner's play. Napoleon and Danton are both puppet figures crushed in a materialist senseless world. Yet in both Büchner and Grabbe there is an element of fascination in the great, dynamic leader who at least stirred men to action. Both writers rebelled against the boredom of their age and against the smug acceptance of bourgeois conventions and respectability. Both anticipated in many ways the 'epic theatre' of Brecht.

IV. RAIMUND AND NESTROY:
THE VIENNESE POPULAR TRADITION

While the Burgtheater supported the classical repertoire, a succession of theatres – Theater an der Wien, Theater in der Leopoldstadt, Theater in der Josefstadt, Kärntnertortheater, Carl Theater – catered to more popular entertainment. This Viennese theatrical tradition had its roots in the strolling players of the seventeenth and eighteenth centuries, the *englische Komödianten* and the Italian Commedia dell' Arte, with emphasis on the clown (Harlekin or Hans Wurst) and on improvisation. (Even Nestroy is said to have preserved a tendency to improvise throughout his career.) By the beginning of the nineteenth century, Vienna had produced its own species of popular play known as the *Wiener Zauberposse* (Viennese farce), which in many respects was the forerunner of our musical comedies in which spoken dialogue alternates with song and dance. Often the writers were themselves (like Shakespeare) actors and directors. Among the prolific writers of popular plays of the period were Gleich (1772–1841), Meisl (1775–1853), and Bäuerle (1786–1859), but Ferdinand Raimund (1790–1836) far surpassed his rivals.

Raimund began with a *Zauberposse* with song and dance modelled on Meisl: *Der Barometermacher auf der Zauberinsel* (1823). Among his best-known works are *Der Bauer als Millionär* (1826), *Der Alpenkönig und der Menschenfeind*, subtitled a 'romantisch-komisches Originalzauberspiel' (1828), and *Der Verschwender* (1834), in which the figure of the beggared grandee still grips the imagination as a picture and symbol of the transitoriness of all earthly possessions. Valentin, the faithful valet, played by Raimund, rescues his pauperized former master who had treated him so unjustly. Higher powers re-establish the fortunes of the reformed Flotwell and the faithful servant is rewarded.

Raimund's work transcends that of his rivals by its higher poetic quality, the universal themes, presentation of characters in depth, and the moral, didactic, and even religious tone. All of these qualities are combined in a mixture of fantasy and realism peculiar to the genre. The world is basically sound and good and the divine power can intervene to correct transgressions. There is thus still a freshness and *naïveté* in Raimund, whose comic elements, as in Molière, appear as aberrations from the healthy norm: the behaviour of the misanthrope or the spendthrift is exposed in a number of exaggerated humorous predicaments and in the end good sense effects a cure, often by the intervention of the divine or of magic. But the vitality and the faith in human and divine goodwill belied a vein of pessimism and despair in Raimund's personality and in the real world as he experienced it. He shot himself after having been bitten by a dog which he believed to be rabid.

Raimund's premature death saved him from being outmoded in his own prime by a newer, more cynical, nihilistic element embodied in his younger rival Nepomuk Nestroy (1801–62). Shortly before his death Raimund passed a poster advertising Nestroy's first great success, *Der böse Geist Lumpazivagabundus oder das liederliche Kleeblatt* (1833), and sadly remarked that he could never have written such a vulgar title. In 1861 the poet Holtei observed: 'Glauben sie mir: Raimund ist nicht an dem Biß eines wütenden Hundes, er ist an Nestroy zugrunde gegangen'.[4] As the title implies, Nestroy parodied the traditional *Zauberposse* and especially its moralistic and supernatural elements. As Heine surged forward on the wave of Romanticism which he assimilated and destroyed, so Nestroy manipulated the manual of the *Zauberposse* as a virtuoso while making fun of it all in the manner of the modern cynic.

The special talents and characteristics of Nestroy are revealed most clearly in his parodies. Hebbel's *Judith* (1840) inspired Nestroy's *Judith und Holofernes* (1849), which devastatingly lays bare the weaknesses of Hebbel's characters. Hebbel's inhuman monster Holofernes who is impelled to destroy all in his path becomes in Nestroy's play a good-natured bourgeois lapsing into Viennese dialect. But the opening chorus sings of his awesome power:

> Holofernes heißt der Held
> Vor dem die ganze Welt
> Und alles, was drauf lebt,
> Erzittert und erbebt.
> Er ist der Feinde Schrecken, Schrecken, Schrecken,
> Tut alles niederstrecken, -strecken, -strecken.
> Blitzstrahl ist sein Grimm, Grimm, Grimm,
> Donner seine Stimm, Stimm, Stimm!
> Weil er uns sonst niederhaut,
> Preisen wir ihn alle laut!

Later Nestroy's Holofernes soliloquizes on his own greatness: '... noch hab' ich keine Schlacht verloren; ich bin die Jungfrau unter den Feldherrn. Ich möchte mich einmal mit mir selbst zusammenhetzen, nur um zu sagen, wer stärker ist: ich oder ich' (I, iii). Especially inviting to Nestroy's parodistic wit is Hebbel's depiction of Judith as a virgin-widow. Nestroy has his Judith reveal the impotence of her husband in rhymed verse punctuated drastically by Holofernes's prosaic comments:

> *Judith:* Der Manasses hüpft vor Wonne, und zärtlich grinst er:
> 'O Judith, ich sehe dich auch in der Finster'.
>
> . . .
>
> Mich schwach nur sträubend, sink ich in ein Fauteuil;
> Da springt er zurück – rührt sich nicht von der Stell.

Unbeweglich – mir graut –
's hat grad so ausg'schaut,
Als hätt' ihm ein Dämon von unten
Die Füß an ein'n Felsen an'bunden.
Ich denk mir: was ist's denn, was treibt er?
Doch in seiner Stellung verbleibt er.
'Willst mich schrecken' – sag' ich – 'genug des Spaßes,
Komm zu deiner Braut, du garst'ger Manasses!'

Holofernes: Na, da wird er doch deutsch – will sagen hebräisch verstanden haben?

Judith: Da sagt er, mit schauerlich starrem Gesicht,
Zehnmal in ein' Atem: 'Ich kann nicht!' –

Holofernes: O du verflixter Manasses!

. . .

Judith: Erst wie er zum Sterben war, hab' ich's übers Herz 'bracht,
Zu fragen: 'Was war es denn in der Hochzeitsnacht?'
'Ja' – sagt er – 'jetzt will ich dir's sagen, du – '
Bumsdi! fall'n ihm die Augen zu.

(xxiv)

So Judith, Holofernes, and the audience never learn the intriguing riddle of Manasses's impotence – but of course Nestroy's Judith is not even a female, but is Judith's young brother Joab in disguise!

Another target for parody was Wagner. Nestroy took full advantage of his opportunities in his *Tannhäuser* (1857) and *Lohengrin* (1859).

In March 1842 Nestroy appeared in one of his greatest successes: *Einen Jux will er sich machen, Posse mit Gesang in vier Aufzügen.* It comes close to farce in its disguises and compromising situations, but the basic theme of the small-town shop clerk stealing away to the big city for a fling still appeals.

Whereas Raimund was born in humble circumstances and ran away from his post as a baker's apprentice to seek his fortune on the stage, Nestroy came from a prosperous bourgeois family and studied philosophy and law at the University of Vienna. He was drawn away from his studies first to opera, in which he sang successfully more than fifty roles, mostly in Mozart, Rossini, and Beethoven's *Fidelio*. Music was an obvious path to his final home in the Viennese popular play, in which song and dance play such a prominent part. The successes of Raimund and Nestroy owe something to the Viennese composers who collaborated with them, such as Wenzel Müller (1767–1835), Josef Drechsler (1782–1852), Adolf Müller (né Schmid; 1801–86).

Raimund and Nestroy appeared with success in their own and in other plays throughout Germany. (An adaptation of Raimund: *The King of the Alps and the Misanthrope* was even played in London at the Adelphi Theatre in January 1831.) Through their acting as well as through their plays, they made the Viennese popular play part of the all-German cultural tradition. Nestroy in particular is credited with amazing versatility in acting and in speaking, so that he could produce the shade of dialect appreciated in Hamburg or Berlin as well as Vienna.

In spite of the biting satire of his plays and parodies, Nestroy was not entirely sympathetic to the Revolution of 1848. His feelings were monarchical and he was passionately devoted to the cause of Greater Austria – but with a liberal orientation. He believed in centralization of power and foresaw the dangerous centrifugal trends inherent in local autonomy in the multiracial Habsburg domains. Although in so many ways the counterpart of the recluse Grillparzer, Nestroy shared the latter's political views. But Nestroy had not pondered politics deeply, as had Grillparzer. Nestroy's response was almost instinctive and all his energy was devoted to theatre-business, which had been hard hit by the disorders in Vienna in the spring and summer of 1848. On 1 July Nestroy restored prosperity to the languishing Carl Theater with the *première* of his *Posse: Freiheit in Krähwinkel* in which he deals devastatingly with Metternich's Vienna (i.e., Krähwinkel). But the play had a retrospective character since the pilloried regime was already a thing of the past. The Viennese penchant for political witticisms pounced on such passages as this:

> Wir haben sogar Gedankenfreiheit g'habt, insofern wir die Gedanken bei uns behalten haben. Es war nämlich für die Gedanken eine Art Hundsverordnung. Man hat s' haben dürfen, aber am Schnürl führen! – Wie man s'loslassen hat, haben s'einem s'erschlagen. Mit einem Wort, wir haben eine Menge Freiheiten gehabt, aber von Freiheit keine Spur!
>
> (I, vii)

The final words spoken by Ultra have an ambivalent twist: '... die Reaktion ist ein Gespenst, aber G'spenster gibt es bekanntlich nur für den Furchtsamen; drum sich nicht fürchten davor, dann gibt's gar keine Reaktion!'

On 26 October Windischgrätz and Jellacic blockaded Vienna and bombarded the suburbs. The city capitulated on 1 November and censorship was restored on the 11th. On 2 December Ferdinand abdicated and young Francis Joseph entered upon his long reign. Many in Vienna were arrested and a few were executed after the capitulation. Despite his outspoken political satire no steps were taken against Nestroy. During the autumn months he had been playing in Graz, Brünn, Prague, and Linz, but at the beginning of February 1849 Nestroy appeared in his new play in the Carl Theater: *Lady und Schneider*.

Nestroy himself wrote more than eighty plays and in his thirty years as an actor in Vienna he is said to have appeared in 879 different roles. Although Raimund had instinctively felt that Nestroy represented something alien which he abhorred, the two actor-director-playwrights are properly linked. They share the fame of universalizing a kind of drama which had local and lowly origins. Their best works became part of the permanent repertoire, not only of the Burgtheater but of theatres throughout the German-speaking world, and their best work has an enduring place in the history of German literature which, without them, would be deficient in comedy. Raimund represents the apogee of the naïve grace and almost Baroque charm of the genre. Nestroy is the greater genius, but, like Heine, he is through his scepticism and cynicism both the culmination and the destroyer of the tradition.

Beneath Nestroy's gaiety and wit one can glimpse the common bond of nihilism, cynicism, and despair which appear generally in more sombre tones in Büchner and Grabbe. In a famous essay of 1912, 'Nestroy und die Nachwelt', Karl Kraus showed how Nestroy penetrated the threadbare façade of a world of apparently unshakeable *Gemütlichkeit*. A penetrating critic surmised that the early loss of his singing voice instilled in Nestroy a sense of transitoriness, existential anxiety, and fear of death. This is reflected in his realistic cynicism which anticipates the 'alienation' technique of Brecht:

> *Stellaris:* Mächtigster Geist!
> *Fatum:* Wer stört das Schicksal in seinem wichtigsten Geschäfte?
> *Stellaris:* Ich, dein Neffe, habe es gewagt. Laß dir erzählen, in welcher Angelegenheit wir deiner Hilfe bedürfen.
> *Fatum:* Ich weiß alles. (Vortretend, für sich.) Ich weiß gar nichts, aber ich bin viel zu faul, die ganze Geschichte anzuhören. Es ist etwas Prächtiges, das Schicksal zu sein, man tut rein gar nichts, und am Ende heißt es bei allem, was geschieht, das Schicksal hat es getan.
> *Stellaris (zu Fatum):* Dürfen wir hoffen?
> *Fatum:* Ja, ja, hofft nur zu![5]

Like Raimund before him, Nestroy in his last years was haunted by the spectre of the growing popularity of a rival, Karl Treumann (1823–77). For six years both served jointly as actor-director-playwright at the Carl Theater, until in 1860 Nestroy retired to live in Graz, where he died of a stroke two years later.

The influence of the Viennese popular theatre is apparent both in Grillparzer's comedy *Weh dem, der lügt* (1838) with its naïve and fairy-like atmosphere, and also in his dream-play, *Der Traum ein Leben* (1834). Even the posthumously published *Libussa* can be linked with the tradition. But with Nestroy's death, the genre began a rapid decline.

V. MINOR DRAMATISTS

The Viennese dramatist Ludwig Anzengruber (1839–89) was a prolific writer in many genres. In some of his dramas we may see a continuation of the Viennese *Volksstück*, especially in the two early works, *Der Pfarrer von Kirchfeld* (1870) and *Der Meineidbauer* (1871). The latter shows tragic developments in peasant life and reveals Anzengruber as a transitional Realist anticipating the Naturalism which was to burst upon the scene in the year of his death.

From today's perspective other German dramatists share with Anzengruber the dubious distinction of minor playwrights whose realistic tendencies are characteristic of the trend. Gustav Freytag is better remembered for his novels than for his realistic comedy *Die Journalisten* (1853). Likewise Otto Ludwig is justly famed for his *Novelle, Zwischen Himmel und Erde*, while the better of his two plays, *Der Erbförster* (1849), hardly towers above the now forgotten plays of Gutzkow (1811–78), Laube (1806–84), and Immermann (1796–1840), all of whom were prolific providers of plays popular in their time.

Nineteenth-century drama is best represented in the contrasting pairs: Grillparzer–Hebbel, Büchner–Grabbe, Raimund–Nestroy. German drama was to flourish once more at the end of the century and in the following century, under the impulse of Ibsen and of Naturalism and then of Expressionism.

NOTES

1. Sten G. Flygt, *Friedrich Hebbel*, New York, 1968, 58.
2. Georg Büchner, *Werke und Briefe* dtv complete edition, 191.
3. *Hebbels Tagebücher*, ed. Friedrich Brandes, II, Leipzig, n.d., 94.
4. Otto Basil, *Johann Nestroy in Selbstzeugnissen und Bilddokumenten,* Reinbek bei Hamburg, 1967, 171.
5. *Die Familien Zwirn, Knieriem und Leim oder Der Welt-Untergangs-Tag*, I, v.

Chapter 3

EPIGONES IN PROSE:
REGIONALISM AND REALISM

THE DEATH OF GOETHE in 1832 is one of the few undisputed land-marks dividing literary epochs. Goethe, whose productivity remained undiminished to the last, bestrode the world of letters like a colossus and he left his mark on every genre: lyric and epic poetry, drama, *Novelle* and novel. Moreover, the last decades of Goethe's life had coincided with the achievements of Romanticism to which Goethe's Classicism was in so many ways opposed. The Romantics had broadened literary horizons and indulged in a variety of experi-mentations, the influence of which extended well into the twentieth century. The literary scene in the 1830s suggests that writers then experienced feelings similar to those of writers in the second half of the twentieth century. Like Alexander the Great they tended to lament that there were no more worlds to conquer. The cataclysmic upheavals caused by Napoleon on the stage of European history left the following generation doubly conscious of the circumscribed limitations of human endeavour. In the real world there were the limits of reimposed particularism under Metternich's aegis and in the world of the imagination all paths seemed to have been explored by the Classic or Romantic poets.

The calm and uneventful tenor of the times is reflected in a litera-ture that focuses on the individual of the middle class – *Bürgertum* – and displays characteristics of Realism and Regionalism or *Heimat-kunst* which produced a subgenre: the *Dorfgeschichte*. The whole period is often subsumed under *Biedermeier*, a term more apt of furniture than literature in which it stresses unduly the solid, virtuous, money-conscious, hard-working *Bürger*.

Biedermeier (originally with 'ai') was the invented name of a philistine character that appeared in 1850 in the *Fliegende Blätter* (an unpolitical, humorous journal founded in Munich in 1844), and the term quickly became a fashionable epithet designating the philistine and apolitical reactionary period 1815–48. If it is true that the popular literature of the age was largely undistinguished and characterized by tendencies towards smug satisfaction, ornamenta-tion, sentimentality, or escapism (Gothic or historical novels), it has become increasingly obvious that strong, vigorous creative currents persisted, even if they were at the time sometimes unrecognized (Büchner, Grabbe) or savagely attacked (Heine). *Biedermeier* seems a very inappropriate term, especially since it can be applied, if at all, only to a fraction – mostly second-rate – of the literature of the period. The term *Vormärz* is therefore coming into general use to designate the whole output of the generation between Waterloo and the March 1848 revolutions in Berlin and Vienna.

The July Revolution of 1830 which saw the end of the elder Bourbons and the elevation of the citizen-king Louis-Philippe caused hardly a ripple in the German states. But if all seemed to continue placid on the surface, the Revolution of 1830 had subterranean reverberations and served as a reminder that revolution was not dead but only somnolent. Authors as diverse as Grabbe and Büchner on the one hand and Stifter and Fontane on the other reveal awareness of revolutionary forces at work.

I. IMMERMANN

The two decades following Goethe's death are summed up by the key-word *Epigonentum*. It was Karl Immermann's massive novel *Die Epigonen* (1836) which directly and consciously bestowed this sobriquet. Immermann (1796–1840) struggled desperately and pro-lifically to assert himself as a writer, and, ironically, he expended his major efforts to prove himself as a dramatist, while his more enduring work was accomplished as a novelist. His collection of plays, *Trauerspiele* (1822), was sent to Goethe but remained un-acknowledged. Immermann struggled to construct dramas from the materials left by others. *Die Prinzen von Syrakus* combines the themes of twins and of hostile brothers of Shakespeare, Schiller, and Tieck. *Edwin* was derived from Shakespeare's *Cymbeline*. A planned Hohenstaufen cycle resulted in only one completed play: *Kaiser Friedrich II* (1828). The historical themes and milieux and the re-working of Classic and Romantic materials failed even to indicate the path towards Realism which Immermann followed in his fiction.

He worked for twelve years on the vast novel *Die Epigonen, Familienmemoiren in neun Büchern*. In a much-cited passage from one of his letters, Immermann declared that this novel was intended to treat the blessings and tribulations of being born in a late age:

Unsere Zeit, die sich auf den Schultern der Mühe und des Fleißes unserer Altvordern erhebt, krankt an einem gewissen geistigen Überflusse. Die Erbschaft ihres Erwerbes liegt zu leichtem Antritt uns bereit, in diesem Sinn sind wir Epigonen. Daraus ist ein ganz eigentümliches Siechtum entstanden, welches durch alle Verhältnisse hindurch darzustellen, die Aufgabe meiner Arbeit ist. Das Schwierigste bei derselben ist..., aus

diesem verwünschten Stoff ein heiteres Kunstwerk zu bilden, denn der
Abweg in ein trübes Lazarettgeschichte liegt sehr nahe.

(Letter to his brother Ferdinand, April 1830)

Few readers today will find satisfaction in reading this *Zeitroman*
which is nevertheless strangely contemporary in depicting crumbling
layers of society: an aristocracy gazing backwards, having lost all ties
to reality, a new caste of entrepreneurs and capitalists enslaved to
property, a young generation making vain revolutionary gestures,
imitators of Byron, vociferous but timid stand-pat upholders of
things as they are, demagogues, hypocritical pietists, vacillating con-
verts. The book's realism is starkest in its fearless peering into chaos,
but the individuals themselves are strangely lifeless marionettes.

Immermann's next novel, in four volumes, *Münchhausen, Eine
Geschichte in Arabesken* (1838–39), has a complex structure in which
the popular but fantastic, braggadocio Münchhausen-arabesques
enfold an interior story, involving down-to-earth figures of Oberhof,
a farm firmly rooted in Westphalia and thus pointing to Regionalism and the *Dorfgeschichte*. Immermann is more successful in
this realistic milieu than in the Romantic 'arabesques'.

Immermann's first novel, *Die Papierfenster eines Eremiten* (1822),
shows him still enthralled by both Goethe and Romanticism. The
Novelle, Der neue Pygmalion (1825), both in theme and execution
marks a long stride towards Realism which is carried even further
in *Der Karneval und die Somnambüle* (1829). Both in his character
and in his works Immermann is representative of a late and a transitional epoch.

II. ALEXIS

Willibald Alexis (born Wilhelm Häring in Breslau 1798) had no
roots in Prussia. His father's family came from Brittany, his mother
from Switzerland. Like Immermann, Alexis represents a transitional
stage in the development of Realism leading to Fontane, whose
career is similar in so many ways. For Alexis too wrote poetry –
especially ballads (including the martial 'Fridericus Rex') and travel
books; he was active as a journalist and he finally wrote novels depicting past and present. From the German perspective he resembles
Sir Walter Scott, whose influence he acknowledged and whose work
he translated. Even though Alexis's realism in his historical novels is
far greater than Scott's, he has not succeeded in attaining a place in
world literature.

After translating Scott's *The Lady of the Lake* (*Die Jungfrau vom
See*, 1822), Alexis published a three-volume novel *Walladmor* (1823),
with the subtitle 'freely adapted from the English of Walter Scott'.

He attributed his next novel, *Schloß Avalon* (1827), also to Scott and this was widely believed although it was his own work.

The best novels of Alexis are based on historical episodes in Prussian history: *Der falsche Woldemar* (1842), *Die Hosen des Herrn von Bredow* (1846), *Ruhe ist die erste Bürgerpflicht oder Vor fünfzig Jahren* (5 vols., 1852). The latter illustrates how the historical novelist frequently has his eye on the contemporary scene. Alexis gave vent to his indignation at reactionary conditions in Prussia under Frederick William IV by re-evoking a similar picture of Prussian enfeeblement half a century earlier when Frederick William III capitulated to Napoleon. It is a work of social and political criticism and significant also for its realistic depiction of Berlin.

Isegrimm (1854) depicts the peasants and nobles of the lands east of the Elbe still free of corrupting influences and (in Alexis's view) the future cradle of Prussian greatness. *Dorothee* (1856) deals with the last years of the Great Elector, but already shows signs of Alexis's failing strength. His last fifteen years were plagued by illness and he died in 1871.

III. MÖRIKE

The fame of Eduard Mörike (1804–72) rests chiefly on his poetry which transcends any limits of Regionalism or *Epigonentum*. His one completed novel, *Maler Nolten* (1832), also towers above the prose works of his contemporaries. Through the influence of the Romantics and of Goethe, Mörike's originality shines undimmed. This is no doubt because the novel, like most of his poetry, reflects his personal problems and predicaments. The psychological probing in depth and the clear awareness of human inconstancy and weakness give a realistic core to the action, which has so many affinities with Romanticism. Essentially a *Bildungsroman* dealing with an artist, *Maler Nolten* treats the conflicting claims of the higher, spiritual, or artistic realm and the world of everyday material existence. It is probable that Mörike could not have developed his sensitivity and psychological penetration without a neurotic or pathological element in his own life which made him receptive to all the dark tones of the unconscious. While *Maler Nolten* is one of the greatest novels in German literature, and while it has original elements – especially those which reflect the author's own deepest conflicts – it shows the influence of Goethe's *Wilhelm Meister* and *Die Wahlverwandtschaften*, and of the leading Romantics, Tieck, Hoffmann, Jean Paul, Brentano, and Eichendorff. The latter's habit of breaking the prose with numerous lyrical poems is an especially obvious influence on Mörike's novel.

In shorter prose forms Mörike was not prolific. After his *Märchen-novelle, Der Schatz* (1835), came *Der Bauer und sein Sohn* (1839), *Das Stuttgarter Hutzelmännlein* (1853), and his undisputed master-piece, *Mozart auf der Reise nach Prag* (1855).

Mörike's spiritual affinity with Mozart, the profound emotions aroused in him by *Don Giovanni,* and his similar capacity for uncon-scious, spontaneous creation have been noted by many critics.[1] Our grandfathers may have been charmed by the *Biedermeier* elements: the almost sentimental elegiac re-creation of Rococo elegance. More recent critics are fascinated by the structural and symbolic finesse of the *Novelle*[2] or by its musical analogy to sonata, symphony, or even to the opera *Don Giovanni* itself.[3]

Whether the seeming casualness and ease of construction mirror Mozart's (or Mörike's) character with traits of playfulness and full-ness of ideas, or whether the apparent looseness is an artistic mask for underlying taut control and Apollonian form – just as deeper themes lie close beneath the charming Rococo surface – these ques-tions the reader should consider and resolve for himself. But the critical trend is towards crediting Mörike with manifold subtleties and control.

Lighthearted gaiety is one of the many facets of Mozart's char-acter, revealed first by his spilling the perfume of his wife Constanze as they travel by coach to Prague for the *première* of *Don Giovanni.* Stopping for lunch at an inn, Mozart wanders into the adjoining garden where he absentmindedly plucks and slices an orange destined to play a role in the marriage of Eugenie, niece of Count von Schinzberg. The latter insists on fetching Madame Mozart and detaining them both as honoured guests. Constanze chats with the ladies, revealing both her practical preoccupations and her husband's multifaceted personality: sometimes gay, *insouciant,* sometimes gloomy and depressed.

Meanwhile music increasingly fills the day: Mozart expresses his appreciation of Eugenie's recital of Susanna's aria from *The Marriage of Figaro* and then plays a concerto which Eugenie has just been practising. Mozart describes a scene witnessed years before in Naples: maidens and youths in two fishing-boats tossing oranges to and fro, while his ear was filled with Neapolitan folk-tunes. This scene had returned to his mind as he absentmindedly plucked the orange and simultaneously inwardly evolved from the Italian tunes the duet of Masetto and Zerlina which he had needed to complete the first act and which he now hands as a wedding-present to Eugenie.

At this point the Count has the orange-tree carried into the salon. Mörike develops the history of the tree as a symbol of the age of Rococo. Eugenie had long nursed it as the legacy of an aunt who had received it from a friend at the French court before the cultural atmosphere had been destroyed by the French Revolution. But it had begun to wither and Eugenie had lost all hope for its recovery. Her uncle, the Count, gave it into the special care of a gardener who nursed it back to health. For the first time it bears fruit – nine in number – thus inspiring the young Count Max to relate the story in verses calling upon the nine muses. Since Mozart has severed one of them, Max alters his poem's finale to include Mozart in it as the figure of Apollo, god of poetry and music and protector of the muses.[4]

The polarities underlying every aspect of this miniature masterpiece are nowhere more apparent than in the contrast between the effortless creation from serene reminiscence under the orange-tree and the dark demonic aspects of creation, also spontaneous, of the finale which Mozart, contrary to his custom, was driven to compose under the spell of the Commendatore's statue. Mörike has Mozart re-create this moment:

> Er löschte ohne weiteres die Kerzen der beiden neben ihm stehenden Armleuchter aus, und jener furchtbare Choral 'Dein Lachen endet vor der Morgenröte!' erklang durch die Totenstille des Zimmers. Wie von entlegenen Sternenkreisen fallen die Töne aus silbernen Posaunen, eiskalt, Mark und Seele durchschneidend, herunter durch die blaue Nacht.[5]

After the unbearable tension of this account of *Don Giovanni*'s end and Mozart's confession that he had asked himself whether, if he were to die that night, the thought of his unfinished score would allow him any peace in the grave, Mozart serenely leads his hearers back to a normal conversational tone. With each new revelation Eugenie has become more concerned about the revered composer:

> Es ward ihr so gewiß, so ganz gewiß daß dieser Mann sich schnell und unaufhaltsam in seiner eigenen Glut verzehre, daß er nur eine flüchtige Erscheinung auf der Erde sein könne, weil sie den Überfluß, den er verströmen würde, in Wahrheit nicht ertrüge.

(pp. 620–1)

Mozart expresses a childlike *joie de vivre* at the parting gift from the Count of a carriage, in which the couple proceed on their journey drawn by two black horses. The *Novelle* ends with the poem 'Denk' es, O Seele' (see below, p. 64), which enhances the themes of the immanence of death in life and the problematic genesis of works of art.

In spite of Benno von Wiese's caution against reading too many symbols into the work,[6] it is difficult to refrain from seeing Mozart's journey to Prague as symbolic of life's journey, with its mingling of pain and pleasure, the mundane and the spiritual, despair and creative ecstasy. According to Farrell, 'Mörike designates an image as a symbol only when the association has a somewhat arbitrary character as in the case of the orange-tree and the games'.[7] But Farrell goes on to observe quite correctly that many realistic details never-theless assume the function of symbols. This *Novelle* is an interesting example of later critics discovering unsuspected layers of meaning and symbolism in realistic works of *Biedermeier* and Poetic Realism. Yet this can be overdone, for example by Hermann Pongs.[8]

Despite the fascinating monumental qualities of his early Romantic novel, *Maler Nolten*, most modern readers are likely to regard the Mozart-*Novelle* as Mörike's supreme achievement in prose: a work of genius transcending characteristics of *Biedermeier*, Poetic Realism, and all 'schools' to provide intimate insights into the psychology and the spirit of two creative artists: the musician and the poet.

IV. AUERBACH

Mörike had many Swabian traits, but his genius was as universal as that of his Swabian predecessors Schiller and Hölderlin. The most typical representative of the regional subgenre, *Dorfgeschichte*, was also a Swabian, Berthold Auerbach (1812–82), but nevertheless an outsider as a Jew (real name Moyses Baruch) who once aspired to be a rabbi and then became a *Burschenschaftler* in Tübingen. Find-ing many careers closed to him, he became a writer, publishing books on modern Jewish writers and on Spinoza and Moses Mendelssohn.

Shaken by the death of his father and moved by nostalgia for the village in the Black Forest where he had spent his childhood, Auerbach wrote the four-volume *Schwarzwälder Dorfgeschichten* (1843–54). These are not all realistic either in psychological motiva-tion of characters or in milieu, but in those stories which he based on memory and on his own experience he presented worthy models: *Der Tolpatsch, Tonle mit der gebissenen Wange, Lenhold.*

V. DROSTE-HÜLSHOFF

The most famous and the best *Dorfgeschichte* appeared a year before Auerbach's first volume: *Die Judenbuche* (1842), a single prose masterpiece by a poetess of the first order, Annette von Droste-Hülshoff (1797–1848). *Die Judenbuche* illustrates once more how a great work of genius is almost certain to burst any preconceived forms or limitations. To be sure it has all the characteristics of the *Dorfgeschichte*: concentration on a narrowly limited locality (a hilly area of Westphalia), characters who are peasants or in a similar lowly status in the social hierarchy, realistic dialogue and description. But Droste-Hülshoff's prose tale develops the brooding power of a Greek tragedy in which an avenging Nemesis overtakes and punishes the hubris of the human protagonist. It is a masterpiece of German Realism which probes the depths of the unconscious and which uses the real forests and fields and peasant huts to conjure up a dark, foreboding atmosphere.

On the form of *Die Judenbuche* Benno von Wiese disagrees with Walter Silz's description of it as an 'Entwicklungsnovelle'[9] – a formulation evocative of the 'Entwicklungsroman' and overlooking the compactness of narrative style which, with ballad-like sudden leaps 'von Gipfel zu Gipfel', produces 'so etwas wie eine elektrische Kette'.[10]

The stark realism of the terse dialogues and of certain descriptions – such as the dangling, rotting corpse at the end – forms the earthy substance out of which the symbolism grows like 'die Judenbuche' itself. Von Wiese states: '*Die Judenbuche* ist ein unerschöpfliches Beispiel für die Möglichkeit echter Symbolik innerhalb des realistisch-epischen Stils, die man keinesfalls mit einem gewollten "Symbolismus" verwechseln darf'.[11]

Even earlier critical editions customarily included the acknowledged source – *Geschichte eines Algierer Sklaven* (1818) – and a comparison of the two texts illuminated the poetess's intentions as well as her narrative power. Since 1925 the rediscovered earlier versions and working manuscripts have been available,[12] but only in 1968 did Heinz Rölleke use this material to cast new light on the basic theme, images, and motifs.[13]

We follow the hero (or antihero), Friedrich Mergel, from childhood to his death, but only in highlighted summits of action or dialogue. His twenty-eight-year absence in Turkish slavery is passed over in a few words. The basic theme is the relationship of good and evil and the fallibility of human judgements.

The village and the surrounding forests exude evil. Friedrich's mother, Margret, had suffered under her brutal, drunken husband, whose body is carried home early in the story. But Margret, though she wants her son Friedrich to grow up to be good, shares the villagers' acceptance of the criminal activities of the 'Blaukittel' timber-thieves. And she also allows her son to be taken by her brother Simon Semmler, who is heavily implicated in the 'Blaukittel' and who has denied the paternity of his illegitimate son, Johannes Niemand. As Friedrich follows his uncle Simon, his mother Margret 'sah den beiden nach, wie sie fortschritten, Simon voran, mit seinem Gesicht die Luft durchschneidend, während ihm die Schöße des roten Rocks wie Feuerflammen nachzogen'.[14] Rölleke shows how manuscript A contains more satanic allusions: 'Simon voran ... (die spitze des dreyeckigten) Hütchens einem Horne gleich in die Höhe ... während die Schöße des Rocks wie Flammen hinter ihn herzogen und er war noch gespenstiger und unheimlicher als gewöhnlich'.[15]

In the final version of the story much remains obscure, but nevertheless accessible to the sensitive reader. A comparison of passages such as those just quoted leaves one marvelling at Droste-Hülshoff's finely tuned aesthetic judgement.

It has been noted that most of the action and dialogue takes place at night and relates to the Brederholz where Friedrich's father was found dead under an oak.

Psychological motivation is not lacking: Friedrich's pride is hurt by the forester Brandes whom he sends on a false track to his death. The 'Wendepunkt' and the final ascendancy of evil in Friedrich's life may be observed in the brief following scene, when he rises early on Sunday to go to confession. Although he rises before dawn to escape from Simon's house to the confessional, the tempter, his uncle, stands in his way:

> 'Friedrich, wohin?' flüsterte der Alte. 'Ohm, seid Ihr's? Ich will beichten gehen'. – 'Das dacht ich mir; geh in Gottes Namen, aber beichte wie ein guter Christ'. – 'Das will ich', sagte Friedrich. 'Denk an die zehn Gebote: du sollst kein Zeugnis ablegen gegen deinen Nächsten'.– 'Kein falsches!' – 'Nein, gar keines; du bist schlecht unterrichtet; wer einen andern in der Beichte anklagt, der empfängt das Sakrament unwürdig'.[16]

Friedrich does not go to confession and he has denied knowledge of Simon's axe, the instrument of murder.

Friedrich's arrogance is expressed in his abuse of his illegitimate cousin, Johannes Niemand, whose theft of a half-pound of butter at a village wedding mortifies Friedrich, the dominating dandy. Immediately after this, Friedrich tries to regain attention and prestige by displaying a silver watch. A rival asks whether it is paid for. The wedding has just ended with the distinguished presence of the 'Gutherrschaft' when the Jew Aaron appears to demand of Friedrich the ten dollars owing on the watch. Three days later on a stormy night Aaron's wife calls upon Herr von S. for justice, for her husband's body has been found beneath the beech-tree. Friedrich and his double Johannes have disappeared. The Jewish community buy the tree and carve in it a Hebrew inscription which is not revealed until the end of the story. After an interval of twenty-eight years, a broken old man calling himself Johannes Niemand returns to the village. Suspicion had meanwhile been diverted from Friedrich Mergel by the 'confession' of Lumpenmoises that he had killed a Jew named Aaron. Hearing of this clearance of Friedrich's name, the decrepit 'Johannes' 'horchte gespannt auf . . . "Also ganz umsonst", sagte er nachdenkend, "ganz umsonst so viel ausgestanden!" '[17]

The decrepit Johannes-Friedrich avoids the Brederholz on his errands for Herr von S. until his decaying corpse is found hanging from the beech-tree by the son of the murdered Brandes, now forester himself. The last words translate the Hebrew: 'Wenn du dich diesem Orte nahest, so wird es dir ergehen, wie du mir getan hast'. These words stand in a strange relationship to the motto at the beginning: 'Richtet nicht, auf daß ihr nicht gerichtet werdet'. The diverting of suspicion from Friedrich through Lumpenmoises's 'confession' and the remarriage of Aaron's widow seem intended to enhance the abyss which yawns between human and divine justice.

Lotte Köhler has drawn attention to the changing narrative perspectives, beginning with objective descriptions of the forest and village inhabitants. Very soon this sovereign narrative view yields to that of the local inhabitants into whose doubts and uncertainties the narrator and reader are drawn: 'Aus solcher Perspektive lassen sich keine sicheren Feststellungen machen, so daß nun Formulierungen wie "es hieß", "man meinte", "soll gesagt haben" das Berichtete ins Reich der Vermutungen schieben'.[18] The third perspective emerges from the dialogue scenes – which the authoress records as if present herself.

Johannes's physical resemblance to Friedrich is attributed to their family traits as cousins. But he is also a symbolic mirror and simply disappears from the story when Friedrich's guilt and fall are fulfilled. Margaret Mare has suggested that he receives Friedrich's gift of the 'Holschenvioline' and retains this child's toy 'because he is in point of fact an innocent'.[19] He is both a mirror of Friedrich's lost innocence and the butt of Friedrich's ever-increasing arrogance and hubris.

Henel introduces a very modern reading by suggesting that Annette's art lies in her very obscurity and that the tale does not show the link between crime and punishment, but rather that truth and reality lie beyond the range of human intelligence.[20]

The realistic element is enhanced by the dates which precisely mark the events. Yet there is an inconsistency in that Friedrich, pretending to be Johannes, shows up in the village on Christmas Eve 1788 and is found hanged seven months later in September of the same year! Was Annette guilty of a careless oversight or was she moved to end the tale before the modern age which began with the French Revolution in 1789, as Rölleke assumes?[21] If Rölleke is right, the guilt and isolation motifs are enhanced by their confinement to an epoch when order and faith were generally taken for granted. Benno von Wiese points out that Friedrich is severed from integration even in the dubious criminal 'Gemeinschaft' of villagers and 'Blaukittel': 'es ist ihm bestimmt . . . nur noch einsam als verlorene Seele in der Welt zu sein'.[22]

It is strange that in the age of *Biedermeier* and Poetic Realism two works stressing existential guilt and isolation should emerge. Of these Ludwig's *Zwischen Himmel und Erde* ends on an optimistic note of appeasement, whereas Droste-Hülshoff denies even Christian burial

to Friedrich: 'Die Leiche ward auf dem Schindanger verscharrt'.
Even in death he is cast out of the human and divine order.

VI. LUDWIG

Otto Ludwig (1813–65), whose lifelong dramatic efforts failed to
establish his reputation in the theatre, possessed a narrative talent of
greater power. His few prose works depict his native Thuringia.
A longer work, the novel *Heiteretei* (1855), was followed by *Zwischen
Himmel und Erde* (1856), which brought him a fame that was not
only unexpected but even unwanted, since he never ceased to regard
himself as primarily a dramatist. Critical opinion is divided on the
question whether *Zwischen Himmel und Erde* is a novel or *Novelle*.
By its length and its interior psychological concentration it inclines
to the novel, but through its concentration on a single plot and
theme and its opening and closing frames, it has the hallmarks of a
classical *Novelle* (for discussion of *Novelle*-form see below, pp. 94–6).
The fact that the central figure, Apollonius, and most of those
around him are upright citizens of a small provincial Thuringian
town lends some *Biedermeier* atmosphere and an affinity with the
Dorfgeschichte. The deep-rooted regionalism of this story resounds
in the first paragraph of the interior story proper as the narrator
describes the feelings evoked in the hero approaching his home-town
after years of absence and hearing from a distance the bells of St
George: 'Heimat! Was liegt in diesen zwei kleinen Silben! ... Im
Gedanken Heimat umarmen sich all unsre guten Engel'. Ludwig
glimpsed the ideal of a happy and fruitful life in the middle ground
between heaven and earth.

The opening and closing scenes present the roofer Apollonius
presiding as an old man and a pillar of the community over his
prosperous business and over his sturdy nephews who give every
sign of becoming worthy successors. Between these scenes we go back
more than thirty years to the story proper, in which we learn how
Apollonius's brother Fritz, sent to woo Christiane for his shy and
honourable brother, behaves basely and falsely in deceiving both
Apollonius and Christiane in order to marry the latter himself.

Some years later, returning from successful business enterprises in
Cologne, Apollonius is held in the family home by the pressing
worries of his blind father (Fritz is ruining the business) and by the
commission forced upon him by the town authorities to repair the
endangered steeple of St George's Church. Three hair-raising episodes
occur high 'between heaven and earth'. The first is when the aged
blind father climbs high up in the scaffolding to enjoin his eldest son
Fritz to feign an accident and fall to his death to save the family

from disgrace. It is one of the many ironies embedded in the work that the blind father sees more than anyone else, and when word had arrived that a roofer had fallen to his death from a neighbouring village church, the father, perceiving the machinations of his evil son, had at once believed the victim to be Apollonius. Fritz had in fact partly cut the safety ropes of his brother, but it was another worker who thereby fell to his death. When the steeple and roof repairs of St George are nearly completed, Fritz engages in a desperate struggle with his brother: 'Wirf mich hinunter, oder du sollst mit!' Thinking of his father, Christiane, and her children, Apollonius decides to live and lets Fritz plunge to his death. Forced into this moral (but not criminal) 'fratricide', Apollonius is left with an inner guilt which may be one reason for his not marrying Christiane.

In the third episode lightning strikes the steeple in the middle of the night during a wild November storm. The fire seems inaccessible, especially in the darkness and the howling, icy gale, and not only the church but the whole town is threatened. Through snow, wind, and lightning, Apollonius, with superhuman strength, scales the tower, confines and extinguishes the fire.

Neither now nor earlier after Fritz's death will he do what everyone, including his father and the whole community, expect: marry the still-beloved widow of his brother. Instead he lives as a fraternal protector, helping Christiane to raise her sons. The money presented by grateful townsfolk Apollonius applies to the erection of a civic hospital.

From this sketchy résumé of the plot, the story seems full of external action and the failure to consummate the union (thwarted earlier by Fritz) with Christiane (which they both desire and which all the world expects) seems to stand inadequately motivated.

But the basic theme is internal: namely isolation. As Johannes Klein has pointed out, the isolation of the characters goes so far that no figure in the *Novelle* really knows anything about anyone.[23] Moreover, Lillyman has demonstrated convincingly that the leitmotivs which form a striking element in the structure enhance this central theme ironically.[24] Thus Fritz's characteristic and identifying leitmotiv: 'Ich bin einer, der die Welt kennt und mit der Art umzugehen weiß, die lange Haare hat und Schürzen trägt' develops almost cosmic ironic proportions. Far from knowing the world and especially those with long hair and aprons, Fritz misunderstands everyone because he attributes his own evil motives to those with whom he comes in contact. When Fritz causes Apollonius to dance at the ball, he is sure that his brother, whom he considers an awkward dreamer, will make a laughing-stock of himself. When forced to admit that Apollonius dances well, Fritz takes to the floor himself, sure that he will triumph over his brother:

Aber der Undankbare [Apollonius]! Er ließ sich nicht überglänzen. Fritz Nettenmair tanzte jovial und wie einer, der die Welt kennt und mit der Art umzugehen weiß, die lange Haare hat und Schürzen trägt; der Bruder war ein steifes Bild dagegen ... der tanzte durchaus weder jovial, noch wie einer, der die Welt kennt und mit der Art umzugehen weiß, die lange Haare und Schürzen trägt; und dennoch blieben alle Blicke auf ihm haften; und Fritz Nettenmair übertraf vergeblich sich selbst.[25]

It is true, as Lillyman remarks, that this is not the objective perspective of the narrator, but a false, ironic, and subjective view as seen by Fritz's distorted eyes. But Lillyman does not go on to ponder the possible metaphysical implications which underlie not only this action of Apollonius but his whole life. What was it about Apollonius which drew people's attention whether he danced badly or not? His name and that of Christiane certainly seem to carry the widest associations. It may be going too far to suggest that Apollonius symbolizes Apollonian form, control, and restraint and Christiane Christian devoutness. *Caritas* and concern for others run deep in both. If they live separate lives within the family, it seems that the author needed this most striking renunciation of marital union as the culmination of his theme of isolation. If it is true that no human being can know any other outside himself, then in such moral and metaphysical isolation, high moral ideals and actions are more than ever necessary to help us in our paths between earth and heaven.

At the end of the *Novelle*, as the aged Apollonius sits in his well-ordered garden looking at the steeple-roof of St George and the still beautiful matronly face of Christiane peers at him through the shrubbery, the author introduces some moralizing reflections which point the lesson of good works:

Die Glocken rufen es, das Grasmückchen singt es, die Rosen duften es, das leise Regen durch das Gärtchen flüstert es, die schönen greisen Gesichter sagen es, auf dem Turmdach von Sankt Georg kannst du es lesen: Von Glück und Unglück reden die Menschen, das der Himmel ihnen bringe! Was die Menschen Glück und Unglück nennen, ist nur der rohe Stoff dazu; am Menschen liegt's, wozu er ihn formt. Nicht der Himmel bringt das Glück; der Mensch bereitet sich sein Glück und spannt seinen Himmel selber in der eignen Brust. Der Mensch soll nicht sorgen, daß er in den Himmel, sondern daß der Himmel in ihn komme. Wer ihn nicht in sich selber trägt, der sucht ihn vergebens im ganzen All. Laß dich vom Verstande leiten, aber verletze nicht die heilige Schranke des Gefühls. Kehre dich nicht tadelnd von der Welt, wie sie ist; suche ihr gerecht zu werden, dann wirst du dir gerecht. Und in diesem Sinne sei dein Wandel:

Zwischen Himmel und Erde!

Through the slightly irritating *Biedermeier*-didactic tone of this ending, one can glimpse the basic existential isolation and despair and the necessity therefore of creating one's own heaven within and doing good for others. The Greek philosopher Apollonius of the first century A.D. was regarded as a magician and miracle-worker by his contemporaries. Within the realistic provincial setting, Ludwig's Apollonius has performed almost a miracle in bringing his family through a generation of crisis and of existential isolation to restore external order and prosperity, but not without inner guilt and renunciation of marital happiness.

Isolation is not the sole theme, just as realism, irony, and leitmotiv do not exhaust the modes of this remarkable work. It was H. Boeschenstein[26] who pointed to the central moral theme and to the symbolism concentrated in the role of Apollonius. In his conclusion Boeschenstein raised the question, 'ob die vielbesprochene Reparatur des Kirchendaches nicht symbolhaft die Erneuerung des Christentums andeutet, die Ludwig für notwendig erachtet?'[27]

More recently Heinz Wetzel has interpreted the work as a secularization of the Christian doctrine of salvation.[28] In doing so he has demonstrated new symbolical elements in milieu and character: old Herr Nettenmair as a God-figure, Apollonius hanging from the steeple in the attitude of crucifixion.

Wetzel's interpretation sheds new light on Apollonius's guilt and vow of celibacy:

> Daß er ... den Selbstmord des Bruders zuläßt, setzt ihn dem Selbstvorwurf aus, seine Entscheidung sei von dem unbewußten Wunsch beeinflußt worden, Christiane zu besitzen. Durch diese Handlungsführung wird Apollonius potentiell in eine Schuld verstrickt, die zwar in Anbetracht der Umstände und nach konventionellen Moralbegriffen kaum ins Gewicht fiele und nur in seinem eigenen Bewußtsein bestünde. Da ihm aber die Ehe mit Christiane eine Bestätigung dafür wäre, daß er den Rettungsversuch am Bruder nur seiner eigenen geheimen Wünsche wegen unterlassen hat, ist ihm die Anfechtung zugleich eine Chance, sich über jene konventionellen Moralbegriffe zu erheben: Überwindet er die Versuchung, Christiane zu heiraten, so entgeht er nicht nur jener Schuld, sondern er erhält sich dadurch zugleich die Möglichkeit, sein Gelübde des Altruismus zu erfüllen.[29]

These references to the unconscious and to the metaphysical-religious sphere add new dimensions, but is it necessary to deny the importance of the isolation theme? It too can be seen as an essential feature of a world that needs to be restored, although this theme would appear to be more restricted (principally to the evil brother Fritz) than earlier critics claimed. As Wetzel correctly points out, Christian morality is to be placed on a new, purely secular basis through the exemplary achievement of Apollonius.[30] In this respect Ludwig hardly goes beyond the outlook of *Biedermeier* and Poetic Realism. It is rather the boldness and the subtlety of literary techniques and the interwoven complexity of themes which make this work a minor classic.

VII. GOTTHELF

The work of Jeremias Gotthelf (the pseudonym of Albert Bitzius, 1797–1854) exemplifies *Heimatkunst* and *Dorfgeschichte* and yet is uninfluenced by Auerbach who was writing not far away at the same time. Gotthelf's work portrays a narrow segment of his native Switzerland: the peasants of the Bernese hinterland, among whom he spent his life. In 1832, at the age of thirty-five, Bitzius became pastor of the Reformed church at Lützelflüh in the Emmental where he remained to the end of his days. Most of his works present an additional barrier in the extensive use of Bernese dialect. His greatness transcended all regional limitations and Ernst Alker even claims that Gotthelf surpasses Grimmelshausen and Stifter and that he can be compared only with Cervantes, Tolstoy, Dickens, and Balzac.

His life was lived in perpetual tension: with his parishioners, with the church hierarchy, with school authorities, with literary critics, and with politicians of both Right and Left. Although he attacked left-oriented radicalism and perceived the destructive tendencies in the modern spirit, he was barely tolerated among conservatives.

The main impulse of his first work was the resentment of a man who refused to be a mere puppet as member of a local school board: *Der Bauern-Spiegel oder Lebensgeschichte des Jeremias Gotthelf: Von ihm selbst beschrieben* (1837). In the shape of a pseudo-auto-biography, Gotthelf gave a moving depiction of peasant life in Canton Berne between 1820 and 1830. As a Swiss and as a preacher, Bitzius could not refrain from didacticism, but if this is a flaw, it is overshadowed by the power of the work.

In his third book, *Uli der Knecht* (1841), Gotthelf shifted from first- to third-person narration, becoming more objective and less didactic. *Uli* remains one of his most popular works, with its vivid characters, realistic detail, and its eulogy of life on the land. Here, as elsewhere, Gotthelf is particularly successful in probing the depths of his female characters.

Among his more than fifty stories some are of dubious merit, but others are magnificent achievements. Despite the narrow regional milieu and despite the use of dialect, his works were published in Berlin and he was at first held in higher esteem beyond the Swiss borders. Gottfried Keller recognized the greatness of his compatriot and compared Gotthelf's master *Novelle, Elsi, die seltsame Magd*, with Goethe's *Hermann und Dorothea*.

Surprising, in view of the author's irascible temperament, are the Christian humility and moderation which appear as the dominant traits in *Hans Joggeli der Erbvetter* (1848), wherein a middle course is steered between asceticism and worldliness. Although much has been made of Gotthelf as a precursor of Naturalism (extended use of dialect, calling a spade a spade, etc.) his orientation was basically different. He was fascinated with man and especially with his striving spiritual potential. This spiritual dimension is evident in this passage from *Hans Joggeli*:

> Wie der Baum seine Wurzeln in die Erde geschlagen hat, seine Aeste in der Luft entfaltet, seine Krone nach seiner Kraft gen Himmel treibt, aus Erde, Luft und Himmel seine Nahrung saugt, bei guter Nahrung gesund bleibt, blüht und Früchte trägt, so soll der Glaube im Herzen wurzeln, hinaus ins Leben reichen, hinauf-, Gott entgegenstreben, aus Gott, Leben und Herz, aus dieser Dreifaltigkeit soll er täglich, stündlich Nahrung saugen, unmittelbar, fast bewußtlos, fast ohne Mühe, dem Baume gleich; dann bleibt der Glaube lebendig, schön wird er bleiben, süße Früchte wird er tragen.[31]

The most discussed and perhaps the greatest of Gotthelf's *Novellen* is *Die schwarze Spinne* (1842). The author's vocation as pastor and his Christian faith led inevitably to allegorical interpretations based on Catholic doctrine denying the full beatific vision to unbaptized children. Rationalistic interpreters saw in the 'black spider' an un-enlightened stage in the progressive development of man. The influence of psychoanalysis led later critics to see in the 'black spider' a female mother-symbol. Probably none of these allegorical or one-sided interpretations does justice to the poetic achievement of Gotthelf. In broader terms one can claim that in this poetic vision, Gotthelf depicts the world in a perilous situation, for mankind is constantly threatened. It is by no means established that evil is punished and good rewarded. So-called earthly justice is the work of fallible human hands. The devil can seize power in this world and the innocent are victimized along with the guilty. It seems to be a mystery of divine justice that only the sacrifice of the innocent has expiatory power. The plague (yet another interpretation) of the 'black spider' in the Emmental is finally extirpated by the self-sacrifice of the hitherto too gentle Christen:

> Er aber betete Tag und Nacht zu Gott, daß er das Übel wende, aber es ward schrecklicher von Tag zu Tag. Er ward es inne, daß er gutmachen müsse, was er gefehlt, daß er sich selbst zum Opfer geben müsse, daß an ihm liege die Tat, die seine Ahnfrau getan. Er betete zu Gott, bis ihm so recht feurig im Herzen der Entschluß emporwuchs, die Talschaft zu retten, das Übel zu sühnen, und zum Entschuß kam der standhafte Mut, der nicht wankt, immer bereit ist zur gleichen Tat, am Morgen wie am Abend.
>
> (XVII, 89)

If the work is correctly interpreted in some such broad general terms, it is easy to see the relevance and the fascination which this masterpiece holds for the modern world. Although the outer frame of the *Novelle* opens and closes in a mood of serenity, the interior story conjures up an overwhelming atmosphere of black despair and demonic power.

Gotthelf belongs to the world and to all ages, not merely to his peasant parishioners of the Emmental, nor can he be confined to the narrow limits of a minor subgenre, the *Dorfgeschichte*. He must be ranked among the great writers of the following age of Poetic Realism; Keller, Stifter, Raabe, Storm, and Fontane. Gotthelf was a favourite author of the Nazis, who overemphasized the conservative factor and the element of 'Blut und Boden' inherent in his *Heimatkunst*. For such misguided or one-sided followers, Gotthelf ought not to be blamed, any more than Nietzsche in similar circumstances.

NOTES

1. Cf., e.g., Margaret Mare, *Eduard Mörike: his Life and Work*, London, 1957, 215–33.

2. Cf., e.g., K. K. Polheim, 'Der künstlerische Aufbau von Mörikes Mozartnovelle', *Euphorion*, XLVIII (1954), 41–70.

3. R. Immerwahr, 'Narrative and "Musical" Structure in "Mozart auf der Reise nach Prag"', *Studies in Germanic Languages and Literatures in Memory of Fred O. Nolte*, ed. E. Hofacker and L. Dieckmann, St Louis, 1963, 103–20; and same author's 'Apocalyptic Trumpets: The Inception of Mozart auf der Reise nach Prag', *PMLA*, LXX (1955), 390–407.

4. Cf. Helga Slessarev, *Eduard Mörike*, New York, 1970, 110–20.

5. *Sämtliche Werke I*, Munich, 1967, 616.

6. *Die deutsche Novelle von Goethe bis Kafka*, Düsseldorf, 1962, I, 213–237.

7. R. B. Farrell, *Mörike: Mozart auf der Reise nach Prag*, London, 1960, 27.

8. ibid., 25.

9. Walter Silz, *Realism and Reality*, Chapel Hill, 1954, 36–51.

10. Von Wiese, op. cit., I, 156.

11. ibid., 159.

12. Karl Schulte-Kemminghausen, *'Die Judenbuche' mit sämtlichen jüngst wieder aufgefundenen Vorarbeiten der Dichterin*, Dortmund, 1925; repr. *Annette von Droste-Hülshoff: Sämtliche Werke*, ed. Clemens Heselhaus, Munich, 1952; 4th rev. edn., 1963.

13. 'Erzähltes Mysterium: Studie zur Judenbuche der Annette von Droste-Hülshoff', *DVLG*, XLII (1968), 399–426.

14. Annette von Droste-Hülshoff, *Werke in einem Band*, ed. Heinz Rölleke, Berlin, 1970, 245.

15. op. cit., 404. Manuscript A: an earlier version unpublished in the poetess's lifetime. Cf. also Emil Staiger, *Annette von Droste-Hülshoff*, 2nd ed., Frauenfeld, 1962, 58.

16. *Werke in einem Band*, 263. Interpreters who read the work only as a criminal story quite plausibly point to the murder of Aaron and ensuing flight of Friedrich as the turning-point. But on a deeper plane the tipping of the scales from good to evil seems to lie here.

17. ibid., 278.

18. Lotte Köhler, 'Annette von Droste-Hülshoff' in *Deutsche Dichter des 19. Jahrhunderts*, ed. B. v. Wiese, Berlin, 1969, 239. See also Edson Chick who detects five different narrative 'voices': 'Voices in Discord: Some Observations on Die Judenbuche', *GQ*, XLII (1969), 142–57.

19. Margaret Mare, *Annette von Droste-Hülshoff*, Lincoln (Nebraska) and London, 1965, 258. The 'Holschenvioline' is a toy made of a 'Holzpantoffel'.

20. 'Annette von Droste-Hülshoff. Erzählstil und Wirklichkeit' in *Festschrift für Bernhard Blume*, Göttingen, 1967, 146–72.

21. op. cit., 415.

22. op. cit., 165.

23. *Geschichte der deutschen Novelle*, 2nd edn., Wiesbaden, 1954, 173–8.

24. N. J. Lillyman, 'The Function of the Leitmotifs in Otto Ludwig's *Zwischen Himmel und Erde*', *Monatshefte*, LVII (1965), 60–8.

25. *Zwischen Himmel und Erde*, Frankfurt a.M., 1858, 55–6, quoted Lillyman, op. cit., 63.

26. 'Zum Aufbau von Otto Ludwigs *Zwischen Himmel und Erde*', *Monatshefte*, XXXIV (1942), 343–56.

27. ibid., 355.

28. Heinz Wetzel, 'Otto Ludwigs *Zwischen Himmel und Erde*: Eine Säkularisierung der christlichen Heilslehre', *Orbis Litterarum*, XXVII (1972), 102–21.

29. ibid., 110.

30. ibid., 119.

31. *Sämtliche Werke*, ed. R. Hunziker and H. Bloesch, Erlenbach-Zürich, 1936–37, IX, 72–3.

Chapter 4

HEINRICH HEINE AND
DAS JUNGE DEUTSCHLAND

THE ENGLISH and French in the nineteenth century regarded Heine as the greatest German poet after Goethe and Schiller. In Germany Heine remained a controversial or denigrated figure until after the Second World War. Heine's fame at home and abroad long rested on his earlier poetry – especially *Das Buch der Lieder* (1827). The nineteenth-century reader generally accepted the Romantic elements – including copious sentimentality – as genuine. Renewed interest in Heine has revealed the extent to which even his earliest love lyrics are permeated by a cynical irony, sometimes overt, more often subtly embedded. It is a moot question whether the close textual criticism is destructive which reads ironic or cynical twists into lyrics which were previously accepted at face value. D. H. Lawrence pointed to this in 'Du bist wie eine Blume':

> One can see the elderly gentleman laying his hands on the head of the pure maiden and praying God to keep her for ever so pure, so clean and beautiful – in his vulgar sense of clean and pure – for a few more years, then she'll be an unhappy old maid, and not pure nor beautiful at all, only stale and pathetic.[1]

One need not agree entirely with Lawrence and yet one must concede the possibility of *double entendre* in much of the early poetry. 'Du bist wie eine Blume' leaves one with an uneasy feeling, owing partly to its too perfect, too symmetrical form, with its consciously inverted triplets: 'so hold, so rein, so schön'. On the whole it seems that the heightened consciousness of the present-day reader adds a dimension to this poetry rather than detracts from it.

Heine was the first Jewish poet of prime importance in German literature. He was born in Düsseldorf in 1797 – in time to experience in his boyhood the sleepy little *Residenzstadt* of the duchy of Jülich-Berg. As a Jew, Heine was aware of the less idyllic aspects of the narrow confines of this principality which was swept away in Napoleon's wake. The French occupation stamped Napoleon indelibly in Heine's mind as the heroic liberator, for the *code napoléon* removed all restrictions on Jews. Heine's birthplace, along with most of the Rhineland, was given to Prussia at the Congress of Vienna. Even in Heine's lifetime, the little town was to begin its metamorphosis into a dynamic industrial megalopolis. Heine was basically a modern, urban poet and in his early Romantic verse the nature-settings have almost the quality of stage-props.

Heine developed a prose style which gave to German something of the elegance, wit, and lucidity of French without sacrificing the strength and depth of German. His first prose work, *Die Harzreise* (part of *Reisebilder* I, 1826), showed much more clearly than his early poetry the revolutionary trend of his cynical wit: 'The Hanoverian aristocracy are asses who talk of nothing but horses'.[2]

The July Revolution of 1830 in France found Heine depressed and at loose ends. His father had just died and the professorial chair in Munich, to which he aspired, had gone to another. He had no prospects in Germany and so he went into voluntary exile in the French capital where he spent the rest of his life, except for two short visits to Hamburg. A city-dweller at heart, Heine described how much he felt at home in Paris, this largest, gayest, most intellectual and progressive of European cities, in a letter of 24 October 1832 to Ferdinand Hiller: 'Fragt Sie jemand, wie ich mich hier befinde, so sagen Sie: wie ein Fisch im Wasser. Oder vielmehr, sagen Sie den Leuten, daß, wenn im Meere ein Fisch den anderen nach seinem Befinden fragt, so antworte dieser: ich befinde mich wie Heine in Paris'. Here, however, the most troublesome of the complex ambiguities of his nature brought him into difficulties. He came not only as a poet and prose artist of stature but, so it seemed, as a dedicated radical recruit to the band of political exiles. For several years he seemed to accept this role and the contacts with various revolutionary circles, but the clash between artist and polemicist was bound to appear.

Ironically, it may be said that Metternich created the literary school known as *Das junge Deutschland* by the law which he persuaded the Federal Diet to pass in December 1835, banning the writings of the school known by this name and specifically listing Heine, Karl Gutzkow, Ludolf Wienbarg, Theodor Mundt, and Heinrich Laube. The term 'Junges Deutschland' had occurred in the dedication of Wienbarg's *Aesthetische Feldzüge* (1834) and in earlier correspondence between Gutzkow and Laube, but it was the *Bundestag* decree which gave it currency.[3]

From his point of view, Metternich was right in perceiving the threat to the Establishment from these militant liberal nationalists, some of whom were outright republicans. They belonged to, and addressed themselves to, a young generation no longer willing to accept a privileged social order and political particularism and autocracy. But many of these individuals were unaware of their allegiance to a 'school' until Metternich gave them a common cause. Their work, as well as the fall of the elder Bourbons in 1830, served as a reminder that the revolution was not dead but merely dormant. They represent not only the enlightenment of the previous century and the 'liberty, equality, fraternity' of the glorious Revolution of 1789, but also the influence of the 'young Hegelians'. Hegel offered not only an arsenal for conservative upholders of the Prussian state and the *status quo*, but also a storehouse of fermenting ideas for the radical Left. The dynamic overcoming of the present through a dialectical progress provided the springboard for Karl Marx, who may also be ranked with *Das junge Deutschland* in the most extended use of the phrase, along with others unnamed in the *Bundestag* decree, such as the poets Freiligrath, Herwegh, Dingelstedt, and the critic Ludwig Börne. Apart from Marx – who as a literary artist was by no means the least talented – and Heine, 'Young Germany' is mainly of historical interest, since these writers not only kept alive the smouldering embers of revolt, but also very largely conditioned the attitudes of the liberal-nationalists elected to the Frankfurt Parliament in 1848. Posterity has awarded poetic laurels to Heine alone and his artistic genius could not be confined to one school nor dedicated to a specific socio-political programme.

As Heine had earlier attacked the aristocratic poet Count von Platen wittily but viciously (alluding to Platen's homosexuality in *Die Bäder von Lucca, Reisebilder*, III, 1829), so he now attacked the radical Ludwig Börne after the latter's death in 1837, with scurrilous allusions to his liaison with Frau Wohl: *Heinrich Heine über Ludwig Börne, Eine Denkschrift* (1840). Heine's book on Börne is one of his prose masterpieces, although it is confusing because of its shifting perspectives, and it is full of incisive and prophetic comments on European art and society. The publication created a scandal and provoked a duel between Heine and the second husband of the former Frau Wohl. Before facing his challenger, Heine married his illiterate mistress 'Mathilde' (Crescentia Eugénie Mirat) in order that she might be legally provided for, should he succumb. To his friend Weill, Heine intimated his awareness of the troubled matrimonial waters on which he was now embarking: 'That terrible Frau Wohl has had her revenge. But I will have mine. After leaving the church, I made a will, leaving everything to my wife. I left it to her, however, on one condition – that she marry again immediately after my death. In that way, I shall be sure at least one man is sorry I am no longer alive'.[4] Both duellists acted like gentlemen born to the tradition; Heine fired in the air and Herr Strauss's bullet merely grazed Heine's hip.

Ludwig Börne (born Löb Baruch in the Frankfurt ghetto) had been one of the most influential and respected of the German radical exiles and this affair illustrates Heine's alienation from them.

Of Heine's voluminous prose, mention must be made of *Die*

romantische Schule and *Zur Geschichte der Religion und Philosophie in Deutschland* (1834–35). These and many other works appeared either simultaneously or earlier in French editions, so that Heine played a vital role as interpreter between France and Germany. His book on Romanticism is, of course, also a reckoning with a chapter of his own past. He pillories the backward look and the Romanticized Middle Ages, painting a ludicrous portrait of Uhland, poet of knightly chivalry and political reformer in the Württemberg legislature:

> ... und da sein Pegasus nur ein Ritterroß war, das gern in die Vergangenheit zurücktrabte, aber gleich stätig wurde, wenn es vorwärts sollte in das moderne Leben, da ist der wackere Uhland lächelnd abgestiegen, ließ ruhig absatteln und den unfügsamen Gaul nach dem Stall bringen. Dort befindet er sich noch bis auf den heutigen Tag, und wie sein Kollege, das Roß Bayard, hat er alle möglichen Tugenden und nur einen einzigen Fehler: er ist tot.[5]

The extant chapters of Heine's unfinished novel, *Der Rabbi von Baccharach*, indicate that this genre just missed a potential master.

The form of the long narrative poem *Atta Troll, ein Sommernachtstraum* (1843) is a fantastic parody of Freiligrath's *Der Mohrenfürst*. The content is also mainly a satiric attack on the political poetry of the day. Heine's mock-epic is typical of his highly conscious yet apparently casual versification, written in unrhymed trochaic tetrameter four-line stanzas, which seem almost prosaic and casual and yet have a carefully calculated artistry. The fusion of animal fable with satire and the fantastic situations and adventures justify Heine's calling it 'das letzte freie Waldlied der Romantik'. The companion piece *Deutschland, ein Wintermärchen* (1844) – occasioned by a trip to Hamburg – has amusing and satirical episodes, but lacks the strength and coherence of the animal epic.

Heine also parodied Dingelstedt's *Lieder eines kosmopolitischen Nachtwächters* in the poem 'Bei des Nachtwächters Ankunft zu Paris' (1842). Heine's nightwatchman also voices his own caustic criticism of German backwardness:

> Nicht oberflächlich wie Frankreich blüht es,
> Wo Freiheit das äußere Leben bewegt;
> Nur in der Tiefe des Gemütes
> Ein deutscher Mann die Freiheit trägt.
>
> . . .
>
> Die Konstitution, die Freiheitsgesetze,
> Sie sind uns versprochen, wir haben das Wort,
> Und Königsworte, das sind Schätze,
> Wie tief im Rhein der Niblungshort.

In these years occurred Heine's collaboration with Karl Marx, in whose paper *Vorwärts* some of Heine's most revolutionary poems were published, including the incomparable 'Die schlesischen Weber' (1844).

Heine's health had been steadily deteriorating and on his last walk he was caught up in the turbulence of the Revolution of 1848. He sought refuge in the Louvre where he reports – with dramatic self-persiflage and perhaps with conscious symbolism – that he collapsed at the feet of the Venus de Milo. He was paralysed (probably from syphilis) and was carried to his 'mattress grave' where he spent his last eight painful years, writing (later dictating) his greatest poetry: *Romanzero* (1851), *Gedichte 1853 und 1854,* and the posthumously published *Letzte Gedichte* (1869).

His painful personal situation, the Revolutions of 1848 and their aftermath, the rising tempo of industrial and commercial developments, the dislocations of society, and the creation of a displaced urban proletariat, all these factors combined to produce a pessimistic tone in the late poetry. The aristocracy was a ghost of the past. For the entrepreneurs – the *Großkapitalisten* – Heine had no more liking than he had for the communist alternative which he perceived lurking in the wings from which it was to erupt to seize power temporarily in the Paris Commune of 1871. Although pessimistic in tone, the poems are by no means without Heine's ironic wit, now more frequently of a macabre nature, as in 'Rhampsenit' or 'Vitzliputzli':

> Dort auf seinem Thronaltar
> Sitzt der große Vitzliputzli,
> Mexikos blutdürstger Kriegsgott,
> Ist ein böses Ungetüm,
>
> Doch sein Äußres ist so putzig,
> So verschnörkelt und so kindisch,
> Daß er trotz des innern Grausens
> Dennoch unsre Lachlust kitzelt –

It has been claimed that Heine lacked variety in his versification. The earlier poems use predominantly the folk-song or ballad stanza and in his late poetry he favoured the unrhymed trochaic tetrameter four-line stanza. But he used these forms frequently for deliberate parodistic purposes and he occasionally used successfully poetic structures as diverse as the Petrarchan sonnet ('Mein Tag war heiter . . .') and the dithyrambic free verse of the North Sea cycles. In fact he was the first German poet to use free rhythms and bold new word-formations to convey the changing moods of the ocean. 'Ritter Olaf', 'Der Dichter Firdusi', and 'Der Apollogott' are triptychs in which Heine varied the verse form in each of the three sections, creating little masterpieces in which form and content reinforce each other with maximum effect. But undoubtedly Heine was less interested in the formal elements than, for instance, his rival Graf von Platen. Heine was an innovator in the spirit and content of poetry rather than in form, combining, often simultaneously, contradictory or ambivalent moods and enlarging the sphere of poetry to include every kind of subject from the ridiculous to the sublime. He was an innovator in treating prosaic themes in poetry (e.g., 'Jammertal') – even in writing sometimes intentionally prosaic poetry – and in expanding the range of vocabulary and imagery. Before Baudelaire, Heine experimented with the poem in prose ('Hymnus'). His impact on German literature was so great that the Nazis could expunge his name but not the familiar poems, many of them set to music by Schumann and a host of other composers. The Hitler Youth song-book contained 'Die Lorelei' and attributed it to an anonymous author!

Heine's prose served successive generations as a model and such perceptive critics as Nietzsche and Karl Kraus[6] were aware of this legacy as well as of the debt owed to Heine by posterity for his acute diagnosis of the malaise of modern man. The war which he foresaw and dreaded between France and Germany was to come in 1870, but this, he said in *Lutezia* (1854):

> ...wäre nur der erste Akt des großen Spektakelstückes, gleichsam das Vorspiel. Der zweite Akt ist die europäische, die Weltrevolution, der große Zweikampf der Besitzlosen mit der Aristokratie des Besitzes, und da wird weder von Nationalität noch von Religion die Rede sein: nur *ein* Vaterland wird es geben, nämlich die Erde, und nur *einen* Glauben, nämlich das Glück auf Erden.... Es wird vielleicht alsdann nur *einen* Hirten und *eine* Herde geben, ein freier Hirt mit einem eisernen Hirtenstabe und eine gleichgeschorene, gleichblökende Menschenherde! Wilde, düstere Zeiten dröhnen heran...[7]

Metternich may have indirectly established *Das junge Deutschland* as a literary school, but it was Heine who gave it immortality, ambivalent and loose as were his ties to it.

NOTES

1. 'Pornography and Obscenity' in *The Portable D. H. Lawrence*, New York and Toronto, 1954, 661.
2. Louis Untermeyer, *Heinrich Heine*, London, 1938, 306.
3. The federal apparatus of 1815 was ineffectual in almost every area and censorship was no exception. This law was partially effective because Prussia supported Austria in the attempt to implement it. Even so, Heine's cunning publisher, Campe, in Hamburg, contrived to publish and circulate Heine's works quite widely.
4. Untermeyer, op. cit., 256.
5. Heinrich Heine, *Werke und Briefe*, ed. Hans Kaufmann, Berlin, 1961, V, 146–7.
6. Kraus's attitude to Heine is deeply ambiguous since he charges Heine with responsibility for inaugurating tendencies which developed into the 'feuilletonistic' style which Kraus deplored. Even such negative criticisms pay tribute to the importance of Heine.
7. *Werke und Briefe*, VI, 433.

Chapter 5

LYRIC POETRY IN THE FIRST HALF OF THE CENTURY

IN NO AREA of literature was the influence of the past – of Goethe and of Romanticism – greater than in the lyric. Here, however, the legacy had a productive rather than inhibiting effect, perhaps because Goethe and the Romantic poets had made this genre pre-eminent and had opened up so many new avenues of development. It is also true that the most typically lyrical poetry is highly subjective and does not lend itself so readily to epigonal imitativeness. But primarily it was the presence of genius which distinguished the lyric of this age. In addition to Heine, four poets claim the highest laurels: Mörike, Platen, Droste-Hülshoff, and Lenau.

I. EDUARD MÖRIKE (1804–75)

All four lyricists of the *Vormärz* (age of Metternich) were problematic personalities, although two of them seemed outwardly to lead idyllic, *Biedermeier* lives. This is certainly true of the greatest, Mörike, who prepared for the Lutheran ministry at the Tübinger Stift and served as pastor in successive country parishes (ten years in Cleversulzbach), his mother and sister jointly, and then his sister, keeping house for him. He had always felt uneasy within the church and retired from the ministry when still in his forties, married late in life, and eked out his small pension for fifteen years by lecturing on literature in a girls' school in Stuttgart. He felt this post, too, a burden which he was glad to relinquish. After his marriage at the age of forty-six to Margarete von Speth, a Catholic, who bore him two daughters, Mörike's sister continued to keep house for the family as she had done before. Finally Margarete tired of being merely a wife and divorced the poet. But Mörike's deepest and most painful experience was undoubtedly his youthful infatuation for Maria Meyer – 'Peregrina' of the poems. When he met her, he was a theological student at Tübingen and she was a tavern waitress – albeit a quite untypical one. Her employer had found her unconscious; no one knew whence she came; and the mystery was heightened by a religious aura, since it was reported that her parents had disowned her because she had

joined a dissenting sect. She was beautiful and she was saintly:
Mörike was fascinated. Even after he discovered that the girl was a
cheat, he broke off the affair only with great suffering which quivers
not only in the Peregrina-cycle but again and again in later poems.
The free rhythms of the sixth Peregrina-poem are a direct confession:

> Ein Irrsal kam in die Mondscheingärten
> Einer einst heiligen Liebe,
> Schaudernd entdeckt' ich verjährten Betrug.
> Und mit weinendem Blick, doch grausam,
> Hieß ich das schlanke,
> Zauberhafte Mädchen
> Ferne gehen von mir.

Mörike is often classified as a late Romantic partly because of his
frequent portrayal of unhappy love – not only in 'Peregrina' but, for
example, in the unforgettable 'Das verlassene Mägdlein' – and because of his awareness of dualisms, of the dark, demonic, irrational
forces (personified in the immortal ballad 'Der Feuerreiter'), and
because of his dwelling on the contrast between night and day, symbolizing death and life. But although these Romantic traits are strong
in many poems, Mörike strove to overcome the dualisms and demons
in himself and in the world, in the quest of classic calm. He has a
spiritual affinity with John Keats who also achieved a fusion of the
Classical and Romantic worlds.

In the poem 'Um Mitternacht' (1827), Mörike attained Classical
harmony on the basic Romantic theme of night and day, death and
life, a harmony symbolized by the balanced scales:

> Ihr Auge sieht die goldne Waage nun
> Der Zeit in gleichen Schalen stille ruhn.

The poem achieves simultaneously an effect of unity and contrast by
the division into two equal stanzas, each of which consists of two
parts rhythmically different, one of restful, regular iambs and the
other a lively, hopping and skipping mixture of iambs and anapaests.

'Auf eine Lampe' (1846) shows Mörike closest to Classical serenity
and perfection of form, using the stately trimeter of Greek tragedy.
The poem is constructed symmetrically of three parts of three lines
each and a single concluding line which reads: 'Was aber schön ist,
selig scheint es in ihm selbst'.[1] Keats's 'Ode on a Grecian Urn' –
despite difference in length and verse (Keats uses an elegiac stanza) –
ends on a similar note:

> 'Beauty is truth, truth beauty', – that is all
> Ye know on earth, and all ye need to know.

Both poems share the elegiac lament for a lost golden age of beauty
and harmony, evoked by the object contemplated. Mörike begins:

'Noch unverrückt, o schöne Lampe . . .', while Keats's opening lines read:

> Thou still unravish'd bride of quietness,
> Thou foster-child of Silence and slow Time
>
> . . .
>
> Heard melodies are sweet, but those unheard
> Are sweeter.

The poem 'Denk es, O Seele' with which Mörike concludes his best-known *Novelle, Mozart auf der Reise nach Prag* (1855), presents striking images of death (black horses) in the midst of life which is but a flash in the vast night of eternity.

'Am Rheinfall' (1846) conveys the danger of the thundering masses of water threatening to obliterate the puny human figure. As the poem proceeds, the poet (and with him the reader) transcends the peril to revel in plunging movement – the waves now appearing as Apollo's steeds. Then in the last two lines he is overwhelmed again by *Angst* – this time not produced by external physical forces but from the seething id within. Yet all this power and dynamic energy is contained, not as one might expect in free rhythms, but in the rigid confines of the Classical hexameter distich. Through art the poet has mastered and imposed form on both external and internal chaos.

Most of Mörike's poetry was composed before his marriage in 1851. His domestic infelicity and divorce a dozen years later coincided with renewed productivity. One of these late poems has been analysed and eulogized by W. F. Taraba[2] who defines the theme as 'experience of death' in epistolary form: 'Erinna an Sappho'. The free verse in which it is composed suggests dissolution and death, while within the free rhythms are embedded snatches of classic forms and metres, including the distich and the Sapphic ode. In a certain formal sense, it is therefore the opposite of 'Am Rheinfall'.

The serious tone of the poems mentioned so far applies to only part of Mörike's diverse output. He wrote many gay poems celebrating *Wanderlust*, continuing this Romantic theme but giving it a more realistic imprint, recording nature as it is: 'Septembermorgen', 'Fußreise', 'Jägerlied', 'Auf einer Wanderung'. The famous ballad 'Schön Rohtraut' was composed in the garden at Cleversulzbach as the poet meditated on the strange and mellifluous name which he had chanced upon in his reading and which stimulated him to invent the story. Although the ballad treats the potentially tragic theme of love which cannot be consummated because of difference of social status, the story is conveyed in a resigned but buoyant and cheerful mood. On occasion Mörike went further in displaying an earthy sense of humour in such poems as 'Scherz' and 'Häusliche Szene'. The latter shows a side of Mörike which links him with the *Bieder-*

meier of other Swabian poets, with *Heimatkunst*, and with Poetic Realism.

II. AUGUST VON PLATEN (1796–1835)

August Graf von Platen-Hallermünde had the misfortune to be born in an age when the social function of the aristocrat was becoming highly problematic, especially if unsupported by property, office, or money. Conscious of being an outsider, he strove to carve a niche for himself through poetry. He worked assiduously at the drama and achieved at least greater success than Heine in this genre – although his plays are book-dramas rather than stage-pieces. *Die verhängnis-volle Gabel* (1826) was a witty satire on the popular fate tragedies. In *Der romantische Oedipus* (1829), Platen gaily parodied what he took to be Immermann's Romanticism. He knew only the latter's *Cardenio und Celinde*.

From 1810 until 1814 Platen was a page at the Royal Bavarian court and then an officer, but without experience at the front and with no understanding for the niceties of garrison life. King Maximilian I of Bavaria protected him, giving him constantly renewed leave from military duty, while he studied for sixteen semesters successively law, philosophy, and science in Würzburg and in Erlangen (where he revered his teacher Schelling). During this time he acquired some knowledge of a dozen languages, but never completed any of the academic studies which he had embraced. His diaries reveal his struggle with his homosexuality, which reinforced his sense of re-jection by society and drove him into a nomadic existence in Italy where he died, worn beyond his years, in Syracuse.

Platen's importance as a lyric poet is sometimes underrated, possibly because of the Romantic stress on subjective feeling which tends to dominate this genre in German literature. In an age which tended to equate lyric poetry with *Erlebnis*, Platen reasserted the claims of *Gedankenlyrik*, in which coincidence of form and content combine to give a pregnancy and universality and even an extra dimension to the thought expressed. It is sometimes forgotten that Goethe made *Gedankenlyrik* respectable with his epigrams and his *Gott und Welt* philosophical poems. Platen's connections are back-wards to the Enlightenment (Lessing and Pope) and forward to Conrad Ferdinand Meyer, Stefan George, and Rilke. His search for chiselled, formal perfection in verse became a model for George.

Platen, the poet of formal perfection, has another little-known side: in the *Polenlieder* of 1831 and the *Briefwechsel zwischen einem Berliner und einem Deutschen* (both held up by censorship and pub-lished posthumously in 1839) he shows himself to be as radical as

Heine. The *Briefwechsel* presents reactionary Prussian attitudes in the *Berliner* which are countered by the liberal *Deutscher*. Two stanzas from his *Berliner Nationallied* may illustrate his radical verse:

> Zehnmalhunderttausend Knuten
> Hau'n im Notfall tüchtig ein,
> Und Europa wird verbluten,
> Wird unendlich ruhig sein!

> Untertänigkeit erwarte
> Jeder Herrscher wie der Zar,
> Ausgenommen Bonaparte
> Weil er nicht von Adel war.

Although noted for the cultivation of Classical and exotic forms, *terza rima*, ghazals etc., Platen is pre-eminent in the sonnet. His pessimism and despair as expressed in sonnet 68 ('Wer wußte je das Leben recht zu fassen?') seem close to Schopenhauer's philosophy of the Will: yet it is highly unlikely that the latter's *Die Welt als Wille und Vorstellung* (1819) had come to the poet's attention, for the philosophy of pessimism had to wait for a later generation. It is probably a case of the *Zeitgeist* manifesting itself independently. The sestet reads:

> Denn jeder hofft doch, daß das Glück ihm lache,
> Allein das Glück, wenn's wirklich kommt, ertragen,
> Ist keines Menschen, wäre Gottes Sache.

> Auch kommt sie nie, wir wünschen bloß und wagen:
> Dem Schläfer fällt es nimmermehr vom Dache,
> Und auch der Läufer wird es nicht erjagen.

In his intuitive self-identification with decay, decadence, and death, Platen anticipated Thomas Mann's preoccupation with the relationship of art, decadence, and death. Platen's famous lines

> Wer die Schönheit angeschaut mit Augen,
> Ist dem Tode schon anheimgegeben,
> Wird für keinen Dienst auf Erden taugen

could serve as a motto for *Der Tod in Venedig*. Platen's Venice had been conquered by Napoleon and its Republican Lions of St Mark (trophies from Constantinople) carried to Paris. Although the lions were restored to St Mark's Square, the republic was not restored. Instead Venice was ceded to Austria by the Congress of Vienna and the lagoon-city sank still further into decay and corruption. Not until Cavour and Napoleon III drove Austria out of Lombardy in 1859 and Bismarck drove Austria out of Germany in 1866, did Austria give up her Venetian province which then entered the new kingdom of Italy. The fourth of Platen's *Sonette aus Venedig* (1825) expresses his awareness of Venice's ghostly prolongation of life – a city moribund if not dead:

Venedig liegt nur noch im Land der Träume
Und wirft nur Schatten her aus alten Tagen,
Es liegt der Leu der Republik erschlagen,
Und öde feiern seines Kerkers Räume.

Die ehrnen Hengste, die, durch salz'ge Schäume
Dahergeschleppt, auf jener Kirche ragen,
Nicht mehr dieselben sind sie, ach, sie tragen
Des korsikan'schen Überwinders Zäume.

Wo ist das Volk von Königen geblieben,
Das diese Marmorhäuser durfte bauen,
Die nun verfallen und gemach zerstieben?

Nur selten finden auf der Enkel Brauen
Der Ahnen große Züge sich geschrieben,
An Dogengräbern in den Stein gehauen.

The Venetian sonnets represent his finest achievement in form and content, but unforgettable among his ballads is the portrait of Charles V, abdicating to end his days as a simple monk, in the poem entitled 'Der Pilgrim vor St. Just' which ends with the couplet:

Nun bin ich vor dem Tod den Toten gleich
Und fall' in Trümmer wie das alte Reich.

Despite his veneration of antiquity, Platen gives a curiously sympathetic picture – no doubt because it celebrates death in the midst of life – of Alarich the Goth, who sacked Rome and then died at the age of thirty-four and was buried, according to legend, in the bottom of the Busento River which had to be diverted for the purpose ('Das Grab im Busento'). Platen was inspired, as was Goethe, by Hammer-Purgstall's translations from the Persian Hafiz and he published two slim volumes entitled *Ghaselen* (1821, 1824). Platen's lyrical output was not great in quantity but rich in quality, especially in formal perfection. He obviously anticipated the mid-century movement of aestheticism, *l'art pour l'art*, and of Poetic Realism; and he left a legacy of identification of decadence and beauty.

III. ANNETTE VON DROSTE-HÜLSHOFF (1797–1848)

'Die Droste', as she is called, Germany's greatest nineteenth-century poetess, like Platen of noble birth, was depicted by earlier biographers as having led an idyllic, protected life in the seclusion of her family's country estate in Westphalia or on Lake Constance. This security seemed symbolized by the Catholic faith by which she lived and died. But we now know that she clung to her religion as a last desperate defence in a world in which she anticipated the existentialist *Angst* of modern man. Even her later 'geistliche Lieder' (*Das geistliche Jahr*, 1840) are strewn with melancholy doubts and questioning of faith itself.

Unattractive in appearance, composed of a curious compound of masculine and feminine traits, Annette found in her art, as well as her religion, an outlet for the fear, despair, and frustration of life. She was also unusually short-sighted and it has been suggested that this had a twofold effect in her poetry: the precise observation and description of close detail on the one hand and the vaguely disturbing undefined contours of more distant objects on the other.

She was educated to a degree exceptional for women of her epoch, partly by the blind Münster professor, Christoph Bernhard Schlüter. She studied half a dozen languages, history, mathematics, science, and music. In her own literature she was drawn more to Klopstock, Matthisson, Hölty, and the Hainbund-poets than to the more recent Classical and Romantic writers, but her vision was enlarged by knowledge of Shakespeare, Percy's *Reliques of Ancient English Poetry* (1765), Scott, and Byron.

From 1826, after her father's death, she led an even lonelier life on her mother's country estate in Westphalia, interrupted only by occasional travels and by sojourns on Lake Constance. When nearly forty, she experienced the most searing passion of her life – without at first being conscious of the perilous shift from maternal to erotic feeling for her ward and protégé, Levin Schücking. The pain of this love and of the final parting was responsible for some of her most moving poems, such as 'Durchwachte Nacht' or the opening stanza of 'Am Turme' (1841), which surprises by the fierceness of the passion:

> Ich steh' auf hohem Balkone am Turm,
> Umstrichen vom schreienden Stare,
> Und lass' gleich einer Mänade den Sturm
> Mir wühlen im flatternden Haare;
> O wilder Geselle, o toller Fant,
> Ich möchte dich kräftig umschlingen
> Und, Sehne an Sehne, zwei Schritte vom Rand
> Auf Tod und Leben dann ringen!

One is struck not only by the depth of passion but by the masculinity of its expression, and the poem ends on a note of lament for the restrictions then imposed upon ladies:

> Wär' ich ein Mann doch mindestens nur,
> So würde der Himmel mir raten;
> Nun muß ich sitzen so fein und klar,
> Gleich einem artigen Kinde,
> Und darf nur heimlich lösen mein Haar
> Und lassen es flattern im Winde!

When Schücking married in 1844, Annette addressed to the couple the moving poem 'Lebt wohl':

> Lebt wohl, es kann nicht anders sein!
> Spannt flatternd eure Segel aus,
> Laßt mich in meinem Schloß allein,
> Im öden geisterhaften Haus.
>
> Lebt wohl und nehmt mein Herz mit euch
> Und meinen letzten Sonnenstrahl;
> Er scheide, scheide nur sogleich,
> Denn scheiden muß er doch einmal!

The poem goes on to strive for solace in nature, in religion, and in art, but the reader feels, nevertheless, how desperate this attempted sublimation is:

> Verlassen aber einsam nicht,
> Erschüttert, aber nicht zerdrückt,
> Solange noch das heil'ge Licht
> Auf mich mit Liebesaugen blickt.
>
> . . .
> Solange noch der Arm sich frei
> Und waltend mir zum Äther streckt,
> Und jedes wilden Geiers Schrei
> In mir die wilde Muse weckt.

The poem 'Feuer' may be compared with Mörike's 'Der Feuer-reiter'. Both personify the destructive and demonic power of fire. Whereas Mörike's ballad rises to a crescendo of demonic fury only to subside and end on a note of harmony, Droste's poem ends with fire castigating the human race represented by the blacksmith:

> O, hätt' ich dich, o könnte ich
> Mit meinen Klauen fassen dich!
> Ich lehrte dich den Unterschied
> Von dir zu Elementes Zier,
> An deinem morschen, staub'gen Glied,
> Du ruchlos Menschentier!

The poem 'Der Heidemann' (a personification of the autumn and spring mists on the moors) combines acutely realistic descriptions of foreground objects with their threatened obliteration by the approach of the demonic 'Heidemann'. Her nature poems of the heath are deemed masterpieces, combining realistic depiction of the desolate north German plain with impressionistic, sometimes demonic undercurrents. Her *Heidebilder* are in the same vein as the later realistic ones of Storm and the impressionistic pictures of Liliencron.

IV. NIKOLAUS LENAU (1802–50)

Droste's *Heidebilder* also link her with Lenau, whose moors were the Hungarian puszta where he roamed in his boyhood. Like Droste, Lenau was the progeny of aristocrats and was born near Temesvar in Hungary. His real name was Nikolaus Niembsch Edler von Strehlenau and he inherited – perhaps from his profligate father who died when the poet was a child – a neurotic strain which led to a final mental collapse in 1845.

The family had come from Silesia and after his father's early death, Lenau's mother was left to bring up her only son in poverty. She doted on him and spoiled him. When she at last allowed him to leave her, a rich grandfather in Vienna supported him at university – in Vienna, Pressburg (Bratislava), and Heidelberg. Lenau studied in turn law, agriculture, medicine, but gave up his academic career when a small legacy from his grandmother enabled him to live for poetry, which he had begun to write at the age of nineteen. He had met Grillparzer and Anastasius Grün in Vienna, and some of the Swabian poets (Uhland, Schwab) in excursions from Heidelberg. Through his contacts with the Swabians he met and fell in love with Charlotte Gmelin. But he shrank from marriage, writing to his friend Schwab: 'Ich habe nicht den Mut, diese himmlische Rose an mein nächtliches Herz zu haften'. The engagement was broken off in 1832, but this hopeless love inspired some of his greatest poetry: 'Mein Stern', 'Waldgang', 'Scheideblick', and above all the *Schilflieder* for which he is best known. Here Lenau is closest to the Romantics with the theme of ill-starred love reflected empathetically in nature: night, stars, sadly murmuring water, and rustling reeds. The *Schilflieder* remind us of Heine's early Romantic *Lieder*, except that Lenau is desperately sincere, while Heine frequently wore a mask to mock what he regarded as stale Romantic poses. Lenau's poems prove that in the hands of a genius giving deepest expression to himself no form need be *passé*. Hermann Hesse's adolescent protagonists in the novel *Unterm Rad* read Lenau's *Schilflieder* aloud, as they lie in the reeds near the pond in which a schoolmate had recently drowned himself. Despite the unifying theme of mourning for lost love which links the poems, the moors are reflected in varying moods and metres, now storm-tossed:

> Durch den Himmel wild
> Jagen Blitze, bleich;
> Ihr vergänglich Bild
> Wandelt durch den Teich.

At other times the moors are motionless:

Auf dem Teich, dem regungslosen,
Weilt des Mondes holder Glanz,
Flechtend seine bleichen Rosen
In des Schilfes grünen Kranz.

Hirsche wandeln dort am Hügel,
Blicken in die Nacht empor;
Manchmal regt sich das Geflügel
Träumerisch im tiefen Rohr.

Weinend muß mein Blick sich senken,
Durch die tiefste Seele geht
Mir ein süßes Deingedenken,
Wie ein stilles Nachtgebet.

Years before, as a student in Vienna, Lenau had had a liaison
with a poor girl who bore a child. Lenau suspected that he was not
the father, but the affair had left its mark upon him.[3] Now with the
breaking of his engagement to Charlotte, Lenau determined to go to
America,[4] not to settle there as was the aim of most *europamüde*
émigrés, but to gather new experience for poetry, for which he
thought five years might suffice. The poems written in America are
not all inspired by local scenes. 'Der Postillon' is European in background and is one of his best-known poems, leaving the reader in
uneasy doubt about the answer to the postilion's horn saluting his
dead comrade in the grave. Two Niagara poems hinge on suicide.
'Das Blockhaus' ends with inevitable death. The poems written at
sea, grouped under the collective title *Atlantica*, are good but represent no advance on Heine's North Sea cycles. The projected five
years in America shrank to eight months and when Lenau landed
at Bremen, he found himself famous, for the poems published on
the eve of his departure (1832) had met with sensational success.

Lenau continued his nomadic existence. In Vienna he fell in love
with the wife of a friend, Sophie Löwenthal, and in 1839 he was on
the point of marrying the singer Karoline Unger.[5] In 1838 his *Neue
Gedichte* had appeared. The poems inspired by Sophie are masterpieces reflecting the deepening gloom now engulfing him: 'Der
schwere Abend', 'Traurige Wege', and 'Tod und Trennung'. His
Faust (1836, revised 1840) is one of three epic-lyric works reflecting
his own downward path through loss of faith (he had been born
Catholic) to utter pessimism and despair. For Lenau death was not a
Romantic release which was yearned for, as with Novalis. It was the
last terror of all. His pessimism might be termed Byronic, but it
would have been the same had Byron never existed. Moreover,
Byron's pessimism was a half-consciously worn cloak, in part a pose.
With Lenau it went to the core of his being and his *Weltschmerz*
seems strangely in tune with late twentieth-century trends. The
literary and psychological problem of his pessimism is enthralling,

and he is, of course, a great poet not because of the fascination of his pessimistic *Weltanschauung*, but because of his poetic power to mould this pessimism into poetic masterpieces. The pair of sonnets entitled 'Einsamkeit' I and II begins with the lines:

> Hast du schon je dich ganz allein gefunden
> Lieblos und ohne Gott auf einer Heide,

and this first sonnet continues with successive images of utter isolation and despair. The concluding sonnet follows:

> Der Wind ist fremd, du kannst ihn nicht umfassen,
> Der Stein ist tot, du wirst beim kalten, derben
> Umsonst um eine Trosteskunde werben,
> So fühlst du auch bei Rosen dich verlassen;
>
> Bald siehst du sie, dein ungewahr, erblassen,
> Beschäftigt nur mit ihrem eignen Sterben.
> Geh weiter: überall grüßt dich Verderben
> In der Geschöpfe langen, dunklen Gassen;
>
> Siehst hier und dort sie aus den Hütten schauen,
> Dann schlagen sie vor dir die Fenster zu,
> Die Hütten stürzen, und du fühlst ein Grauen.
>
> Lieblos und ohne Gott! Der Weg ist schaurig,
> Der Zugwind in den Gassen kalt; und du? –
> Die ganze Welt ist zum Verzweifeln traurig.

The way in which phrases and images of the first sonnet are woven into the second and intensified may be glimpsed by the partial repetition and variation of line 2 of the first; 'Lieblos und ohne Gott auf einer Heide' becomes in line 12 of the second: 'Lieblos und ohne Gott! Der Weg ist schaurig'. It is the path to obliteration in loneliness and despair. Human beings are reduced to 'creatures' (*Geschöpfe*) whose paths through life are 'lange, dunkle Gassen' leading to death. The 'thou' addressed evaporates with a vague question and seems to allude to the poet himself rather than to any other human being in this bleak abstract landscape. 'Überall grüßt dich Verderben' prefigures Baudelaire and Trakl. To the contemporary reader it may seem strange to find the theme of dissolution treated within the rigid form of the sonnet. 'Die Hütten stürzen' may remind us of similar phrases – 'Dachdecker stürzen ab und gehn entzwei ... Die Eisenbahnen fallen von den Brücken' – in Jakob van Hoddis's poem 'Weltende' (1911), widely regarded by critics as the first Expressionist poem, since it makes maximum use of disjointed, unrelated images to reinforce the dissolution theme. Yet the structural sonnet form by its contrast with the theme may enhance the impact. Wolfdietrich Rasch, on the other hand, has pointed to the limp last line, suggesting that the poet gave up the struggle and succumbed to the overwhelming forces of dissolution and decay which had evoked.[6] In 1845, six years later, madness overtook the poet and he died in an asylum near Vienna in 1850.

V. MINOR POETS OF THE PERIOD

Anastasius Grün (1806–76) was the pseudonym of Anton Alexander Graf Auersperg. This scion of high Austrian nobility was a friend of Lenau and an aristocrat of advanced liberal views, especially in the collection *Spaziergänge eines Wiener Poeten* (1831). Metternich's police uncovered the author of the anonymous volume and Graf Auersperg was confronted with the choice of siding with the prejudices and privileges of his class or making his own way as a professional and revolutionary writer. He chose neither, but a typical Austrian compromise: he married within his class and moderated the tone of subsequent publications. His political idealism had blinded him to the dangers inherent in liberal nationalism for the Habsburg state which he basically supported. His poems are now mostly forgotten and were epigonal in form, derived from models such as Byron, Platen, Wilhelm Müller, and Uhland.

Friedrich Hebbel (1813–63) is not so lightly disposed of, and there are still critics who rate his poetry highly. As one would expect from his dramas, his poetry is mostly of a highly cerebral, conscious, controlled nature – in a certain sense *Gedankenlyrik* even where intended as *Gefühlslyrik*. This places him close to Platen and comparison with the latter shows how forced and constrained Hebbel's verse is. Undoubtedly a few of Hebbel's poems deserve the place which they still hold in many anthologies. The best of them are, ironically, nature poems and poems in which genuine feeling predominates: 'Abendlied', 'Waldbilder', 'Sommerbild'; and several familiar ballads: 'Der Heideknabe' and 'Das Kind am Brunnen'. In the nineteenth century Hebbel's stature as a lyric poet was much higher – perhaps because his contemporaries either liked, or were unconscious of, the epigonal character of most of his verse which was deliberately modelled on Schiller, Matthisson, Uhland, and Goethe.

It is difficult to do justice to Friedrich Rückert (1788–1866), who lived too long and wrote too much. Had he died or ceased writing earlier, he could be classified with the late Romantics, as he often is. The best poems look back with longing at the joys of youth and continue to show the influence of *Des Knaben Wunderhorn*. His first book of poems appeared in 1814 (*Deutsche Gedichte*), the second in 1817 (*Kranz der Zeit*), and by 1838 he had published his *Gesammelte Gedichte* in six volumes.

Outwardly idyllic and bourgeois, his life was fraught with tensions. For a soul so conscious of middle-class duties and diligence, it
was a wrench to shift careers from law to classical philology and
finally to oriental studies. Unable to establish himself as *Dozent*, he
could not resolve to become a schoolmaster, and when he finally
received a chair, he felt his professional duties a burden. He tried
diligently to compete in all poetic forms. In 1839 he anticipated
Matthew Arnold by publishing *Rotem und Suhrab*, a narrative
poem based on an episode from Firdusi's *Shah-Nama*. His translations and *Nachdichtungen* (e.g., *Nal und Damajanti* (1828) from the
Mahabharata) are notable achievements. Typical of his bourgeois
background is the careful preservation of every verse he wrote, so
that some genuine lyric gems tend to be buried under the mass of
diligently constructed academic verse in the twelve volumes of
Gesammelte poetische Werke (1867–69).

It was an age of many diligent rhymesters of high and low estate,
and it is interesting to conjecture the responsibility of Goethe, *der
Dichterfürst*, for stimulating emulation from high and low. His
grandson Wolfgang von Goethe (1820–53) vacillated between an
inferiority complex and pride in his inherited name. His own
Gedichte (1851) appeared under the name Goethe writ large and
without other name or initial. Many poets whose original talents
were limited became worthy translators. Alongside the pedantic,
hard-working bourgeois Rückert, one may mention King John of
Saxony (1801–73), who published under the pseudonym Philalethes
an esteemed iambic translation of Dante's *Divina Commedia* (1839–
1848), a worthy competitor of Karl Streckfuß's translation in *terza
rima* (1824–26).

The political poets – *Das junge Deutschland* – have been mentioned in their ambivalent relations with Heine (above, pp. 57f.). One
of them, especially by comparison with others such as Herwegh and
Dingelstedt, was a poet first, before he became a politician. Ferdinand
Freiligrath (1810–76) brought to German poetry a spectacular splash
of colour in exotic settings which he often combined with brutal
realism (*Schauerpoesie*). He also gave new life to long-discredited
forms such as the alexandrine by using them to create new and
startling effects. His conversion to politics occurred suddenly in 1844 –
perhaps instigated by a visit from Hoffmann von Fallersleben, author
of the words of 'Deutschland über alles' (1841) – when Freiligrath
renounced the pension which had been conferred on him two years
earlier by Frederick William IV. The converted evangelist outdid
others in zeal – and he was a better poet too. *Glaubensbekenntnis*
(1844) and *Ça ira* (1846) did their part in preparing the Revolution
of 1848, but the title of the last volume proved a false prophecy.

NOTES

1. There is possibility of ambiguity owing to the two meanings of *scheinen*: to seem or to shine. Emil Staiger used 'seem' to advance the interpretation that Mörike was a latecomer, an epigone who could only surmise at the essence of life and art, whereas Goethe saw 'die ewige Zier' without being haunted by knowledge of its frailty. This interpretation was at once disputed in 1951 by many, including Martin Heidegger who read *scheinen* to mean 'give off light'. It is also possible that Mörike was conscious of Schiller's doctrine of 'schöner Schein' and he might well have remembered Goethe's line in *Faust* II: 'Die Schöne bleibt sich selber selig'. For a résumé see Ilse Appelbaum, 'Zu Mörikes Gedicht "Auf eine Lampe" ', *MLN*, LXVIII (1953), 328–33.

2. Benno von Wiese (ed.), *Die deutsche Lyrik*, II, Düsseldorf, 1956, 98–102.

3. This affair might be a literary link with Musil's *Tonka*, not because the situation is unusual, for Musil had experienced it himself. What is uncommon and shared by both is the psychological depth of the soul-searching induced in the artist.

4. There may be a literary motivation and connection here. The runaway Moravian monk Karl Postl began to publish his novels and descriptive works in German and English under the pseudonym Charles Sealsfield. His *Die Vereinigten Staaten von Nordamerika* was published by Cotta in 1828 – and a Swabian friend had persuaded Cotta to publish Lenau.

5. Contralto soloist in the first performance of Beethoven's Ninth Symphony in May 1824. At the conclusion, Beethoven, stone-deaf and with his back to the audience, was unaware of the tumultuous applause. Karoline took his hand and turned him round to face the audience.

6. In von Wiese (ed.), *Die deutsche Lyrik*, II, 150–8.

Chapter 6

LIBERAL FAILURE – JUNKER SUCCESS: 1848–90

1. THE REVOLUTION OF 1848

THE FALL OF LOUIS-PHILIPPE in February 1848 provided the spark for revolution in Berlin and Vienna. In Berlin on 18 March the troops had the situation in hand and could have ended the local disturbances at once, if Frederick William IV had not shrunk from shedding more Prussian blood. He ordered the troops to be withdrawn to barracks and the next day made a public appearance swathed in black, red, and gold, proclaiming: 'Henceforth Prussia merges in Germany'. What happened was the opposite: if the king of Prussia surrendered to the Revolution in March 1848, the Revolution surrendered to Frederick William·thirteen months later, and within twenty years the Junker Bismarck was to create the *klein-deutsch* united Empire which, in effect, merged Germany (less Austria) into Prussia.

In Vienna the situation was more serious and the central government confronted nationalist rebellions in Bohemia, Italy, Croatia, and Hungary. Metternich went into exile in England. But military force ultimately prevailed in Vienna, for General Windischgrätz, after subduing Prague, had an army at his disposal. The new central government was under Bach, a pre-March radical won over to the cause of a centralized and reformed Austrian Empire. This ministry, supported by a majority of the Austrian parliament, was determined to rescind the concessions made to Hungary in the early months of the Revolution and to reduce Hungary from an independent state to a province of the Empire. The success of this plan would be as much a defeat for German as for Magyar nationalism, for it was unthinkable that Hungary could be incorporated into a German national state. Early in October the radicals in Vienna tried to prevent the sending of troops to Hungary and on the 6th a second revolution broke out in the capital. The army of Windischgrätz bombarded and entered the city on 6 November. The emperor Ferdinand abdicated in favour of his nephew Francis Joseph (aged eighteen and destined to reign until his death in 1916) and a new ministry was formed under Felix Schwarzenberg, an able but cynical advocate of military power. Hungary was conquered in the summer of

1849 with Russian help (Heine's poem 'Im Oktober 1849' echoes the revulsion felt by German liberal-nationalists).

Meanwhile, in Frankfurt the *Vorparlament* of April had given way to the elected National Assembly which convened on 18 May 1848. There were 831 delegates, but only about 500 took an active part in the sessions in the Paulskirche. The composition shows the burgher bias: 49 university professors, 57 high-school teachers, 157 magistrates, 66 lawyers, 20 mayors, 118 higher officials, 18 doctors, 33 clergymen (divided almost equally between Protestant and Catholic churches) – all told 569 with higher academic training. Of the 116 who admitted to no profession, a few were nobles but far more were bankers, merchants, industrialists. None had experience at the national level, but many had been active in state legislatures. When this assembly's efforts failed, it became fashionable to pour scorn upon them (cf. Heine's poem 'Die Wahlesel'). It is now possible to admire and sympathize with these men of goodwill, knowledgeable, skilled in debate, and imbued with dogged persistence to persevere against odds which were insuperable, for power was in the hands of the Hohenzollerns and the Habsburgs. The liberal archduke Johann of Austria was elected regent of the administration which almost at once had to deal with the Danish proclamation incorporating into Denmark the duchies of Schleswig-Holstein (held by the Danish crown). The local German population revolted and called for help. The Frankfurt administration declared war on Denmark and then looked for troops. Prussia responded, but would not allow Prussian troops to take an oath of allegiance to Archduke Johann. Moreover, Prussia was not anxious to conquer Schleswig-Holstein in the interest of Frankfurt; therefore an early peace was concluded which was unsatisfactory to both parties. In addition, the Prussian force had been defeated in battle by the Danes.

In view of their status in society, it is not surprising that the overwhelming majority of the assembly were monarchists. The crucial division was between *kleindeutsch*, i.e., in favour of a united Germany without Austria (which meant Prussian hegemony), and *groß-deutsch*, who, in turn, were divided between those wishing to include all Habsburg territories and those who would admit only the German portions. The Austrian government fiercely resisted any partition of this sort. Many south Germans and many Catholics of the Rhineland favoured one or other of the *großdeutsch* solutions. Finally, in April 1849, by a narrow margin the assembly voted to invite the king of Prussia to become emperor of the Germans. Frederick William IV declined a crown proffered by democratic hands and not by princes. There was nothing for the remaining delegates to do but to disperse, leaving a vacuum at the centre.

II. ASCENDANCY OF AUSTRIA 1850–62

Despite widespread dislike of Austrian and Russian intervention in Hungary in 1849, the prestige of Austria in Germany reached its peak during the 1850s. The Austrian ministers Bach, Schwarzenberg, and Bruck unified the Austrian state and embarked on a twofold ambitious plan: to save the German communities of eastern and south-eastern Europe by extension of power in the Balkans and simultaneously to revive the German Confederation of 1815 and incorporate all Austria in it. The result would be no conservative Austro-Prussian balance and partnership, but instead Germany dominated by the Austrian Empire and the Austrian Empire run by Germans.

Prussia had taken advantage of Austrian preoccupation in Hungary in 1849 to force the German princes into a defensive alliance: the Erfurt Union. In the autumn of 1850 the elector of Hesse-Cassel, a member of the union, was at odds with his subjects. Prussia prepared to intervene. Austria's Schwarzenberg declared the *Bund* revived and induced the Federal Diet to entrust intervention to Bavaria. Prussian and Bavarian troops met in Hesse and the Austrian army was moved into Bohemia under Radetzky, the victor in two Italian campaigns. Schwarzenberg would have liked war, in order to settle with Prussia once and for all. But Francis Joseph was reluctant to fight a fellow monarch. He met Frederick William IV at Olmütz, where Prussia renounced the Erfurt Union and accepted the reactivated *Bund*.

Early in 1851 Schwarzenberg convened a meeting of German princes in Dresden and proposed inclusion of all Austria in the *Bund* and in the *Zollverein*. The German princes defeated the proposal, as they were no more anxious for Austrian than for Prussian domination.

Despite the diplomatic setback sustained in the Crimean War (1854–56) and the unsatisfactory result of the war with Piedmont and France in 1859 (in which she lost Lombardy), Austria, with her liberal parliament of 1861, enjoyed growing prestige in Germany. This reached its high-water mark with the meeting of German princes convened by Francis Joseph in Frankfurt in 1863, where he proposed a strengthening of the federal authority, involving the voluntary relinquishment of some of their powers by the princes. Bismarck's refusal to allow King William to attend heralded the failure of Francis Joseph's grandiose scheme and the beginning of Bismarck's steps to force Austria out of Germany and Prussia upon Germany.

III. BISMARCK AND PRUSSIA

Even the three-tiered electoral system in Prussia produced a legislature which refused to vote the increased army budget desired by William I (brother of Frederick William IV, regent from 1858, and king from 1861). The Minister of War, von Roon, and the Chief of the General Staff, Moltke, advised the king to invite Bismarck to form a ministry, as a last resort. Bismarck collected taxes and spent the money on the army, using the subterfuge of an existing constitutional *Lücke* in which the executive had to take interim measures. It is doubtful if he could have continued for long on this basis. But he moved swiftly to take advantage of events, first manoeuvring the reopened Schleswig-Holstein question in such a way that Prussia and Austria jointly defeated Denmark in 1864 (thus gratifying national sentiment throughout Germany). Then Bismarck would agree to no final satisfactory disposition of the two duchies, so that war with Austria was provoked in 1866. The German Confederation almost entirely supported Austria (except for some north German states at the mercy of Prussia). Taylor claims that Bismarck never aimed at uniting all Germans in a single national state and that Bismarck himself in retrospect and his eulogizers combined to create the myth of Bismarck the unifier.[1] There is no doubt an element of truth in this. Bismarck aimed primarily at glorifying the Hohenzollern dynasty and his Junker class. But in the process, he gave the Germans what seemed to them a *kleindeutsch* national state, but was in reality a prostrate Germany under Prussia.

Thus after the Six Weeks' War ended with the defeat of Austria at Königgrätz (Sadowa), Bismarck imposed gentle terms upon Austria, while he treated harshly those German allies of Austria whose territory stood in the way of Prussian power: the annexation of Hanover and Hesse-Cassel made Prussian territory continuous from the Belgian-French border to the Baltic at Memel. Also among the spoils were both the twin duchies of Schleswig-Holstein. In addition Hesse-Nassau and Frankfurt were annexed (the latter in pique against the Habsburg predilections of this free city). The few remaining states north of the Main entered into the north German confederation with Prussia.

France was alarmed at the growing power on her northern border and Bismarck worked on French fear, using the candidacy of a collateral Hohenzollern prince for the Spanish throne, in order to provoke France into declaring war first – which he did by editing and giving to the press the Ems telegram. The south German states rallied to the 'defence' of Germany and the Prussian armies speedily disposed of the French. In January 1871 at Versailles, the king of Prussia was proclaimed *Deutscher Kaiser*.

IV. *Die Gründerjahre*

The winning of Germany by Prussia altered the balance of power not only in Germany but in Europe. We are not concerned here with Bismarck's diplomacy in the concert of Europe. Within Germany his position was, at first, almost unassailable. He had proved that 'Macht geht vor Recht'. By sheer force he had brought together disparate elements into a system dominated by Prussian Junkers. The Reich consisted of twenty-five states (and the Imperial domain of Alsace-Lorraine), but of 397 seats in the Reichstag, Prussia elected 236. However, as we have seen, Prussia herself was a conglomerate of diverse components. In the nineteen years of Bismarck's chancellor-ship, he had increasingly to resort to various expedients, playing off Ruhr capitalists against agrarian Junkers, liberals and social demo-crats against the ultramontane Catholic Centre party.

Bismarck was wise enough to wish not to become involved in over-seas adventures, foreseeing that colonies would become economic and military liabilities. He knew that the strength of his Prussianized Germany derived from her central position as a land-based power in Europe.[2] It was partly as a result of his internal political difficul-ties that he attempted to divert attention and win popular support by reluctantly participating in the partition of Africa and by annex-ing the Bismarck Archipelago and the Marshalls in the Pacific. After Bismarck's retirement, German influence in the far east was extended by annexation of the Marianas, the Carolines and a portion of the Samoas and by a foothold in China (Tsingtao). The African colonies, Togo, the Camerouns, German South West Africa and German East Africa (1884–85), outstripped the Portuguese who had been estab-lished in Angola and Mozambique for nearly five centuries. The German colonial regimes, like the Dutch, brought law and order and efficient administration.[3]

The Age of Bismarck and of the Prussian triumph finally found an artist of genius in Fontane. But no one can read these late novels without discerning the atmosphere of irony, decadence, and scep-ticism which gives these works their peculiar charm. Fontane was aware that the 'Founding Years' were wrapped in funeral shrouds. Of course only a few, like the wise old Fontane, were aware of the obsolescence of Bismarck's Junkers. One of Fontane's Junker char-acters exclaims: 'Wir wirken nur noch wie Eulen bei Tageslicht'.

The decay of the social and political order on which the Reich was founded was concealed by the accelerated tempo in commerce and industry which preoccupied most people. Conrad Ferdinand Meyer, a Swiss, was a genuine admirer of Bismarck and the Prussian achievement, but this played little part in his sensitive Symbolist poetry and received only oblique reflection in his historical novels and *Novellen.* Nietzsche, who spent almost all his mature life in Switzerland, regarded Bismarck's Germany with vitriolic scorn and scepticism.

V. PHILOSOPHICAL CURRENTS

In the 1850s and 1860s the materialist philosophy of Ludwig Feuerbach (1804–72) and Ludwig Büchner (1834–99) corresponded in a general way to the materialist outlook fostered by accelerating commerce and industry. Haeckel's and Ostwald's materialism was disguised by the dignified title of Monism. Faith in science tended to replace religious or philosophical ideals. Helmholtz, Kirchhoff, Hertz, Röntgen, Max Planck, and, in the following generation, Albert Einstein, contributed to man's knowledge and control of his physical environment. As early as 1872, however, Emil du Bois-Reymond gave his famous lecture 'On the Limits of the Knowledge of Nature' ending with an *ignorabimus* in the face of the ultimate source of life and being. This coincided approximately with counter-materialist trends centred on neo-Kantian and neo-Hegelian revivals. Neither the materialist philosophies nor the material conditions of life were conducive either to religious revival or to new advances in idealistic philosophy.

The scientific method was increasingly applied to history and Treitschke was followed by Leopold Ranke whose historicism also focused on the state. Theodor Mommsen (1817–1903) brought to his history of Rome the nineteenth-century scientific spirit based on evidence, especially archaeological. (The award of the Nobel Prize for Literature to Mommsen in 1902 may have been an indirect tribute to his fellow 'Schleswiger' and lifelong friend Theodor Storm, but the award to a historian created a precedent for Winston Churchill.) There was one historian – and philosopher of history – a Swiss 'outsider', whose influence on philosophical and historical thought was profound: Jacob Burckhardt (1818–97), whose massive studies of Greece and of the Renaissance in Italy shifted the centre of interest from politics to culture and society. Still more influential, in the next age, was Burckhardt's *Weltgeschichtliche Betrachtungen* (published posthumously 1905), which probed historical crises and diagnosed the malaise of western Europe. It is quite probable that Nietzsche knew the ideas of the *Betrachtungen* (which formed the substance of Burckhardt's lectures) when they were both professors in Basel in the 1870s and on intimate terms. The prevailing materialism and scientific positivism had another counter-current in the growing influence of Schopenhauer.

VI. ARTHUR SCHOPENHAUER (1788–1860)

Schopenhauer was born in Danzig. His merchant father's early death left his widow and son independently wealthy and the family moved to Weimar where Frau Schopenhauer conducted a literary salon and wrote second-rate novels. Arthur quarrelled violently with his mother whose literary pretensions he scorned.

His *magnum opus*, *Die Welt als Wille und Vorstellung*, first published in 1819, remained unnoticed until a new edition with a second volume of exegesis appeared in 1844 and at once began to exert growing influence. It is a strange compound of idealist and materialist elements: idealist in banishing all the 'real' world to transient imperfect individualizations cast off by the Will which is the *Ding-an-sich*; materialist (and scientific) in the wealth of biological, psychological, and empirical data with which the system is illustrated and buttressed. The *Wille zum Leben* is a blind force acting in all organic and inorganic nature. Man is never satisfied, for the achievement of one aim involves simultaneously a shift to another desire. In this doctrine one can glimpse incipient ingredients not only of Nietzsche but of Freud's libido and Bergson's *élan vital*. The pessimist finds in Schopenhauer confirmation of the worthlessness of all effort – and this aspect found an echo in many after the failure of liberal-national aspirations in 1848–49. More important for art and literature was the aesthetic theory: release from the relentless drive of the Will through artistic or intellectual creativity (on the highest level) or through contemplation of works of beauty (on a lower level). The affinity with Kant's aesthetic doctrine of disinterestedness is evident.

Schopenhauer's relationship to Idealism is apparent from the debt owed to Plato and to Kant. But Hindu and Buddhist ideas also found direct and indirect expression in his work, reminding us of the profound impact of the East on Goethe, Platen, Rückert, and many Romantics. The most important Asiatic ingredients in Schopenhauer are resignation and contemplation. The real world is an illusion; ultimate reality (Schopenhauer's 'Will') is concealed from us behind the veil of Maya. We are dupes, for life in this world is full only of vain deceits and lies. We have the choice only between perpetual frustrated striving and absolute boredom in this worst of all possible worlds.

Wagner was enthralled by Schopenhauer's doctrine of the Will and his aesthetic theory. He was immediately aware of the sexuality in the driving Will and he composed *Tristan und Isolde* (1859) under the immediate impact of Schopenhauer.

The original date of publication, 1819, reminds us that Schopenhauer shares with Hegel the honour of being one of the last to erect a complete philosophical structure. Despite the fact that Schopenhauer erected his system in conscious opposition to Hegelianism, the two sometimes seem close. Hegel declared that Nature is 'das Aus-sich-heraustreten der Idee, daher nicht Freiheit, sondern Notwendigkeit und Zufälligkeit', and this seems almost a statement of Schopenhauer's individuation. Both are dynamic, but Hegel's dynamism operates through the dialectic, Schopenhauer's through the unremitting drive of the Will. Hegel's tendency is Western-oriented, activist, and optimistic; Schopenhauer's is Eastern-oriented, quietist, and pessimistic.

Schopenhauer's influence continued among Symbolist and *fin-de-siècle* poets of the 1880s and 1890s and found definitive expression in Thomas Mann's *Buddenbrooks*.

NOTES

1. op. cit., 102.

2. Karl Haushofer in the 1930s expounded his geopolitical theories proclaiming the primacy of the land-based power of Eurasia – theories which led Hitler to assume that by conquering Russia he would control the world, without laboriously building a colonial empire.

3. German colonialism in Africa, lasting barely thirty years, left little legacy. It is therefore in the nature of a curious footnote to history to observe that Adolf Friedrich, duke of Mecklenburg (1873–1969), the last German Governor of Togo (1912–14) was fêted by the Togolese on revisiting the former colony half a century later!

Chapter 7

FRIEDRICH NIETZSCHE:
PHILOSOPHER AND POET

LIKE SCHOPENHAUER before him, Nietzsche (1844–1900) was long disregarded by his contemporaries, but since all his works were composed before his mental collapse (medical evidence points to tertiary syphilis) in 1889, they fall into our period. Like Schopenhauer, but in even higher degree, Nietzsche was not only a philosopher but a literary genius. Unlike Schopenhauer, Nietzsche developed, after his first book, a fragmentary style, analogous to his unsystematic thought, and the aphorism or capsule comment became his favourite mode of expression. One could even claim that paradox – deliberate contradiction – was utilized by Nietzsche as both a literary device and as an instrument to provoke the intellect (a kind of pre-Brechtian *Verfremdungstechnik*). Any attempt to claim Nietzsche for a particular ideology is to do violence to his genius and his integrity (as the Nazis did).

Nietzsche began as a disciple of Schopenhauer and of Burckhardt. Eventually Nietzsche turned the tables on Schopenhauer, making out of the latter's world-denying pessimism a world-affirming glorification of action, of life itself. The Will – the life-force – in Schopenhauer was something abhorrent to be denied by de-individuation and return to the original oneness, or to be temporarily suspended by release through art or contemplation. Nietzsche saw as the essence of all life the Will to power. Especially in his acute analysis of the motivation of the creative artist, Nietzsche felt he had tripped up Schopenhauer:

> Sie [die Kunst] ist ihm [Schopenhauer] die Erlösung vom 'Willen' auf Augenblicke – sie lockt zur Erlösung für immer ... Insbesondere preist er sie als Erlöserin vom 'Brennpunkte des Willens', von der Geschlechtlichkeit, – in der Schönheit sieht er den Zeugetrieb *verneint* ... Wunderlicher Heiliger! Irgend jemand widerspricht dir, ich fürchte, es ist die Natur. *Wozu* gibt es überhaupt Schönheit in Ton, Farbe, Duft, rhythmischer Bewegung in der Natur? was *treibt* die Schönheit heraus? – Glücklicherweise widerspricht ihm auch ein Philosoph. Keine geringere Autorität als die des göttlichen Plato (– so nennt ihn Schopenhauer selbst) hält einen andern Satz aufrecht: daß alle Schönheit zur Zeugung reize, – daß dies gerade das proprium ihrer Wirkung sei, vom Sinnlichsten bis hinauf ins Geistigste ...[1]

84

Whereas Schopenhauer's aesthetic doctrine seems related to Kant's 'disinterestedness', by rising above or shutting out the drive of the Will, Nietzsche's acute perception is already an anticipation of Freud's sublimated libido: displaced sexual energy drives to creative expression. Thus Nietzsche's artists are not withdrawn saints but prime expositors of the life-affirming Will to power.

This relatively late insight was foreshadowed in Nietzsche's first book: *Die Geburt der Tragödie aus dem Geiste der Musik* (1871), in which Nietzsche gave an entirely new interpretation of the highest achievements of the Greeks. He saw twin drives: Apollonian and Dionysian. The Dionysian is the underground, irrational, intuitive (and basically sexual) drive to creation in music and tragedy. Nietzsche's interpretation of the Greeks was scorned in his time and later vindicated by scholars. Some readers of Nietzsche failed to note that in his interpretation the greatness of the Greeks resulted from the interplay of *both* Apollonian and Dionysian elements and depended on the rational (Apollonian) power to impose form on chaos. Here is perhaps a link with the Hegelian dialectic. It was at this time that Nietzsche's hopes for regaining the tragic mythical world centred on Wagner's music dramas. Many elements later combined to turn the admiring Nietzsche into Wagner's most devastating critic, but his ire was directed mainly at Wagner's glorification of Christian humility and saintliness in *Parsifal* (1877).

In his *Unzeitgemäße Betrachtungen* (1873–76) Nietzsche excoriated the smug assumption that the military victory of Prussianized Germany over France implies any superiority of German culture:

Vieles Wissen und Gelernthaben ist aber weder ein notwendiges Mittel der Kultur, noch ein Zeichen derselben und verträgt sich nötigenfalls auf das beste mit dem Gegensatze der Kultur, der Barbarei, das heißt: der Stillosigkeit oder dem chaotischen Durcheinander aller Stile.[2]

The aristocratic bias in Nietzsche's thinking now comes to the fore. Mediocrity seems more apt to survive than 'the single higher specimens'.[3] Hence Darwinian natural selection will not generate bigger and better philosophers, artists, or saints, but only bigger and better brutes. A key problem Nietzsche never solved is: who decides what is a 'higher specimen'. This work also contains his reckoning with Schopenhauer and ends with a glorification of *Richard Wagner in Bayreuth*. In 1876 began his disillusionment with Wagner, and in 1879, partly owing to deteriorating health, he resigned his chair of classical philology in Basel (to which he had been called at the age of twenty-five). Henceforth Sils Maria in the Oberengadin became his favourite mountain retreat.

In *Menschliches, Allzumenschliches* (1878–80), dedicated to Voltaire, Nietzsche hailed science and reason, and began the 'Umwertung aller Werte', replacing the concepts 'good' and 'evil' with 'beneficial' and 'harmful' (to life and the Will to power). *Morgenröte* (1881), as the title indicates, heralds the dawn of a new system of values, replacing the 'harmful' ethics of Christianity. *Die fröhliche Wissenschaft* (1881–86) glorifies the Dionysian principle, but as Kaufmann rightly points out,[4] the use of the term 'Dionysian' has undergone change since *Die Geburt der Tragödie*, where it was glorified in balance with 'Apollonian'. Now it stands for the thinker who does not retire into Schopenhauerian passivity, but participates directly in life.

Ironically, Nietzsche was by now almost completely isolated and ignored, except by a handful of admiring friends (including Peter Gast, the musician, and Overbeck who later collaborated with Frau Förster-Nietzsche in 'editing' her brother's works). Nietzsche's personal isolation finds poignant expression in one of his most moving poems:

Vereinsamt

Die Krähen schrein
Und ziehen schwirren Flugs zur Stadt:
Bald wird es schnein. –
Wohl dem, der jetzt noch – Heimat hat!

Nun stehst du starr,
Schaust rückwärts, ach! wie lange schon!
Was bist du Narr
Vor Winters in die Welt entflohn?

Die Welt – ein Tor
Zu tausend Wüsten stumm und kalt!
Wer das verlor,
Was du verlorst, macht nirgends halt.

Nun stehst du bleich,
Zur Winter-Wanderschaft verflucht,
Dem Rauche gleich,
Der stets nach kältern Himmeln sucht.

Flieg, Vogel, schnarr
Dein Lied im Wüstenvogel-Ton! –
Versteck, du Narr,
Dein blutend Herz in Eis und Hohn!

Die Krähen schrein
Und ziehen schwirren Flugs zur Stadt:
Bald wird es schnein. –
Weh dem, der keine Heimat hat!

Images, vowel coloration, and rhythm combine to reinforce the lament which comes from the depths of the poet's soul: the loss of 'Heimat' and exposure to the desolate wastes of space and time in utter isolation. The Romantic myth of nature-empathy is exploded:

the crows seek the warmth of the city whereas the poet takes a contrary course: 'versteckt sein blutend Herz in Eis und Hohn'. The black feathers of the crows conjure up associations of death, transience, loneliness, and pain.[5] The apparent dialogue makes all the greater impact because it is obviously self-communing. Bold word formations – 'schwirr' as an adjective, 'Wüstenvogel-Ton', 'Winter-Wanderschaft' – are striking, but most striking of all is the variation in the near-repetition of the first stanza at the end: 'Wohl dem, der jetzt noch – Heimat hat' becomes 'Weh dem, der keine Heimat hat!' This final contrast is prepared for by the brutal juxtapositions, vowel shifts, and images in the second last stanza: 'Flieg, Vogel, schnarr/ Dein Lied im Wüstenvogel-Ton!' The last line drives home the theme with an overwhelming impact. It may be true that much of Nietzsche's poetry is strained, but there are gems such as this – and the poem 'Venedig' – which figure in most anthologies.

Nietzsche's poetry may be considered in the following ways: (1) that it is derivative in form and of secondary quality and importance; (2) that it is significant only in relation to his philosophy or expository prose; (3) that it is not altogether derivative, is of high quality, and must be interpreted independently. The last view seems to be gaining ground.

'Vereinsamt' (1884) used the conventional rhyming quatrains – but with some startling new effects. More characteristic of Nietzsche's poetry is his use of the unrhymed free rhythms or 'ode' which was also not new, of course, having been handed down from Klopstock through Goethe and Hölderlin to Heine (in his North Sea cycles). When Nietzsche's odes are compared, say with Heine's, certain differences may be observed: a discontinuity of imagery and syntax which may place Nietzsche among the precursors of Impressionism and Expressionism. The poem 'Venedig' illustrates the impressionistic touch:

> An der Brücke stand
> jüngst ich in brauner Nacht.
> Fernher kam Gesang:
> goldener Tropfen quoll's
> über die zitternde Fläche weg.
> Gondeln, Lichter, Musik –
> trunken schwamm's in die Dämm'rung hinaus ...
> Meine Seele, ein Saitenspiel,
> sang sich, unsichtbar berührt,
> heimlich ein Gondellied dazu,
> zitternd vor bunter Seligkeit.
> – Hörte jemand ihr zu? ...

A few bold touches of darkness and light and a snatch of a gondolier's song in the distance – but what is quivering at the end of the poem is not the water or rays of light or the music, but the poet's heart.

The last line concludes with a gentle but more poignant allusion to his loneliness than 'Vereinsamt'.

Nietzsche's best-known – and perhaps his best – poetry consists of the nine 'Dionysos-Dithyramben' which previously were printed at the end of *Also sprach Zarathustra* and were ascribed to Zarathustra, whereas it is, of course, Nietzsche speaking with his own poetic persona. Schlechta has done a service in his edition by separating the two works. It may be claimed that all nine dithyrambs must be read and interpreted as a whole. If we do this, we find that there is a central theme: the poet and his position in the world. We are next struck by the wide divergence in tone and imagery from one poem to the next, corresponding to the moods of ecstasy and despair evoked by the poet's fate. We may note that no. 6, 'Die Sonne sinkt', has a balance and gentleness lacking in the others. But Nietzsche's tortured soul could not end on this note and the final poem reflects in its title the thematic dichotomy of the whole cycle: 'Von der Armut der Reichsten'. An excerpt from the first dithyramb will serve as an example. Its theme is the poet and truth and it is treated with bitterness, staccato disconnected rhythms, broken expressions leaping across chasms from one image to another:

> 'Der Wahrheit Freier – du?' so höhnten sie –
> 'Nein! nur ein Dichter!
> ein Tier, ein listiges, raubendes, schleichendes,
> das lügen muß,
> das wissentlich, willentlich lügen muß,
> nach Beute lüstern,
> bunt verlarvt,
> sich selbst zur Larve,
> sich selbst zur Beute,
> *das* – der Wahrheit Freier? . . .
>
> Nur Narr! Nur Dichter!
> Nur Buntes redend,
> aus Narrenlarven bunt herausredend,
> herumsteigend auf lügnerisch Wortbrücken,
> auf Lügen-Regenbogen
> zwischen falschen Himmeln
> herumschweifend, herumschleichend –
> *nur* Narr! *nur* Dichter! . . .'

In his study of the 'Dionysos Dithyramben' W. D. Williams goes beyond the claim to rank Nietzsche as an important link with Impressionist and Expressionist poetry and suggests that here poetry is moving in a direction 'analogous to non-representational art', consisting of 'linguistic constructs which create a whole system of relationships which are not necessarily applicable to the real world'.[6]

Also sprach Zarathustra (1883–84) is Nietzsche's best-known work and in its way a prose masterpiece – or rather a poem in prose.

The underlying irony consists in the fact that Nietzsche uses his ecstatic colourful Biblical-prophetic language and imagery in order to attack Christian 'slave morality' and calls upon his followers (who did not exist – one of Nietzsche's last works is reported to have sold twenty-five copies in the first edition) to surmount the blows of fate, overcome all obstacles, to arrive at the future *Übermensch*. Despite – or because of – its poetic quality, this book is not the best introduction to Nietzsche's thought. Kaufmann argues with some force that the cruel, militaristic, 'blond beast'-vocabulary of Nietzsche in this work is symbolical and that Nietzsche was anything but a racist,[7] and of course Nietzsche's praise of the Jews must have been very embarrassing for the Nazis. Nevertheless, the life-affirmation of the *Übermensch* of the future is heralded in shrill tones and jarring images. The man of the future who creatively overcomes all previous prejudices and moralities is confronted in this work with another Nietzschean paradox: eternal recurrence. The clash between the drive to transcendence and eternal recurrence is yet another echo of the Hegelian dialectic.

Another dialectical or seeming paradox in Nietzsche's thinking is apparent in the relationship of sickness and health. His writings abound in references to *Krankheit* and *décadence* (like Heine, Nietzsche prefers the associations of certain French words such as *décadence*, which occurs much more frequently than *Entartung*). The physically incapacitated, the unstable neurotics, the outsiders act as stimulants to pevent a *Verdummung* – a stagnation – of a culture. Greek art and intellect flourished amid general prevalence of homo-eroticism, but Greek motherhood kept infusing new health in each generation, thus prolonging the period of Greek greatness. (Nietzsche was less a misogynist than Schopenhauer, but was far from conceding to women intellectual and artistic equality with males.) The caption of the following aphorism from *Menschliches, Allzumensch-liches* is characteristic of Nietzsche's use of paradox:

Veredelung durch Entartung

...Die abartenden Naturen sind überall da von höchster Bedeutung, wo ein Fortschritt erfolgen soll. Jedem Fortschritt im großen muß eine teilweise Schwächung vorhergehen. Die stärksten Naturen *halten* den Typus *fest*, die schwächeren helfen ihn fortbilden. – Etwas Ähnliches ergibt sich für den einzelnen Menschen; selten ist eine Entartung, eine Verstümmelung, selbst ein Laster und überhaupt eine körperliche oder sittliche Einbuße ohne einen Vorteil auf einer andern Seite.... Insofern scheint mir der berühmte Kampf ums Dasein nicht der einzige Gesichtspunkt zu sein, aus dem das Fortschreiten oder Stärkerwerden eines Menschen, einer Rasse erklärt werden kann. Vielmehr muß zweierlei zusammenkommen: einmal die Mehrung der stabilen Kraft durch Bindung der Geister im Glauben und Gemeingefühl; sodann die Möglichkeit, zu höheren Zielen zu gelangen, dadurch daß entartende Naturen, und infolge derselben, teilweise

Schwächungen und Verwundungen der stabilen Kraft vorkommen; gerade die schwächere Natur, als die zartere und feinere, macht alles Fortschreiten überhaupt möglich.[8]

In any case, Nietzsche declares, we cannot return to a *status quo ante*. Conservative or reactionary efforts are vain, we can only move further into decadence and hope that progress will result (a train of thought in Hesse's thinking in the 1920s, especially in *Der Steppenwolf*):

Trostrede eines desperaten Fortschritts

Unsere Zeit macht den Eindruck eines Interim-Zustandes; die alten Weltbetrachtungen, die alten Kulturen sind noch teilweise vorhanden, die neuen noch nicht sicher und gewohnheitsmäßig und daher ohne Geschlossenheit und Konsequenz. Es sieht aus, als ob alles chaotisch würde, das Alte verlorenginge, das Neue nichts tauge und immer schwächlicher werde.... Wir schwanken, aber es ist nötig, dadurch nicht ängstlich zu werden und das Neu-Errungene etwa preiszugeben. Überdies *können* wir nicht ins Alte zurück, wir *haben* die Schiffe verbrannt; es bleibt nur übrig, tapfer zu sein, mag nun dabei dies oder jenes herauskommen. – *Schreiten* wir nur *zu*, kommen wir nur von der Stelle! Vielleicht sieht sich unser Gebaren doch einmal wie *Fortschritt* an: wenn aber nicht, so mag Friedrichs des Großen Wort auch zu uns gesagt sein, und zwar zum Troste: 'Ah, mon cher Sulzer, vous ne connaissez pas assez cette race maudite, à laquelle nous appartenons'.[9]

Again in the *Nachlaß der Achtzigerjahre* we read Nietzsche's note:

Grundeinsicht über das Wesen der *décadence*: was man bisher als deren Ursachen angeschen hat, sind deren Folgen.
Damit verändert sich die ganze Perspektive *der moralischen Probleme.*
Der ganze Moral-Kampf gegen Laster, Luxus, Verbrechen, selbst Krankheit erscheint als Naivetät, als überflüssig:- es gibt keine 'Besserung' (gegen die Reue).
Die *décadence* selbst ist nichts, *was zu bekämpfen wäre*: sie ist absolut notwendig und jeder Zeit und jedem Volk eigen....[10]

The foregoing *aperçus* have, perhaps, more obvious relevance to the late twentieth than to the late nineteenth century. They have been quoted, partly to illustrate elements in Nietzsche's thinking which throw light on contemporary problems, and partly to indicate something of the background relationship of Nietzsche's twin concepts of sickness and decadence in Thomas Mann's works through which runs as leitmotiv the following reflection of Nietzsche's:

Es sind die Ausnahme-Zustände, die den Künstler bedingen: alle, die mit krankhaften Erscheinungen tief verwandt und verwachsen sind: so daß es nicht möglich scheint, Künstler zu sein und nicht krank zu sein'.[11]

The two masterpieces of his last phase are *Jenseits von Gut und Böse* and *Zur Genealogie der Moral* (both 1886). The often contradictory aphorisms render difficult or impossible any attempt at thematic summary. They should be read as *Streitschriften* (polemics) – the second is so called in its subtitle – as far-ranging, probing thrusts at the chinks in the armour of contemporary society and its underlying assumptions and values.

In *Der Fall Wagner, Nietzsche contra Wagner*, and *Götzendämmerung* (1888), Nietzsche pilloried Wagner as the false idol and continued to 'philosophize with the hammer' which he wielded in fierce *Kulturkritik*.

Nietzsche was ruthless in his criticism of German prose:

> Wenn man von Goethes Schriften absieht und namentlich von Goethes Unterhaltungen mit Eckermann, dem besten deutschen Buche, das es gibt: was bleibt eigentlich von der deutschen Prosa-Literatur übrig, das es verdiente, wieder und wieder gelesen zu werden? Lichtenbergs Aphorismen, das erste Buch von Jung-Stillings Lebensgeschichte, Adalbert Stifters Nachsommer und Gottfried Kellers Leute von Seldwyla, —und damit wird es einstweilen am Ende sein.[12]

As we have shown, Nietzsche's relationship to Schopenhauer is highly ambivalent. So is his later criticism of Wagner, who along with Schopenhauer is regarded as hostile to life. Schopenhauer is the ascetic aesthete, withdrawn from life, while Wagner is a licentious and false aesthete, catering to the masses. Wagner's style is 'Verzichtleistung auf Stil überhaupt. Was liegt an aller Erweiterung der Ausdrucksmittel, wenn das, *was* da ausdrückt, die Kunst selbst, für sich selbst das Gesetz verloren hat'.[13]

At the end of *Nietzsche contra Wagner*, something of the ambivalence of Nietzsche's relationship to Wagner is revealed. Nietzsche felt his hopes and aspirations and his friendship betrayed: 'Denn ich hatte niemanden gehabt als Richard Wagner'.[14] Wagner, since the summer of 1876, moved step by step into everything Nietzsche despised, such as nationalism and anti-semitism.

The rise of Wagner and the founding of the Wilhelmian Reich are linked:

> die Bühne Wagners hat nur eins nötig – *Germanen*! ... Definition des Germanen: Gehorsam und lange Beine ... Es ist voll tiefer Bedeutung, daß die Heraufkunft des 'Reichs' zusammenfällt: beide Tatsachen beweisen ein und dasselbe – Gehorsam und lange Beine. – Nie ist besser gehorcht, nie besser befohlen worden.[15]

To Nietzsche, Wagner and the Reich are two aspects of the same cultural phenomenon, namely decadence, the nature of which is concealed from the masses by apparent outward success: 'Richard Wagner, scheinbar der Siegreichste, in Wahrheit ein morsch gewordener verzweifelnder décadent...'[16] On the last page of this work one becomes aware of Nietzsche's savage criticism not only of Wagner but of the whole epoch which he symbolized:

Wie boshaft wir nunmehr dem großen Jahrmarkts-Bumbum zuhören, mit dem sich der 'gebildete' Mensch und Großstädter heute durch Kunst, Buch und Musik zu 'geistigen Genüssen', unter Mithilfe geistiger Getränke, notzüchtigen läßt! Wie uns jetzt der Theaterschrei der Leidenschaft in den Ohren wehtut, wie unserm Geschmacke der ganze romantische Aufruhr und Sinnen-Wirrwarr, den der gebildete Pöbel liebt ... fremd geworden ist!

No mention has been made of *Der Wille zur Macht*, which was long considered Nietzsche's most important book. Karl Schlechta finally proved beyond doubt in the 1950s that Nietzsche's sister had published this after Nietzsche's death, with an arrangement and even substance not of Nietzsche's making. This fraudulent book in Schlechta's edition has disappeared and the genuine fragments appear under 'Aus dem Nachlaß der Achtzigerjahre'.

In 1890 Nietzsche was virtually unknown. Ten years later, at his death in Weimar, carefully selected by his sister as the *Kulturstätte* of a Nietzsche-cult, he was already widely known and admired. Frau Förster-Nietzsche and her team of partly coerced editors cannot take all the credit for making Nietzsche famous in this decade. A Germanophile French outsider, André Gide, became Nietzsche's champion in the 1890s and was profoundly influenced by Nietzsche's *dicta:* 'Werde der du bist! Gefährlich leben!' Nietzsche would have appreciated the crowning irony of his career: that a Frenchman had to teach the philistines of Wilhelmian Germany that they had overlooked a phenomenon of signal importance in German life and letters. In his spiritual autobiography *Ecce Homo*, written on the eve of his insanity, Nietzsche had compared himself with that Franco-phile German, Heine:

Den höchsten Begriff vom Lyriker hat mir *Heinrich Heine* gegeben.... Und wie er das Deutsche handhabt! Man wird einmal sagen, daß Heine und ich bei weitem die ersten Artisten der deutschen Sprache gewesen sind – in einer unausrechenbaren Entfernung von allem, was bloße Deutsche mit ihr gemacht haben.[17]

It is obvious that Nietzsche did not regard himself as a 'mere German' but as a good European.

Nietzsche is still a force to be reckoned with in Western culture – and probably will be for some time to come. But whatever may be the final verdict on Nietzsche's ideas, he will forever remain among the giants of German literature. Indeed, the overwhelming power of his literary style makes him suspect to philosophers, especially in the English-speaking world.

NOTES

1. *Götzendämmerung: Streifzüge eines Unzeitgemäßen*, aphorism 22 (Karl Schlechta: *Friedrich Nietzsche*, Munich, 1966, II, 1003).

2. ibid., I, 140.

3. Burckhardt shared Nietzsche's fascination with historical greatness.

4. Walter Kaufmann, *Nietzsche: Philosopher, Psychologist, Antichrist*, 3rd ed., rev. and enlarged, New York, 1968, 129.

5. cf. F. N. Mannemeier in von Wiese, *Die deutsche Lyrik*, II, 245–54.

6. In A. Closs (ed.), *Reality and Creative Vision in German Lyrical Poetry*, London, 1963, 85–99.

7. op. cit., 358.

8. Schlechta, ed. cit., I, 583.

9. ibid., I, 598.

10. ibid., III, 820.

11. ibid., III, 715.

12. Schlechta, ed. cit., I, 921–2. It is odd that this is the only mention of Stifter by Nietzsche, whereas the other names occur fairly frequently. Ingeborg Beithan (*Friedrich Nietzsche als Umwerter der deutschen Literatur*, Heidelberg, 1933) cites in addition several references from letters including one to his friend, the composer Peter Gast: 'Sehr lieb ist mir zu hören, daß Sie Stifters Nachsommer nicht kennen; ich verspreche Ihnen etwas Reines und Gutes ... Ich selbst kenne ihn seit kurzem' (213). Beithan attributes much of the 'Umwertung' of Stifter to the single reference.

13. Schlechta, ed. cit., I, 836.

14. ibid., II, 1054.

15. ibid., II, 926.

16. ibid.

17. ibid., II, 1088–9.

Chapter 8

POETIC REALISTS IN PROSE

I. THE GERMAN NOVEL AND *Novelle*

As we have seen, bourgeois pragmatism and materialism are reflected in the preference for prose over verse in the writings of *Das junge Deutschland, Epigonen,* and *Heimatdichter.* Gotthelf had in both forms of prose fiction transcended limits of Regionalism and Annette von Droste-Hülshoff, Grillparzer, Mörike, and Otto Ludwig had each contributed a single master-*Novelle.* In the middle of the century the writers loosely linked in the 'school' of Poetic Realism – embodied in the triumvirate Stifter, Keller, Storm – made the *Novelle* the most representative literary form of the age.

As far as the novel is concerned we have no difficulty in recognizing it as such. But the German novel in the nineteenth century developed a pattern of its own: the *Bildungsroman,* founded on Goethe's *Wilhelm Meister,* the great Romantic novels *Heinrich von Ofterdingen, Franz Sternbalds Wanderungen,* and Mörike's *Maler Nolten.* Despite the popularity of Dickens, Scott, and Balzac in the German-speaking world, the German novel continued to focus upon the protagonist's inner development, until Fontane, at the end of the century, moved into the mainstream of European fiction, portraying society and social problems.

As the name indicates, the *Novelle* can be traced back to Boccaccio, but as developed in Germany it possesses characteristics quite different from the *Decamerone* and from the English-American short story or the French *nouvelle.* This development had hardly begun, before both practitioners of the art and critics attempted to define the genre. The earliest was the great Romantic theorist Friedrich Schlegel, but more influential were Goethe's model (entitled simply *Novelle*) and his famous comment to Eckermann (1827) that the *Novelle* was nothing but 'eine sich ereignete, unerhörte Begebenheit'. Tieck, in his post-Romantic phase, wrote a large number of *Novellen* and made his contribution to theory in insisting upon the turning-point (*Wendepunkt*).

There is perhaps something typically German, perhaps north German, in laying down rules and philosophizing on a literary genre. The Swiss Gottfried Keller, in a letter to Storm (14–16 August 1881), warned him not to bother Heyse (whose visit Storm expected) with

94

theoretical scruples about the *Novelle*, 'denn er muß auf Befehl der Ärzte alle Morgen und Abend eine halbe Flasche Portwein trinken, um seine Vernunft einzuschläfern'. Keller went on to say that, in his opinion, there can be no *a priori* theories for novel and *Novelle* – just as there are none for other genres – but that so-called rules are necessarily derived from characteristics of extant masterpieces. As a writer, one just does one's best.

Storm, however, who was north German and whose career depended more on the *Novelle*, as he wrote no novels, expressed his views to Keller, quoting a preface he had written and not published in 1881:

> ...die heutige Novelle ist die Schwester des Dramas und die strengste Form der Prosadichtung. Gleich dem Drama behandelt sie die tiefsten Probleme des Menschenlebens; gleich diesem verlangt sie zu ihrer Vollendung einen im Mittelpunkte stehenden Konflikt, von welchem aus das Ganze sich organisiert, und demzufolge die geschlossenste Form und die Ausscheidung alles Unwesentlichen ...[1]

Storm's points are well taken: affinity with drama, probing in depth of the human psyche, and a single central theme.

Paul Heyse (1830–1914), who wrote well over a hundred *Novellen* and was awarded the Nobel Prize in 1910, is now, ironically, more known for his theory of the *Novelle* than for his practice. His first major statement was in 1871 in the introduction to *Deutscher Novellenschatz* (edited jointly with Hermann Kurz) and he elaborated thirty years later in his autobiography:

> Denn von einer Novelle ... verlangen wir ... daß sie uns ein bedeutsames Menschenschicksal, einen seelischen, geistigen oder sittlichen Konflikt vorführe, uns durch einen nicht alltäglichen Vorgang eine neue Seite der Menschennatur offenbare. Daß dieser Fall in kleinem Rahmen energisch abgegrenzt ist ... macht den eigenartigen Reiz dieser Kunstform aus ... [dann muß man sich fragen,] ob die zu erzählende kleine Geschichte eine starke, deutliche Silhouette habe, deren Umriß, in wenigen Worten vorgetragen, schon einen charakteristischen Eindruck mache, wie der Inhalt jener Geschichte des *Decamerone* vom 'Falken' in fünf Zeilen berichtet sich dem Gedächtnis tief einprägt.[2]

In addition to the probing of human fate, Heyse points to another characteristic widely represented in Poetic Realism: the framework (*Rahmennovelle*), and he is above all identified with his Falcontheory. However much the latter element may be scorned today, it does mark the tendency towards Symbolism.

We must remember that alongside the *Novelle*, the tale (*Erzählung*) flourished, and that authors, in modesty, frequently published their stories as *Erzählungen*, leaving to readers, critics, or posterity to judge whether or not they were mere *Schriftsteller* or *Novellendichter*. The tale, the sketch, and the short story were destined largely to replace the *Novelle* in the twentieth century, but not before Thomas Mann, Hermann Hesse, Franz Kafka, and Günter Grass had proved that the *Novelle* is not only not dead but capable of new development, especially in psychological depth.

Length is not a reliable guide. A short story tends to have 3,000 to 4,000 words, a *Novelle* ten times as many. But Storm's *Späte Rosen* fills only a few pages while Tieck's *Der junge Tischlermeister* has over four hundred. Obviously *Novellen* can be shorter than short stories and longer than some novels. The organization around a central point and other characteristics are more determinative.[3]

II. ADALBERT STIFTER

The Austrian Stifter (1805–68) has primacy, at least chronologically, over his Swiss and north German rivals, Keller and Storm. His first stories were published (as *Erzählungen*) in various periodicals, beginning in 1840, before the theory and practice of the *Novelle* was far advanced. Stifter called them *Studien* when they appeared in book-form (1844–50), but many are ranked among the great *Novellen* of the century. One of the earliest, *Abdias* (1843), runs to over a hundred pages and depicts the whole ninety-year life of a North African Jew, but does so with concentration on the three women in his life: his mother, his wife, and his only daughter. It opens and closes with speculation on fate: is it *Schicksal*, *Zufall*, or *Fatum* which strikes twice as lightning and once in human guise when the emissary of the Bey of Tunis devastates Abdias's desert-home, leaving his wife dead and a new-born daughter in his arms? Tieck or Heyse might object that there are three turning-points instead of one, but many *Novellen* have more than a single *Wendepunkt*. His second great collection appeared under the title *Bunte Steine* (1853).

Stifter suffered a peculiar fate as an author. After his early successes, his later works were neglected both in his lifetime and subsequently by critics, until a Stifter-renaissance set in after the First World War. Wilhelmian criticism had not been kind nor, on the whole, just to Austrian writers. But the rediscovery of Stifter's greatness rested on several disparate grounds. The serenity and orderliness of Stifter's world exercised a fascination, partly nostalgic, upon the twentieth-century imagination preoccupied by the breakdown of political, social, and religious faith and order. On the other hand, the belated discovery was made that Stifter's world, beneath its surface calm, contained deep counter-currents of anxiety. These factors were combined (not necessarily consistently) with psychoanalytical probing related to his death by suicide, his first frustrated love, and subsequent unhappy marriage. There was no doubt a definite neurasthenic trait in his character, but his suicide has as little bearing on the structures of his imagination as Nietzsche's insanity has to do with his prior thinking. The evidence indicates that he was aware of the mortal nature of his illness (either cancer or cirrhosis of the liver).[4] His depression was deepened by brooding upon the defeat of Austria by Prussia in 1866. He had not been far from the scene of operations, at a Bohemian spa.

Stifter was born in the mountains between Upper Austria and Bohemia and in his years in the Kremsmünster Benedictine Gymnasium he was imbued with humanistic ideals of the Enlightenment. After attending the university in Vienna, he became *Hofmeister* in the household of Baroness Mink and was already (in private) busy writing. The Revolution of 1848 was a deep shock to his belief in organic, orderly (and conservative) growth. He fled to Linz, where he was appointed *Schulrat* in 1850 and for fifteen years worked assiduously at his official duties, labouring to improve education throughout the province for which he was responsible.

His *Novellen* – as well as his two novels – suffered, in the eyes of some critics, from the calm, leisurely pace and from the lengthy, detailed descriptions of nature. The delight in descriptive detail he shares with Keller, Storm, and Raabe and this may be regarded as the common denominator in Poetic Realism. The slow tempo and paucity of action drew the ire of Hebbel, whose temperament preferred violent, drastic action. Hebbel's criticism evoked a reply from Stifter in his famous *Vorwort zu den bunten Steinen*. For him the real subject-matter is not the doings of a person or group of persons who pass across the surface of nature, but nature itself – in its permanent states and in its gradual seasonal changes. For Stifter what is great in nature is permanent, enduring, undisturbed, and he continues:

> So wie es der äußeren Natur ist, so ist es auch in der inneren, in der des menschlichen Geschlechtes. Ein ganzes Leben voll Gerechtigkeit, Einfachheit, Bezwingung seiner selbst, Verstandesgemäßigkeit, Wirksamkeit in seinem Kreise, Bewunderung des Schönen, verbunden mit einem heiteren, gelassenen Sterben, halte ich für groß: mächtige Bewegungen des Gemütes, furchtbar einherrollenden Zorn, die Begier nach Rache, den entzündeten Geist, der nach Tätigkeit strebt, umreißt, ändert, zerstört und in der Erregung oft das eigene Leben hinwirft, halte ich nicht für größer, sondern für kleiner, da diese Dinge so gut nur Hervorbringungen einzelner und einseitiger Kräfte sind, wie Stürme, feuerspeiende Berge, Erdbeben. Wir wollen das sanfte Gesetz zu erblicken suchen, wodurch das menschliche Geschlecht geleitet wird.

'Das sanfte Gesetz' to which Stifter owed allegiance is well illustrated in *Bergkristall* (in *Bunte Steine*), in which the two small children lose their way in the high mountains on Christmas Eve in a snowstorm which descends with gentle stillness. In the vast expanse of ice and snow, the children are minute specks, cut off by the silent curtain of falling snow. They are, of course, in imminent danger of being lost forever and of freezing to death at night in the high altitude. This creates the anti-idyllic, subterranean vein of terror and suspense, as the gentle snow obliterates the world. At night the clouds disperse, revealing the starry beauty of the heavens, but the reader will be aware that the change of weather will entail a drastic drop in temperature threatening these young lives. But nature provides two forms of protection: shelter in the shape of ice-caves and rock-formations (containing the semi-precious stones of the title) and more important a fascinating spectacle of beauty in the northern lights which holds the children enthralled and prevents them from succumbing to the sleep of death. Moreover, the older brother looks after the little sister, doling out bread and coffee and keeping her awake. Nature in its manifold aspects plays the major role, but the mutual concern and helpfulness of the two tiny helpless humans symbolize for Stifter the ideal community. This becomes explicit when the parents and grandparents, representing separate and unfriendly communities, are united with all the inhabitants of both villages in the rescue of the children on Christmas Day.

Stifter was also a landscape-painter and his pictures have some bearing on his writings. In his paintings Stifter obviously preferred the gentle and serene aspects of nature, but a few scenes of violent moods or of stark and foreboding contrasts reflect the presence of the opposite pole. In 1950 his earliest story, *Julius*, was published for the first time. Autobiographical allusions reveal that the author is depicting the psychological tensions evoked by his enforced renunciation of Fanny Greipl. This may have been the turning-point from painting to poetry, for it was literature which provided the catharsis for the artist's tortured soul. At least one critic has wondered whether Stifter might not have become one of the great painters of the century if he had devoted himself exclusively to it.[5]

Most of Stifter's scenes are in Austria, especially in the *Böhmerwald* so familiar to him, and this is what we would expect of the Realist. When he occasionally describes in vivid detail natural environments of which he had no first-hand experience, Stifter may be thought of as inclining more to the 'poetic' than the 'realist'. Yet the scorching desert and the underground dwellings in the Roman ruins in North Africa in *Abdias* seem just as real to the reader as the Upper Austrian countryside in the latter part of the same *Novelle*. Nature has a major thematic and symbolic function and the vivid and realistic descriptions enhance this functional role.

The *Novelle Brigitta* (1844) is of special interest, both because it presents another example of 'realistic' description of a natural environment not directly known to Stifter, the Hungarian puszta, and also because it treats of the progressive aspirations of the Magyars. Western Hungary was familiar to Stifter – at least to the extent that it could be seen from the Danube steamer on his visit to his publisher Heckenast in Pesth. But for the east Hungarian puszta and the Carpathians in the background, Stifter depended on a growing number of sources in the 1820s and 1830s (including the poems of Lenau). As so often with Stifter, *Brigitta* is an *Ehegeschichte* with deeper symbolic meanings. One of these is the problem of recognizing true beauty. Major Stepan Murai[6] marries the land-owner, Brigitta, despite her outward unattractiveness. He then betrays her by succumbing to the external physical beauty of Gabriele and leaves wife and son, who go to live on Brigitta's estate, Maroshely, where Brigitta devotes herself tirelessly to improving conditions of life on the land. Murai spends years abroad and the volcanic activity of Vesuvius (also not witnessed by Stifter) symbolizes his inner turbulence. He returns to a neighbouring estate, Uwar, re-establishes a remote but friendly relationship with his estranged wife, gradually recognizes her inner spiritual beauty, and reinforces her efforts to expand the *Verein* for social, political, and economic progress. When the father rescues the son, Gustav, from wolves on the puszta, both parents are fully reunited – or more properly really united for the first time – over the bed of their recuperating son.

The puszta, as described by Stifter, is stony, scarred by gullies from rains, the habitat of wolves: inimical to man. Brigitta at Maroshely and Stepan Murai[7] at Uwar and other landowners who join their *Verein* improve upon this potentially hostile landscape. Through the portrayal of Hungarian conditions and aspirations and the relationship to the puszta, Stifter symbolizes the need for co-operation and constant effort to improve the conditions of life. The great amount of space devoted to the landscape is not back-ground but intrinsic to the story.

Among the long-neglected late *Novellen* are masterpieces, includ-ing the fascinating and elusive *Nachkommenschaften*. One possible interpretation suggests the autobiographical reflection that Stifter did the right thing in giving up painting, like Friedrich Roderer who tells his story in the first person. The difficulty with such a view is that Roderer does not destroy his paintings in order to write but in order to found a family. Here again a close study of the role of nature may lead to another interpretation. Friedrich is determined to capture in his painting the totality of the desolate moor whose vapours, in the popular imagination, contain mortal illness. He has to record this on canvas before the new owner's filling, clearing, and draining operations obliterate it. But this is the imposition of

healthy, rational control over potential peril and is therefore laud-
able. Friedrich destroys his completed picture and marries the
daughter of the moor-reclaimer. The interior tale – it has also
this element of the *Rahmennovelle* – gives the background of the
Roderers in such a way that Friedrich's problem is enhanced. Peter
Roderer, his future father-in-law, had been as passionately and
onesidedly devoted to literature in his youth, as Friedrich is to
painting. It is necessary for each Roderer to be true to himself
(in Nietzsche's words: 'werde der du bist'), but this also means to
be true to the basic characteristics of all Roderers. That both bride
and groom are Roderers reinforces the theme and points to domestic
felicity. Puzzling is the meaning to be attached to 'die wirkliche
Wirklichkeit' in the context of the turning-point when the moor-
clearing Roderer tells Friedrich that he will abandon painting
entirely (despite his admitted talent and success). Perhaps the ultimate reality in 1864 seemed to lie neither in painting nor poetry,
but in reclaiming and improving the real world around us, in finding
ourselves, in founding a happy marriage based on continuity between forbears and descendants. This and other late works have a
gentle irony and humour which was generally lacking in earlier
Novellen. Perhaps this extends to the relationship between the real
narrator (Stifter = 'founder') and the fictional narrator whose name,
Roderer, suggests 'up-rooter, land-clearer'.

Of Stifter's two novels, the first, *Der Nachsommer* (1857), is a
monument in the history of the *Bildungsroman*. Its monumental
size and slow pace are apt to deter readers, and this is a pity because
Stifter's art is capable of gripping the reader of any age, provided
the reader can shut out the surrounding world for a fortnight and
surrender to the spell of the real-ideal world in which the 'Bildung'
of Stifter's Heinrich is accomplished. There is some truth in the
charge that Stifter's *Bildungsroman* is epigonal in echoing Goethe's
Humanität[8] and even as regards the role played by the cultured
aristocracy: Baron Risach and Gräfin Mathilde. But Heinrich and
his merchant father are also independently wealthy and cultured
and are accepted naturally in Risach's milieu. The marriage between
Heinrich and Gräfin Mathilde's daughter, Natalie, seems entirely
fitting and natural.

Heinrich Drendorf is 'educated' through slow stages – analogous
to nature's 'gentle law' – and nature in all its aspects combines with
science and art in the educative process. The symbol of the rose
plays a central part: the love between Heinrich and Natalie grows
and unfolds gently like the opening buds covering Risach's 'Rosenhaus'.

'In the afternoon they came unto a land/In which it seemed
always afternoon' – the mature mellifluous perfection and stasis of

Tennyson's 'Lotus Eaters' suggests the Indian-summer atmosphere of Stifter's novel. But Tennyson's short poem is usually paired with his 'Ulysses', which embodies the opposite pole of constant restless striving:

> How dull it is to pause, to make an end,
> To rust unburnish'd, not to shine in use!
> As tho' to breathe were life!
> .   .   .
> One equal temper of heroic hearts,
> Made weak by time and fate, but strong in will
> To strive, to seek, to find, and not to yield.

At the beginning of *Faust*, the Lord in Heaven proclaims: 'Es irrt der Mensch, solang er strebt'. Stifter allows no mistakes to mar the perfectly guided unfolding of his hero Heinrich. Keller's 'grüner Heinrich', by contrast, arrives at his Indian-summer maturity after experiencing conflicts, errors, deaths, suffering, and guilt. The Goethean mantle generally bestowed on Stifter by critics is only partially valid. There is the shared Classical ideal of order and harmony and even a similarity in prose style, but conflicts seem to be excluded from the world of *Der Nachsommer*, although, as we have seen, there are palpable and powerful subterranean currents in other works of Stifter.

Worried by the Revolutions of 1848 and the aftermath which seemed to point to the break-up of the unity of the Habsburg domains, Stifter deliberately planned his novel to show what life could be and ought to be:

> Ich habe eine große einfache sittliche Kraft der elenden Verkommenheit gegenüber stellen wollen ... Ich habe ein tieferes und reicheres Leben als es gewöhnlich vorkommt, in diesem Werke zeichnen wollen und zwar in seiner Vollendung.[9]

Stifter is therefore from the beginning conscious of his aim, which is both didactic and utopian – or rather idyllic, for he placed the setting back some thirty years, before the recent revolution and before the impact of industrialization. Heinrich Drendorf's home is in the city, obviously Vienna, and he is constantly returning home. But the environment in which his 'Bildung' takes place is rural: either the unspoiled nature of his mountain journeys to acquire geological specimens, to survey, or to sketch, or else it is the perfectly planned and tended garden of Risach's exquisitely appointed 'Rosenhaus'.

The difference between Stifter's novel and Goethe's *Die Wahlverwandtschaften* is here revealed. Goethe's novel is electric with tensions and polar conflicts in which the garden plays a predominant symbolic role, but Goethe has two 'gardens': the formal one by the

'Stammschloß' tended lovingly by Charlotte and the rugged un-
shaped terrain surrounding the new 'Lustschloß' reflecting the
uncontrolled passion of Eduard for Ottilie. The phenomena of
nature are ambivalent in Goethe. In Stifter's novel the threatening
'Gewitter' which impels him to take refuge in the 'Rosenhaus'
never takes place. Destructive and disturbing forces seem to be
banished from this idyllic retreat.

Pascal states: 'There is not only no passion in the book; there is
no psychological probing'.[10] In a sense this is certainly true, especially in comparison with the *Bildungsromane* of Keller and Goethe.
And yet from the authorial perspective, Stifter is constantly shaping
and developing his protagonist. For example, Heinrich has passed in
Risach's 'Rosenhaus' countless times the statue on the marble stairs,
but without deeper awareness. One day ascending the stairs, he is
struck by its rare beauty illuminated by alternate shadows and
lightning flashes from the skylight. The point is that Stifter waits
until Heinrich is ripe for this aesthetic experience. The dialogue
which ensues between Baron Risach and Heinrich may serve also
as an example of the elevated conversational tone in this novel:

> 'Warum habt Ihr mir denn nicht gesagt', sprach ich weiter, 'daß die
> Bildsäule, welche auf Eurer Marmortreppe steht, so schön ist?'
> 'Wer hat es Euch denn jetzt gesagt?' fragte er.
> 'Ich habe es selber gesehen', antwortete ich.
> 'Nun, dann werdet Ihr es um so sicherer wissen und mit desto größerer
> Festigkeit glauben', erwiderte er, 'als wenn Euch jemand eine Behauptung
> darüber gesagt hätte'.
> 'Ich habe nämlich den Glauben, daß das Bildwerk sehr schön sei',
> antwortete ich, mich verbessernd.
> 'Ich teile mit Euch den Glauben, daß das Werk von großer Bedeutung
> sei', sagte er.
> 'Und warum habt Ihr denn nie zu mir darüber gesprochen?' fragte ich.
> 'Weil ich dachte, daß Ihr es nach einer bestimmten Zeit selber betrachten
> und für schön erachten werdet', antwortete er.
> 'Wenn Ihr mir es früher gesagt hättet, so hätte ich es früher gewußt',
> erwiderte ich.
> 'Jemanden sagen, daß etwas schön sei', antwortete er, 'heißt nicht
> immer, jemanden den Besitz der Schönheit geben. . . .'
>
> (II, 2)

Perhaps the modern educational psychology of 'doing' and
'finding out for oneself' is a little too obvious here. But on a deeper
psychological level, why had Heinrich lived with this 'Mädchenge-
stalt' for years without deeper awareness? Surely because in the
meanwhile he has met Natalie and love for her is germinating within
him with the organic slowness which marks the whole tempo of this
novel.

This incident leads Baron Risach to narrate at considerable
length how he had acquired the statue from an Italian estate

undergoing modernization. Only years later had he discovered that original Greek marble lay beneath the plaster-of-Paris exterior. The mystery of this covering is unaccountable, but the marble figure now gleams with its original freshness and glory. This is a lengthy anecdote with interesting details and sidelights. It is revealing, for example, that Risach, after the discovery of the marble beneath the gypsum, journeys to Italy to explain the circumstances and to pay the additional not inconsiderable extra sum demanded by the vendor – an example of candour and honesty rare among art-dealers in any age! The deeper import of the story must surely lie in the tentative suggestion that classical beauty can be regained and retained in our lives.

That Risach may be to some extent modelled on Wilhelm von Humboldt (1767–1835) seems first to have been recognized by Blackall.[11] Humboldt, the friend of Goethe and Schiller, upholder of the Classical 'Humanitätsideal' and of 'Ordnung', after a distinguished career as diplomat and minister, retired to cultivate his estate at Tegel, where he wrote *Briefe an eine Freundin* to Charlotte Diede, who published them in 1847. In his *Lesebuch* (1854), intended for use in the schools, Stifter included several passages from Humboldt's *Briefe*. This is yet another link with Classicism.

The hinge upon which the novel turns (and the title) is revealed only in the fifth chapter of the third and last book: 'Rückblick'. Risach now tells of the early springtime love between himself and Mathilde. We learn how their mutual affection had been too long concealed from the family (for Risach was then a man of humble circumstances engaged as tutor to Mathilde's brother), and how Risach had then, against Mathilde's wish, confided their love to her mother, who had demanded a lengthy separation. Several years later Mathilde had married Count Tarona and after his death had settled on the neighbouring estate, Sternenhof, with her daughter Natalie and her son Gustav. Risach had served his country for many years at home and abroad and had been ennobled. He had then retired to cultivate his estate, the Asperhof. Coming to visit him after so many years and to ask his pardon for rejecting him, Mathilde had known by the roses covering the façade that she was indeed forgiven. Risach had taken Gustav as his 'Pflegesohn' and for many years Risach and Mathilde have enjoyed a happy 'Indian summer' without any real summer preceding it.

Risach and Mathilde erred in their youth. The young people, Heinrich, Gustav, and Natalie, are to be spared false steps. This is the reason for the organic slow *Entwicklung* of the protagonist and for the painstaking pedagogic devices of his chief mentor Risach. So, if the reader has not, like Tennyson's lotus-eaters, 'swooned with the languid air', he will realize that there are errors and confusions and deeper psychological motivations in the book after all. But he may well complain that these significant elements of plot have been too long withheld.

J. P. Stern has raised further questions on Stifter's handling of this material, asking what the nature of the sin was which Risach spent his life expiating and which Heinrich is to avoid:

> Disobedience and breach of trust towards her parents? This is the burden of their accusation, this is what Risach feels guilty of. But Mathilde, when he told her of her parents' decision and of his readiness to give her up, had charged him with the opposite fault – with a lack of passion, and with timidity. It is with her that he broke faith (she tells him), it is their love he betrayed. And when, with the passage of intervening years, she grew contemptuous of him, it was not because he had shown too much passion but too little. Was he wrong in his weakness or she in her strength?[12]

Stern concludes that Stifter's intention was to show Risach's eventual triumph in this life after his weakness revealed by the retrospective *Novelle* of the rupture between himself and Natalie: 'What we are once more left with is Stifter's strange and relentless *will* to harmony and perfection, a will that shrinks from self-knowledge and replaces the true consequences of an experience by a made-up world'.[13] Stern admits that for most critics, including Emil Staiger,[14] Stifter's intention and realization are one. Stern goes so far as to wonder 'whether Nietzsche can have had Stifter in mind after all, whether he of all readers could have failed to notice the signs of the magnificent contrivance'.[15]

Contrived or not, *Der Nachsommer* has magnificent qualities. How does such a work, constructed to such a degree on idyllic or utopian premises, fit into the category of Poetic Realism? While it is more poetic than realistic, the realism is there too in the precise and detailed descriptions of persons and especially things, both artifacts and natural objects, for nature and beauty (i.e., art) are the twin forces moulding character.

Despite the first-person narration, there is far less of Stifter himself in Heinrich or in Risach than there is of Keller in *Der grüne Heinrich*. Whereas 'green Henry's' attempt to become a painter proves to be a false step, Heinrich Drendorf's landscape-painting is one of the many positive steps in his organic 'Bildung'. Whereas Keller's protagonist finds ultimate fulfilment in 'Staatsdienst', Risach discovers, after years of service to the state, that his true inclination is artistic.

That *Der Nachsommer*, which strives to depict perfection, is itself imperfect is clear. Only Risach is portrayed as a fully rounded character. Heinrich's parents and his sister are silhouettes, and it seems likely that Stifter introduced them because the family is the bastion of order. In spite of its faults, it has been praised by such diverse critics as Hermann Hesse, Karl Kraus, and Ernst Bertram. The latter wrote: 'Wie ein unwahrscheinliches Eiland von Klarheit, Stille, naturhafter Einfalt, gütiger Strenge, seliger Ordnung, so liegt die Landschaft dieser Kunst da'.[16]

Stifter's second novel, *Witiko* (1865–67), aimed to do for the state what *Der Nachsommer* had done for the individual and the family. This 'Bohemian Iliad' is set in the twelfth century, but it was Stifter's intention thereby to obtain objectivity and perspective denied by later historical periods. The hero of the novel is really the people, ancestors of the Czechs, under their feudal overlord Witiko.

Thomas Mann claimed to be one of the few who had read *Witiko* to the end and assigned it with typical irony to the category 'Langweiligkeit höchster Art'.[17] Mann's letters and diaries reveal a lifelong preoccupation with Stifter. Recuperating after a pneumothorax in a Chicago hospital in 1946, Mann wrote:

> Außerdem beschäftigte Adalbert Stifter mich wieder einmal aufs angelegentlichste. Ich las seinen *Hagestolz* wieder, den *Abdias*, den *Kalkstein*, den ich 'unbeschreiblich eigenartig und voll stiller Gewagtheit' fand.... Man hat oft den Gegensatz hervorgekehrt zwischen Stifter's blutigselbstmörderischem Ende und der edlen Sanftmut seines Dichtertums. Seltener ist beobachtet worden, daß hinter der stillen, innigen Genauigkeit gerade seiner Naturbetrachtung eine Neigung zum Exzessiven, Elementar-Katastrophalen, Pathologischen wirksam ist, wie sie etwa in der unvergeßlichen Schilderung des Schneefalls im Bayerischen Wald, in der berühmten Dürre im *Heidedorf*, und in den vorhin genannten Stücken beängstigend zum Ausdruck kommt. Auch die Gewitter-Verwandtschaft des Mädchens im *Abdias*, ihr Anzüglichkeit für den Blitz, gehört in diesem unheimlichen Bereich. Wo fände man dergleichen bei Gottfried Keller? ... Stifter ist einer der merkwürdigsten, hintergründigsten, heimlich kühnsten und wunderlich packendsten Erzähler der Weltliteratur, kritisch viel zu wenig ergründet.[18]

Thomas Mann has intuitively seized upon the subterranean demonic elements in Stifter which struck responsive chords within him. Even in political and social attitudes, Stifter was far from reactionary, as has been sometimes claimed. He was very conscious of the accelerating tempo of change, as the words of Freiherr von Risach testify:

> Wie wird es sein, wenn wir mit der Schnelligkeit des Blitzes Nachrichten über die ganze Erde werden verbreiten können? ... Wie weit das geht, wie es werden, wie es enden wird, vermag ein irdischer Verstand nicht zu ergründen. Nur das scheint mir sicher, andere Zeiten werden ... kommen, wie sehr auch, was dem Geiste und dem Körper des Menschen als letzter Grund innewohnt, beharren mag.

III. GOTTFRIED KELLER

Keller (1819–90) is the greatest Swiss writer of the nineteenth century and the one who achieved the widest fame throughout the German-speaking world. He was a gifted poet, but his prose fiction is more significant. His realism is both robustly earthy and highly imaginative and is laced with hearty humour and sparkling irony.

The early death of his father, a master carpenter, left widow, son, and daughter in poverty, although Frau Keller came from a long-established burgher family. Charged as leader in a school escapade, Keller was expelled and left to educate himself – and ultimately countless others through his auto-biographical *Bildungsroman: Der grüne Heinrich*. He wasted years in the study of art, including nearly two years in Munich where he lived penuriously on the pittance his mother was able to send him. Unlike Stifter, who had talent and painted throughout his life, Keller was forced to the realization that he was a failure.

The following years at home in Zürich (1842–48) were the most difficult. He became actively associated with political radicals, and when they came to power in the mild Swiss reflection of the Revolution of 1848, Keller received a travelling scholarship. His *Gedichte* (1846) further justified the award. In Heidelberg he met and heard the famed professor of literature Hermann Hettner, but the major impact upon him was that of Ludwig Feuerbach, whose lectures were held in the Rathaus, for the atheist was not granted university space. The embracing of atheism and materialism can lead to pessimism or to optimism. The latter prevailed with Keller who, having decided that this life is all we have, determined to make the most of it.

There followed five years in Berlin, where he was at first supported by the renewed stipend and then by his mother's remittances and advances from the publisher Vieweg. He had gone to Berlin to become a dramatist and in this too he failed. Nevertheless, the years in Berlin – he called the Prussian capital his 'Korrektionsanstalt' – formed the basis of future success. Between 1853 and 1855 appeared his novel *Der grüne Heinrich* in four volumes and he returned to Zürich with his first *Novellen* which appeared in 1856: *Die Leute von Seldwyla*.

In 1861 Keller was quite unexpectedly appointed to the highest office in the canton: 'Erster Staatsschreiber'. Like Stifter, Keller devoted fifteen years to the meticulous execution of official duties. Even during this term of office two further collections of *Novellen* appeared: *Sieben Legenden* (1872) and volume II of *Die Leute von Seldwyla* (1874). Thwarted in his efforts to marry, Keller remained a bachelor and his embittered sister, Regula, kept house for him.

There is no doubt about Keller's affinity with Goethe: the striving for wholeness, for organic unity of polarities in his nature; Swiss citizen and cosmopolitan, painter and poet, human being and politician, artist and civil servant, atheist and believer (in human potential for good), idealist and realist, defeated in love but eulogizer of women. In view of the recognition which Keller has won throughout the German-speaking world, it is difficult to agree with Alker's denial of ultimate greatness:

> Doch durfte es Keller an letzter Größe fehlen: er hat die Zeitbefangenheit nicht ganz überwunden, er blieb neunzehntes Jahrhundert. Die weltanschauliche Grundlage seiner Persönlichkeit war rissig und schwankend; so wurde er frommer Atheist, politischer Privatmann, konservativer Demokrat, barscher Kulturträger und als Mensch ein prachtvolles, obschon schwieriges Phänomen.[19]

Alker's reasons for his verdict are all sound in themselves, but beg the larger question: is it possible for the individual to transcend the age in which he lives? For Goethe it *was* possible, but perhaps the peculiar concatenation of individual and environmental circumstances cannot recur to make this transcendence possible in every time and place. Certainly Keller was a child of his time, but one of the greatest and most representative – even in the fractured relationship between belief and disbelief.

Keller's *Novellen* are all *Rahmennovellen* – although in some the frame is loose and easily comes away. The two volumes of *Die Leute von Seldwyla* are linked by the fictitious but realistically portrayed Seldwyla: a compound of small-town characteristics, Swiss in a very definite sense, mid-nineteenth-century, and bourgeois, but yet with a wider universal link revealing the foibles and finer qualities universal in man.

Keller's method of composition is illustrated by one of his best-known *Novellen: Romeo und Julia auf dem Dorfe*. The theme came to Keller from a newspaper account of the finding of the drowned bodies of a young couple who had apparently spent the night on a hay-barge drifting downstream. The event occurred in Saxony, but Keller at once related it to Shakespeare and to the local Swiss landscape and character. Some of the worst aspects of the people of Seldwyla are revealed: the sly encroachment on the unclaimed field, the blind rage which brings both sets of parents to disaster, and the *Schadenfreude* of the local populace. This background makes the purity and poignancy of the love of the young couple stand out in relief. Despite the tragic theme and ending, Keller has some boisterous comic scenes in the central section. These are based primarily on the irrepressible *joie de vivre* of young Vrenchen, one of Keller's unforgettable female characters.

Kleider machen Leute is not darkened by a tragic ending; in fact the humour and irony reach a climax in the final paragraph, which states the conventional 'they lived happily ever after' in such an ironic and ambiguous way that we smile inwardly, wondering whether a couple who had ten children in as many years would find life so idyllic! *Kleider machen Leute* has a classical *Wendepunkt* when the framework Seldwylans appear at the Goldachers' party and execute the charades of 'clothes make the man' and 'man makes clothes', leaving Wenzel Strapinski unmasked. Keller took perhaps excessive pains to ensure that Strapinski was an innocent victim and not an intentional impostor. Keller may be criticized for overt didacticism and moralizing in this and other works. Underlying the plot is a deeper meaning: the overcoming of Romanticism. Nettchen develops under the shock of her lover's unmasking from a frivolous, spoiled, romantically inclined girl into a determined, hard-headed woman: 'Keine Romane mehr' she says to Strapinski as she takes him in tow to make a man of him. Much humour and irony in the second half arise from the inversion of the usual male-female relationship. There is in the first part much mockery of the solid citizens of Goldach who insist upon seeing in Strapinski an incognito count and in their bowing and scraping and heaping of favours upon him.

The twin but polar characteristics of poetic imagination and realistic description mark all the stages of Keller's writing. The first volume of *Die Leute von Seldwyla* contains alongside the basically realistic *Romeo und Julia auf dem Dorfe* the *Märchen-Novelle*, *Spiegel das Kätzchen*, in which Keller gave free rein to his fancy. The charm of the talking cat who outwits the town-sorcerer and marries him to the town-witch (concealed by her external existence as a Beguine-nun!) lies in the humanity of the animals whose actions and speeches reflect normal human behaviour, whereas the two human protagonists are grotesque. There is also an inner story narrated by Spiegel – another *Rahmennovelle* – of the life of his mistress spent in pursuit of true love which her wealth denies her.

The *Sieben Legenden* of 1872 are based on Kosegarten's collection of legends of saints. In Keller's presentation the stories take on a quite different aspect. He not only narrates from the standpoint of the sceptical atheist, leading to surprisingly realistic human traits, but he embellishes the tales with roguish, Rococo, poetic imagination.

The two volumes of *Züricher Novellen* (1877) are united by the connecting thread of his native canton, but this tie becomes very thin in several stories, at least three of which are considered unsuccessful. The jewel is *Der Landvogt von Greifensee*, in which autobiographical and historical allusions, poetic fancy, and realistic description and psychology achieve a sublime synthesis. The historical figure of Salomon Landolt and the Zürich of the end of the eighteenth century were to Keller real and not remote, as in the case of the less successful *Hadlaub* and *Der Narr auf Manegg*. *Der Landvogt von Greifensee* has a very complex framework, for between the opening review of Salomon's sharpshooters and the closing party bringing together all five former flames, we are given the whole vivid story of each rebuff in Landolt's love-life, often with a wealth of humour, irony, imagination, and realistic detail. The closing note of renunciation in Salomon's 'Nachsommer' is not unlike the situation between Risach and Mathilde in Stifter's novel.

From a purely formal standpoint *Das Sinngedicht* (1881) marks the high point not only of Keller's *Novellendichtung* but of the genre. The impeccable 'Rahmen' is based on an epigram of Logau reported by Lessing:

> Wie willst du weiße Lilien zu roten Rosen machen?
> Küß eine weiße Galatee: sie wird errötend lachen!

The protagonist decides to test these verses on a holiday journey – with mixed but always interesting results. Keller, the bachelor, again reveals himself as an experienced connoisseur of love and marriage – and shows himself as an eroticist, albeit with a strict moral attitude. Although *Das Sinngedicht* is a sustained unified work, the *Novellen Regine* and *Die arme Baronin* may be ranked above the others.

Keller's 'green Henry' in his great *Bildungsroman* is even more directly autobiographical than Stifter's Heinrich in *Der Nachsommer*.[20] There has been much confusion[21] and debate over the respective merits of the early and late versions. That published in 1853–55 is narrated in the third person, except for the long interpolation of the *Jugendgeschichte*. The ending with Heinrich's death reflects Keller's sense of failure and of moral guilt *vis-à-vis* his mother in 1855. Keller condemned this version and cursed anyone who should dare to republish it in place of the authorized revised version of 1879–80. Both are now widely reprinted. There seems to be no doubt that an element of youthful vigour and freshness has been lost in the revised version which, on the other hand, gains greatly in unity, clarity, and order. The first-person narration is made uniform throughout, chronological sequence is followed, and 'green Henry' survives to devote himself to public service (like his creator), and Judith returns from America to share – at a distance – Heinrich's life. This is another 'Nachsommer'-relationship: renunciation of passion in favour of mellow friendship. Without the revised version, *Der grüne Heinrich* could hardly have become one of the great landmarks of the nineteenth-century *Bildungsroman*.

Over a century passed before Keller's *magnum opus* became

available to the English-reading public, and the anonymous re-
viewer, while praising the translation, is rather critical:[22] 'Certainly
the book is clumsy and much too long. The enormously tedious
digressions ... can become inexpressibly wearisome'. But the re-
viewer goes on to acknowledge that the work will always take a high
place in the distinguished list of German *Bildungsromane*, for Keller
'has the gift ... of breathing life into people and places'.

The earlier sections, especially the evocation of childhood experience, bear the stamp of utter authenticity. The final *Bildungserlebnis*, Heinrich's sojourn in the castle of Count Dietrich and his
relationship with the Count's foundling and ward, Dortchen Schön-
fund, all this was not experienced by Keller but invented in order
to round off the plot and prepare for Heinrich's return to Zürich as
a mature citizen.

Roy Pascal has contributed a considerable amount of evidence
to clear Keller of the charge of episodic digressions.[23] Even the
Meretlein episode – a frank digression – 'tells us, subtly and indirectly, of the problem besetting both Heinrich and his mother',
namely the rebellion of the child against the religious requirements
of the parent.

Underlying the whole work is the theme of the relationship of
dream and reality: the drive to integrate these two poles in order
to arrive finally at a balanced *Weltanschauung*. For Heinrich's
imagination gets him into painful situations which leave a legacy of
guilt. Thus he invents a whole imaginary location and sequence of
events implicating his fellow pupils in teaching him bad words. At
the beginning of this chapter ('Kinderverbrechen', I, 8) the author
tells how he

> spann in der Stille unserer Stube den Stoff zu großen träumerischen
> Geweben aus, wozu die erregte Phantasie den Einschlag gab. Sie verfloch-
> ten sich mir mit dem wirklichen Leben, daß ich sie kaum von demselben
> unterscheiden konnte.

This overactive imagination is then seen at work in his fabrication:
how the accused pupils had led him into a wood (which he describes
in detail although he had never been there) and when he had
refused to say the 'unanständige Wörter', 'banden sie mich an einen
Baum fest und schlugen mich so lange mit den Ruten, bis ich alles
aussprach'. At the end of the chapter we learn that three of the
four, seeing Heinrich bowed down by his guilt, forgave him, while
the fourth who had a hard life never was able to overcome the
deepest hatred for his childish accuser. The uncontrolled imagination is a potential source of grief and guilt, but it is also a necessary
spur in the development of personality. The long painful efforts of
Heinrich to become an artist illustrate this. What is the relationship
of imagination and nature in the mind and in the picture created by

the artist? In Munich when he fills a canvas with grey cobwebs, he approaches the realization of his relative failure as a landscape artist, and yet the efforts have not been in vain, for they have been a powerful educative element in his development.

Anna and Judith symbolize these two elements, and Heinrich, perhaps oddly and yet perhaps with both a symbolical and psychological justification, accepts both simultaneously. He loves the delicate ethereal Anna as if she were not real but an ideal being. This is portrayed with considerable psychological subtlety: he is shy and at a loss for words in the presence of this idolized girl. At the end of the village carnival celebration, 'wir küßten uns ebenso feierlich als ungeschickt' (II, 4). Heinrich in the next chapter describes his turbulent feelings:

> Als ich schlafen ging, spukte und rauschte es die ganze Nacht auf meinen Lippen, durch Traum und Wachen, welche oft und heftig wechselten; ich sank von Traum zu Traum, farbig und blitzend, dunkel und schwül ... ich träumte nie von Anna, oder ich küßte Baumblätter, Blumen und die lautere Luft ... war es, als ob die wirkliche Anna von meinem Lager soeben und leibhaftig wegschliche ...

This description is not only interesting psychologically but is suggestive of the twin theme of imagination and reality. The next morning Heinrich suddenly departs for the city, and Anna is loved at a distance until her death from consumption.

But simultaneously with his spiritual infatuation with Anna runs his innocent but earthy relationship with Judith, the robust young widow of twenty-two: '... indem ich immer an die junge Anna dachte, hielt ich mich gern bei der schönen Judith auf. ... Manchmal traf ich sie am Morgen, wie sie ihr üppiges Haar kämmte'. After a playful wrestling match, the overheated situation between them is cooled by Judith's self-control and Heinrich's innocence:

> Judith saß in tiefen Gedanken versunken und verschloß, die Wallung ihres aufgejagten Blutes bändigend, in ihrer Brust innere Wünsche und Regungen fest vor meiner Jugend, während ich, unbewußt des brennenden Abgrundes, an dem ich ruhte, mich arglos der stillen Seligkeit hingab und in der durchsichtigen Rosenglut des Himmels das feine, schlanke Bild Annas auftauchen sah; ich ahnte das Leben und Weben der Liebe ...'
>
> (II, 2)

The psychological ambivalence and the symbolic implications of Heinrich's double relationship to Anna and Judith are apparent. The death of Anna, however, does not symbolize the eradication of imagination, for Judith disappears from his life also, emigrating to America. Later in Munich the carnival in the artists' colony parallels the village carnival, and the involvement of Heinrich's friend Lys with two women, Rosalie and Agnes, presents a parallel situation.

The foregoing quotations from scenes with Anna and Judith are little changed (the last is retained verbatim) in the later version.[24] Such unchanged passages retain the youthful vigour and freshness of the early version. While the consensus is that the revised version gains greatly in cohesion, unity of style, thematic clarity, not all critics share the unfavourable opinion of the first version. Josef Hofmiller is of this school, and he laments in particular the omission of the scene in which Judith bathes naked before Heinrich in the moonlight in a forest stream.[25]

The reader interested in a detailed comparison may be referred to Beyel, who quotes Keller's changed attitude to eroticism:

> Die Nuditäten müssen selbstverständlich wegfallen; sie stammen aus der Zeit, da dergleichen in der Luft lag, sind völlig unnötig und hindern ein Werk, seinen Weg zu machen; abgesehen davon, daß es die roheste und trivialste Kunst von der Welt ist, in einem Poem den weiblichen Figuren das Hemd übern Kopf wegzuziehn.[26]

An astonishing change of attitude between 1854 and 1879! Part is no doubt a change in social attitudes, but more is inherent in the change in Keller from the outlook of a man of thirty-five to that of a sixty-year-old. But the change in Keller's lifetime is minute compared with the abyss which separates us today from such views. Despite the prudery expressed, Keller's statement is stamped with his robust personality to such a degree that the style seems almost to refute the prim content.

Among the affinities of Keller's novel with Goethe's *Wilhelm Meister* are the theatrical experiences in his childhood. Investigation has indicated that Keller as a child was involved in productions of Mozart's *Zauberflöte* and Schiller's *Wallenstein*,[27] and these in the novel are metamorphosed into Goethe's *Faust* and Schiller's *Wilhelm Tell* respectively. In these transfigurations we can glimpse the integration of imagination and reality which lies behind the best parts of the novel and we can also see the basis for the repeated assertion of critics that Keller represents the continuity of Goethe's Classicism: 'In der Beschränkung zeigt sich erst der Meister'.[28] *Der grüne Heinrich*, despite its similarities with *Wilhelm Meister* in detail and in underlying theme and structure, is no pale imitation. Keller's sturdy independence saved him from any slavish imitation. Moreover, Keller's novel is much more directly autobiographical than *Wilhelm Meister*, so that it may be regarded as in some respects closer to *Dichtung und Wahrheit*, with some elements perhaps from *Faust*. Beyond the surface episode of the *Faust*-performance, the importance of nature as a major formative influence reminds us of the leitmotival nature-theme running through both parts of *Faust* from the opening monologue: 'Wo fass' ich dich, unendliche Natur?' (455) through the awakening to new life in Part II: 'Du,

Erde, warst auch diese Nacht beständig' (4681) to Faust's final desire to confront Frau Sorge on his own:

> Stünd' ich, Natur, vor dir ein Mann allein,
> Da wär's der Mühe wert, ein Mensch zu sein
> (11406–7).

The 'Bildungserlebnis der Natur' in *Der grüne Heinrich* is confined to the unspoiled organic physical world unmarred by nineteenth-century industrialization. As Boeschenstein puts it:

> Keller hat den Mut, seine Bildungsmächte fast ausschließlich aus geistigen Quellen, aus der Kunst, der Sittlichkeit und einer humanen Wissenschaft abzuschöpfen. . . . es ist eine von Zeit zu Zeit gemachte Rückbewegung auf das Naturhafte, Echte hin, die Heinrich Lee vornehmen muß, wenn er sich ins Phantastische . . . verstiegen hat. . . . Die ganze puffende und dampfschnaubende Seite der damaligen Welt, der immer höher stapelnde Handel und Wandel wird unterschlagen und verschwiegen.[29]

The modern reader will decide for himself whether the omission of urban industrialization is a flaw. In the latter part of the twentieth century we may well feel envy and nostalgia for the balance of 'Naturfrische' and 'Humanität' which *Der grüne Heinrich* reveals and which it shares with Stifter's *Der Nachsommer*.

In his second novel, *Martin Salander* (1886), Keller attempted to give expression to his concern at the decline of *bürgerliche Sittlichkeit*. Like Stifter's *Witiko*, which arose from similar motivation but took different form, *Martin Salander* comes under the rubric 'Langweiligkeit höchster Art'. It is overburdened with dry didacticism which Keller himself acknowledged: 'So geht es, wenn man tendenziös und lehrhaft sein will'.[30]

Of the three giants of Poetic Realism, Keller is the only one who achieved front rank in all three genres: novel, *Novelle*, and lyric.

IV. THEODOR STORM

The north German Storm (1817–88) remains a lyric poet even in his prose *Novellen* and he remains much more limited to his Schleswig *Heimat* than either Keller or Stifter. His birthplace, Husum – 'die graue Stadt am Meer' – is never far from the settings of his poetry and fiction. In his time Husum was already decadent – the earlier busy port had been left behind by changing patterns of trade and the harbour had been filled with silt. Son of a lawyer, Storm attended the *Lateinschule* in Husum, took his final year in the Lübeck Gymnasium, studied law in Kiel and Berlin, and returned to practise like his father in Husum. The melancholy mood of his poetry and prose grew out of the retrospective fascination with Husum as well as with the bleak North Sea and the dikes, meadows, and marshes of the coastal plain and the stony *Geest* inland. His anti-Danish stand in the war between Denmark and Prussia (acting on behalf of the Frankfurt parliament) in 1848, led to the withdrawal of his licence to practise and Storm emigrated to Prussia where he served first as an *Assessor* in Potsdam and then as magistrate in Heiligenstadt. When the Austro-Prussian army liberated Husum from Danish sovereignty, the citizens nominated Storm to the vacant post of *Landvogt* in 1865. The annexation of Schleswig by Prussia transformed the last *Landvogt* of Husum into the first Prussian *Amtsrichter des Landbezirkes* Husum in 1867. In 1879 he became *Amtsgerichtsrat*, but retired in the following year to live in a house he had built in the country. He was not ardently pro-Prussian and would have preferred a liberal, federal integration of Schleswig-Holstein into Germany.

Apart from the fifteen-year exile from Schleswig, his life appears uneventful, but was not without problems and afflictions. Three sisters died in 1829, 1847, and 1863. Soon after his happy marriage to his cousin Constanze Esmarch, who bore him seven children, he was irresistibly attracted to a younger girl, Dorothea Jensen – the attraction to very young girls is a prominent motif in his fiction. Constanze befriended Do and made her almost a member of the family. Storm was genuinely shattered by Constanze's death a year after his return to Husum – but in the following year married Dorothea, by whom he had one more child. Storm's eldest son in early life became an alcoholic and caused his father much grief.

Storm wrote more than fifty *Novellen* and although they are all (but one) in some degree *Stimmungsnovellen* in which the melancholy lyrical mood predominates, it is still possible to trace three stages of development which can be only approximately dated. The *Novellen* of the first period are more heavily impregnated with an almost Romantic mood of melancholy memory of lost happiness. *Immensee* (1852) is the most typical and most famous. Like the other works of this period there is a vein of sentimentality which helped to make *Immensee* a late Victorian favourite.

In view of Storm's insistence on the strict form and dramatic affinity of the genre, it may seem odd that he wrote so many *Novellen* which are undramatic and which tend to evaporate in *Stimmung*. But then his pronouncements on form came later in letters to Heyse and Keller.

In his second period he composed problem-*Novellen*: in *Späte Rosen* (1859) his own problem of restoring a marriage which had become shaky; *Drüben am Markt* (1861) and *Abseits* (1863) centre in a more problematic way on his major theme of renunciation; *Auf dem Staatshof* (1858) depicts the tragedy of the last of a decadent family – from this work Thomas Mann derived the creative inspiration for his *Buddenbrooks*; in *Auf der Universität* (1863) Lenore becomes the sacrificial victim of class distinction. All these show an increase in the realistic elements over Romantic. Two personal problems are reflected in *Viola Tricolor* (1873) and *Ein stiller Musikant* (1876): the first presents a second marriage in the Indian summer of life and the second reflects the tragedy of his son's half-talent and destructive tendency. *Draußen im Heidedorf* handles the tension between individual and society.

In his third phase, Storm turned to the historical *Novelle*. This would seem to call for a comparison with Conrad Ferdinand Meyer. But they are not really comparable, for Storm uses the frame to bring the picture of the past into closest intimacy with the reader and he is less concerned with history than with the individual and the family. *Aquis submersus* (1871) is the first and perhaps best of this period, it was Storm's own favourite, perhaps because it re-evokes so much of the earlier *Stimmungsnovellen*: melancholy memory and renunciation.

Storm, like Keller, was an atheist and a fairly typical representative of materialistic *Bürgertum* of the second half of the nineteenth century. But we have seen how Keller's 'Diesseitigkeit' developed into affirmation of life and optimistic faith in man (except at the end). Storm's atheistic materialism seems to have reinforced his tendency to brooding on transience, mutability, and decay of all things. Some of his last works reflect this gloomy despair in high degree, such as *Die Söhne des Senators* (1881) and the earlier *Carsten Curator* (1878), which involves guilt and atonement in the fate of a son. The difficulty of a clear chronological division is evident in the fact that while creating these sharply outlined problem-*Novellen*, some of them suggestive of northern family sagas, Storm continued to write lyrical *Stimmungsnovellen* like the story of idyllic love entwined with the fate of strolling puppet-players: *Pole Poppenspäler* (1875), and artist-*Novellen* in the Heyse-style such as *Psyche* (1876).

In spite of development of greater realism, clearly outlined dramatic situations, and deeply-felt personal problems, it seems that all of Storm's prose (with one exception) has survived the test of time less successfully than Keller's and Stifter's. Despite his formal mastery and the diverse themes of the later *Novellen*, there is an element of sameness. If many of Storm's stories are read together, they tend to blur in one's memory. As we have noted, he is limited both in milieu and atmosphere, for the retrospective melancholy brooding is all too frequent; and for the late twentieth century Storm is burdened with an undeniable streak of sentimentality. It is possible that his fame will shrink still further, perhaps to the level of his once formidable rival, Paul Heyse. Why does he nevertheless form one of the leading trio of Poetic Realists in prose? He continues to hold this position, not because historians of literature have traditionally accorded him this status, but because of the remarkable qualities of his last *Novelle: Der Schimmelreiter* (1888).

Storm had been working on this material when his illness was diagnosed as cancer of the stomach. Storm had demanded that his doctor tell him the truth, but he was incapable of standing up under it and fell into gloomy apathy. A family consultation resulted in another examination by three doctors (one a brother), who pronounced the earlier diagnosis false. Storm rebounded in renewed vigour and he not only spent a happy last summer but went on to complete his *magnum opus*. The breadth, depth, and length of *Der Schimmelreiter* have prompted discussion as to whether or not it should be classed as a novel. This seems quite unnecessary and unfounded. It is true it recounts the whole life of Hauke Haien and takes more than a hundred pages to do so, but so did Stifter's *Abdias*. It is not only a *Novelle* but one in which all the characteristic elements of form reach a high synthesis. Here there is no longer a trace of sentimentality. The characters of Hauke and his wife Elke and their tragic fate are etched indelibly on the reader's memory. Nominally it could fit into the category of the historical or problem-*Novellen* as well as into *Heimatkunst*, but it far transcends such categorization. The complex triple framework carries us back to the middle of the preceding century as Storm remembers how fifty years before he had read the story in his grandmother's house and had never rediscovered it, but had also never forgotten it. The second frame presents the traveller on the dikes on a stormy night in the 1830s when, taking refuge, he hears the interior tale from the local schoolmaster, who narrates while the dike-masters keep watch for a possible break-in of the hostile sea. The interior tale is interrupted at strategic moments – once as the spectral *Schimmelreiter* passes. The interior schoolmaster-narrator is a rational sceptic above local superstitions and yet the undercurrent of uncanny, even demonic, elements gathers cumulative force. It is curious that Storm, whose scepticism is that of the schoolmaster, nevertheless succeeds in building up such an undercurrent of irrational fear, for the supernatural elements are of two kinds: those based on ignorant folk-legend and other elements not so easily explained away, e.g., the apparition of the *Schimmelreiter* to the traveller, the dike-masters, and the schoolmaster, and the ominous prophecies of dying Trin Jans. Some critics speak of Hauke's neglect of wife or family, or imply that the marriage was one of convenience: necessary for Hauke's rise to become *Deichgraf*. To this reader both interpretations seem wrong. It is true that the marriage is motivated by practical considerations on both sides, and in this respect was typical of burgher-society. On the other hand, they were clearly destined for each other. They meet on the common ground of mathematics and 'rechnen' becomes a key leitmotiv, repeated a dozen times. Their marriage-relationship is ideal, for Elke, daughter of the previous *Deichgraf*, understands and supports her husband in all he does. Hauke's love for his wife is movingly revealed in the crisis when she nearly dies after childbirth. The one flaw in their domestic bliss is that the long-delayed child is subnormal. All the more moving is the increased love of both parents for this helpless child and for each other. Hauke, with his wife's support, carries through his plans for a new dike, against the ill-will and superstition of the whole community. It is ironic that the catastrophe results from a momentary relaxation of his vigilance. Weak after illness, he accepts the report of a subordinate on the condition of the old dike which then bursts in the wild storm carrying away Hauke, Elke, and their child. The depiction of the fury of the elements is terrifying. For this work alone Storm will always have a key position in the history of the German *Novelle*.

V. WILHELM RAABE

In recent decades the star of Raabe (1831–1910) has risen, as Storm's has waned. No longer is there any doubt of Raabe's superior stature, and if we have excluded him from the trinity of Stifter, Keller, and Storm, it is because these three are typical representatives of Poetic Realism and of the *Novelle*-genre, whereas Raabe was an individualist at odds with his age and with prevailing literary conventions. In his outer life his unbourgeois tendency is reflected in the fact that, unlike his three rivals, Raabe held no office and had no means of support but his pen.

Born in Brunswick into a burgher family, Raabe at fourteen lost his father. He spent four years apprenticed to a book-store in Magdeburg, failed a later *Abitur*, moved to Berlin, where he attended university lectures and worked on his first rambling novel: *Die Chronik der Sperlingsgasse* (1857). Published at his own expense, this work was successful, partly because it expressed the outlook of the age in which the optimistic materialism of Feuerbach lingered alongside the pessimism of Schopenhauer. Raabe later read Schopenhauer intensively, but was rather proud that his first novel, written when he was twenty-five, anticipated the wave of Schopenhauer-gloom, expressed in the opening line: 'Es ist eigentlich eine böse Zeit'. Later we read: 'Verkehrt auf dem grauen Esel Zeit sitzend reitet die Menschheit ihrem Ziele zu .... Wir wissen nicht, trägt es uns ins Paradies zurück oder aufs Schaffott'.[31] The realism appealed to prevailing trends and Raabe based the novel on his own life and observation in the Spreegasse in Berlin.

In 1862 Raabe married and settled in Stuttgart, where he spent his happiest eight years, participating in literary and social life, finding in Mörike a kindred spirit. In 1870 he moved to Brunswick, where he spent his last forty years, in increasing isolation and poverty.

One of the many difficulties in assessing Raabe lies in the unevenness of his prolific production. Ordinarily a discerning critic can distinguish gold from dross, but Raabe sometimes wrote deliberate parodies, even using for this purpose the *Novelle*-form which he despised. Fritz Martini sees here a link with the twentieth century:

> In anderen Erzählungen spielt er belletristische Klischee's an und nach, sich scheinbar auf sie einlassend, in Wahrheit mit ironischer Pointierung sie als Rahmen und Einkleidung dessen nutzend, worauf es ihm ankam. In anderen wiederum hat er Trivialmotive zu satirischer und parodistischer Wirkung in sein Erzählgefüge eingearbeitet: *Horacker* und *Prinzessin Fisch*. Es liegt ein ersichtlich 'moderner' Zug Raabes in dieser Distanzierung vom vorfabrizierten Erzählschema, das zitiert, parodiert und derart zu einer ihm widersprechenden Funktion gebracht wird.[32]

These tendencies came increasingly to the fore in his late work. Meanwhile we skip the five long novels published in the six years after the *Chronik der Sperlingsgasse* and come to *Der Hungerpastor* (1864) which, although not so intended, has been regarded as first of a trilogy, each consisting of three volumes: *Abu Telfan oder die Heimkehr vom Mondgebirge* (1867) and *Der Schüdderump* (1870). Through the nineteenth century *Der Hungerpastor* was considered Raabe's best work and a worthy example of the *Bildungsroman*. Actually Raabe oversimplified his task in two ways: firstly, by having two protagonists, one good and one evil. The shoemaker's son, Hans Unwirsch, remains unsullied and finds satisfaction in a rural pastorate on the Baltic. Moses Freudenstein (who becomes Dr Theophil Stein) embodies the aggressive evil of modern business.[33] In the second place it is difficult to see 'development' in Hans Unwirsch: things happen to him, but he simply retains his native innocence. This does not quite fit the pattern of the nineteenth-century *Bildungsroman*, but it does make Unwirsch a forerunner of the passive or unheroic hero of a later age.

Barker Fairley claims that the other parts of the so-called trilogy are failures because Raabe set out to write novels of social and political criticism and failed.[34] It is doubtful if he ever had such an intention: 'Einen großen Zeitroman schreibe ich nicht', he wrote to a friend in 1871, adding with characteristic self-irony, 'Ich bin entweder zu dumm oder zu klug dazu'. If the novels are partial failures, it is because not all the characters come to life – Raabe was not at his best in conveying the conversation and character of aristocrats – and because the symbol of the death-cart (Schüdde-rump) is dragged across the scene in the last novel without relevance to events.

The idea of having a figure return from twelve years' slavery in Africa (*Abu Telfan*) to a philistine small town and *Residenz* and to use this as a platform for a broadside against local political and social conditions is certainly tendentious and there is much criticism given in the comparison between sublunary slavery in Africa and the tyranny of submissive burghers in Germany. But the situation is more interesting to Raabe as a vehicle for humour and irony. Basically his own *Weltanschauung* is too problematic for him to take a party-stand. Even towards small-town philistines he is ambi-valent, for he feels certain sympathetic ties.

There is no doubt that the death-cart as a symbol of life in general, and of nineteenth-century society in particular, marks a nadir in Raabe's pessimism – 'Wohl dem, der stark genug ist . . . um zu jeder Stunde dem Nichts in die leeren Augenhöhlen blicken zu können' (*Abu Telfan*, ch. 18). Later, however, Raabe resented this label of pessimism which had been pinned on him. The mellow and sovereign irony of *Stopfkuchen* (1891) represents a personal transcendence of pessimism, although he remained pessimistically critical of the industrialization and urbanization which began with the *Gründerjahre* and which threatened to wipe out a more humane way of life. The transcendence of pessimism is essentially Schopenhauerian: objectification of the Will through Art.

Why were Raabe's late masterpieces so long neglected? There are many possible answers. For most readers the multiple narrative perspectives were too subtle and the modest pseudo-naïve dis-claimers of Raabe were accepted at face value instead of as parts of a subtly complex narrative technique.

Raabe worked on his English so that he could read Thackeray in the original. At the end of Chapter 8 of *Vanity Fair*, Thackeray explained to his readers how he wished to describe men and women as they actually are, good, bad, and indifferent, and to claim a privilege:

> . . . occasionally to step down from the platform, and talk about them; if they are good and kindly, to love and shake them by the hand; if they are silly, to laugh at them, confidentially in the reader's sleeve; if they are wicked and heartless, to abuse them in the strongest terms politeness admits of. Otherwise you might fancy it was I who was sneering at the practice of devotion, which Miss Sharp finds so ridiculous; that it was I who laughed good-humouredly at the railing old Silenus of a baronet – whereas the laughter comes from one who has no reverence except for prosperity, and no eye for anything beyond success. Such people there are living and flourishing in the world – Faithless, Hopeless, Charityless: let

us have at them, dear friends, with might and main. Some there are, and very successful too, mere quacks and fools: and it was to expose such as those, no doubt, that Laughter was made.

It will be obvious that Thackeray and Raabe were kindred spirits. As for the stylistic device of the author stepping out of his narrator-role and letting the reader in on his secrets, this was not new, of course, and Sterne and Jean Paul had prepared the way. Raabe built upon his predecessors to mould readers and characters into a narrative structure of multiple levels and perspectives. An interesting example is *Pfisters Mühle* (1884) which deals with the problem of pollution of a mill-stream. Although the last miller wins his law-suit against the industrial polluters, the old mill is sold, the miller's son has abandoned the family trade for a 'higher' career, and even the helpful scientist and the lawyer, who successfully combined in prosecuting the factory-owners, cannot understand why the miller's family did not invest heavily in the offending industry's shares! The polluted stream and abandonment of the mill represent the *Gründerjahre* and Dr Asche's ambivalent attitude is Raabe's. The inner story is narrated by the last Pfister to his bride. The fact that he takes her for their honeymoon to the deserted mill before it is torn down (to make way for another factory) indicates the whimsicality which abounds in Raabe's work. The bride goes along with the honeymoon, but cannot really accept the nostalgic element in her husband's story. She thus provides a counter-idyllic current. The tale is carefully constructed of so-called mere 'Blätter' and Raabe is engaging in self-persiflage when he has his narrator say at the end:

> Nun könnte ich mich selber literarisch zusammennehmen, auf meinen eigenen Stil achten, meine Frau und alle übrigen mit ihren Bemerkungen aus dem Spiel lassen und wenigstens zum Schluß mich recht brav exer-zitienhaft mit der Feder aufführen.

Obviously the 'Bemerkungen' of his wife and the other participants are essential elements in a complex technique of irony and multiple perspective.

There is much whimsical humour in Raabe's late works, reminiscent of Thackeray, Dickens, Jean Paul, and Sterne, but there are also many links with late twentieth-century grotesque humour, because with Raabe it was basically a release from the unresolved tension between the old and the new. The difference between Raabe and the existential absurdity seen in life after the Second World War has been pointed out by Oberdieck:

> Die Grenzerfahrung der Absurdität des Lebens ... führt nun aber bei Raabe nicht zu einer Weltanschauung der Absurdität. Hier liegt der entscheidende Unterschied zur Moderne. Die Begegnung mit dem Absur-

den ist notwendig, um die Freiheit zu entdecken, die völlige Unabhängig-
keit vom 'man' des Saeculums. Den *Riß im Universum*, die *dunklen
Mächte* muß jeder erfahren, um als Mensch zu reifen (*Alte Nester*...).
Aber das Ganze der Welt ist nicht absurd.[35]

During his long and prolific career Raabe demonstrated diverse
styles and covered a wide range of subject-matter in time and space.
His most popular tale is *Die schwarze Galeere* (1865), with its speed
and dramatic tension set in the war between the Spanish occupying
forces and the Dutch-Flemish population. But even in his historical
tales, Raabe had his own epoch in mind.

Barker Fairley has demonstrated that the true criteria of Raabe's
genius lie in his best late works, of which he singles out nine for
detained analysis, and he has shown the depths which lie behind
the whimsical façade of *Stopfkuchen* (1891).[36] The fatness of the
interior narrator and passive hero, Heinrich Schaumann[37] – nick-
named 'Stopfkuchen' from his schooldays – is a comical front for
the deeper fact that he stays in his 'red redoubt' and the world
comes to him:

> since the 'rote Schanze', with Schaumann sitting there, is just as surely
> the centre of things as the round earth and the circling stars are the peri-
> phery. Everything is concentrated here.... it is scenario and auditorium
> for the tale he tells; it is history and geology; the Seven Years War and
> the giant sloth....'[38]

Schaumann had constantly been called a 'sloth' by his teachers.
Eventually in his retreat he took to fossil-hunting to pare his weight
and ended up with a geological museum including the fossil of a
megatherium or giant sloth. Beneath the humour of this incident
is the reflection that geological time points both backwards and
forwards: Heinrich had been stirred to fossil-hunting by musing
that he might be dug up one day as 'one of the more remarkable
fossils'. There is a similar veiled allusion in Heinrich's excellent
well, which is so deep that it might penetrate to the other hemi-
sphere:

> 'Look, Edward, there it is. It's the same old well and it gives good water.
> The shaft goes pretty deep through the fortifications of Count von der
> Lausitz into the bowels of the earth. I don't think you have any better
> water in Africa'. The reader who fails at this point to complete the seg-
> ment in the book's geometry by extending the chord of the well shaft to
> meet the other end of Edward's arc is missing an opportunity, not to say
> an invitation.[39]

It is also possible to speculate how much self-irony, tinged with
bitterness, may lie in the above allusions. Here was the late Raabe,
a lonely disregarded author, but confident that his late works would
one day be discovered as 'quite remarkable fossils' for they 'penetrate deeply into the bowels of the earth'.

These symbolic allusions also summarize Raabe's place in literature. Now that it has become fashionable (in an esoteric way) to
emphasize the 'modernity of Raabe', we must remember that he
was a transitional figure with at least as many subterranean connections backwards as forwards. Even his language illustrates this.
His narratives are carried on dialogue, which he handles with
versatility and realism, but he also stamps his neo-Baroque idiosyn-
crasies, often with humorous or ironic touches, through figures for
whom such coinage seems realistic or natural. Sometimes he uses
archaic or lengthened forms (siebenzig, Dintenfaß), but sometimes
he invents arresting new compounds (Landdoktorenphysiognomie,
Tischlergesellenherbergskreatur, freudiggrün, grimmigschön). This
language then extends both backwards to the linguistic drolleries
of *Horribilicribrifax* in the seventeenth century and forwards to the
verbal fireworks of Günter Grass.

Among the late works of special merit not yet mentioned are *Das
Odfeld* (1888), *Die Akten des Vogelsangs* (1896), and *Unruhige Gäste*
(1884). The latter has a striking *Wendepunkt* which might qualify it
as a *Novelle*, but for its length and for its multiple focus on four
characters.

Hermann Hesse visited Raabe in 1909 and in his essay 'Besuch
bei einem Dichter' predicted Raabe's future fame 'denn er hat
jenes die Kritik verwirrende Plus, jene Dimension zuviel, die so
schwer einzureihen ist und die sich mit der Zeit doch meistens
durchsetzt'.

VI. CONRAD FERDINAND MEYER

In 1883 Theodor Fontane, in a conversation with Rudolf Lindau,[40]
found contemporary German fiction deficient in comparison with
Turgenev: 'Es fehlt ihr an Wahrheit, Objektivität, Realität. Die
Menschen tun und sagen beständig Dinge, die sie, wie sie nun mal
sind, nie tun und sagen könnten'. Asked if there were not exceptions,
Fontane replied: 'Ja, Keller und den anderen Züricher, den Meyer,
ebenso Storm und Anzengruber lass' ich gelten'.

Meyer (1825–94), 'der andere Züricher', was the opposite of
Keller in almost every respect. Meyer's friend and fellow author,
Louise von François, suggested that Keller viewed life through a
microscope and Meyer through a telescope.

Earlier criticism rated Meyer's prose above his verse, perhaps
misled by Meyer's own verdict on his work. With the passing of time,
his poetry had risen on the scale as the reputation of his *Novellen*
has fallen. It is fitting that we leave the details of his problematic
life to be considered with his poetry in the following chapter, for

Meyer himself declared that he used the form of the historical *Novelle*, in order to conceal himself behind an objective mask. It is curious that Fontane excepted Meyer from his castigation of *Novellen* in which characters 'continually act and talk' as they would never do in real life, for Meyer's language is poetically stylized, having the effect of polished marble. This is the more remarkable when one realizes that his stories are built on dialogue with a minimum of pure description or narration. Fontane was probably aware of the basic psychological, philosophical, or historical realism which underlies Meyer's fiction.

When we look closely at Meyer's statement about hiding behind the mask, we find his remark ambivalent:

> ... je n'écris absolument que pour réaliser quelque idée, sans avoir aucun souci du public et je me sers de la forme de la nouvelle historique purement et simplement pour y loger mes expériences et mes sentiments personnels, la préférant au *Zeitroman*, parce qu'elle me masque mieux et qu'elle distance davantage le lecteur.
>
> Ainsi, sous une forme très objective et éminemment artistique, je suis au dedans tout individuel et subjectif.[21]

There are, then, beneath this artistic and objective form, both 'idées' and 'sentiments personnels'. It has been observed that his *Novellen* are in fact just as much problem-*Novellen* as historical. Beneath the pageant of history we face timeless ethical problems and thus Meyer's stories have some affinity with the *Ideendramen* of Schiller and Hebbel who also used the materials of history. As for the 'sentiments personnels', we shall refrain from a Freudian analysis and simply suggest that the powerful passions and violent deeds of his fiction are compensations emanating from a hesitant, doubt-ridden author. Keller wrote (9 June 1884) to Storm: 'Meyer hat eine Schwäche für solche einzelne Brutalitäten und Totschläge' and Storm remarked on *Jürg Jenatsch* ending in a brutal 'Fleischhauertat'. On the other hand, we find beside the 'great' men of action passive suffering creatures, such as the title figure in *Das Leiden eines Knaben* (1883) or Antiope in *Die Hochzeit des Mönchs* (1884). Thus both the wish-projections and the psychological actuality of the author can be detected behind the historical mask.

The fact that much of his correspondence is in French points to another dichotomy: the attraction both to the southern Mediterranean world and the northern Germanic. The influence of Jacob Burckhardt may be discerned in Meyer's preference for the Italian Renaissance. We find an echo of Schopenhauer in his assertion that only art gives release: 'Die Kunst hebt uns wie nichts anderes über die Trivialitäten dieses Daseins hinweg'. In life he had no firm hold between Mediterranean and German poles until 1866 and 1870 when he became an ardent admirer of Bismarck and even wished

German Switzerland could be incorporated into the Wilhelmian Reich.

His literary skill was achieved, not intuitively, but as a *tour de force*, by an endless process of filing and refining. He endlessly importuned his publisher, Haessel in Leipzig, requiring minor changes: 'das "und wurde Purpur" auch nicht gefällt. Besser wäre: und wurde Flamme', but later the same day, 2 December 1891, another message went out: 'Nein, lieber Freund, muß es weder Purpur, noch Flamme heißen, sondern Glut'. Apart from changes in the manuscript stage, every time a new edition was printed Meyer made extensive revisions, 750 alterations, for example, between the first and second printings of *Die Hochzeit des Mönchs.*

Meyer wrote eleven *Novellen* (if we include *Jürg Jenatsch*, which might be classed as a novel), all published between 1873 (*Das Amulett*) and 1891 (*Angela Borgia*). Through his pages stride the great historical personages: Gustavus Adolphus, Louis XIV, Kaiser Frederick II, Henry II and Becket, Cesare Borgia, Madame de Maintenon, Michelangelo, Raphael, Petrarch, and Dante. To Kögel he wrote: 'Ich nehme gern Helden, die im irdischen Leben hoch stehen, damit sie Fallhöhe haben für ihren Sturz'. The peripeteia-motif and the dramatic affinity are clear. Paul Ernst, himself a *Novellendichter*, in an analysis of Meyer's *Die Versuchung des Pescara* (1887) points to the problem: Italy had reached a stage when a strong man might unite the nation and save it from destruction by becoming king (allusions to nineteenth-century unification of Germany and Italy are unmistakable) and this was Wallenstein's problem too. But Wallenstein was thwarted, committed treason, and perished. Fate, on the other hand, decreed an early death for Pescara. He is aware of this in advance and the temptation is visited upon one mortally stricken. Thus Ernst concludes that the latter is 'novellistisch' and not 'tragisch': 'eine Warnung für die Naiven, welche noch immer durch die scheinbar dramatische, in Wahrheit kunstvoll novellistische Konstruktion Meyers verführt werden, aus seinen Novellen Dramen zu machen'.[42]

For the English reader, *Der Heilige* (1879) is of special interest, not only historically but also in view of T. S. Eliot's dramatization of the material in *Murder in the Cathedral*. Meyer strained historical veracity in order to develop a complex of ethical problems. At the cultured Moslem court of Granada, the Saxon Becket had married a princess who died in childbirth, leaving him with an infant daughter, called variously Grazia, Gnade, Grace, whom he raises in England in an elegant miniature Moorish palace hidden in the forests beyond Windsor! Henry II finds and seduces the girl, causing her death in an encounter with retainers of his embittered Queen Eleanor. Becket appears outwardly to recover from this bereavement and continues loyally to support Henry, not only in his continental conquests, but also in his efforts to curb the power of ecclesiastical courts which afforded the clergy immunity. Elevated, against his will, to the see of Canterbury, Becket's loyalty switches from king to church. But is the motivation revenge for Grace's death? Or is it the higher loyalty to the Kingdom of God and His Vicar on earth? Or is it loyalty to the oppressed Saxons against the Normans? The death of his daughter is an obvious *Wendepunkt*. Thereafter the additional problem of Henry's relationship with his difficult sons worsens and it was Becket who had been their guide and mentor. It is Richard the Lion-Heart who tries to reconcile the exiled archbishop and his father and the failure of this attempt leads directly to Becket's return and his murder in the cathedral. The multiplicity of motives and problems suggests the novel rather than drama. It is also a *Rahmennovelle* narrated by a Swabian former bodyguard of Henry to a canon in Zürich as the bells peal, summoning the populace to Becket's canonization in 1273.

The framework structure is used by Meyer to obtain distance and perspective, whereas Storm used it to narrow the focus and bring things close. In *Die Hochzeit des Mönchs* Meyer achieved a *tour de force* by making Dante – an exile in Verona from Florence – his narrator and by making the characters in his story fit the characters to whom he is telling the story and, in part, making them co-narrators. Furthermore, Dante is supposed to be making up his story as he goes along, based on an epitaph he has noted in a cemetery: Hic jacet monachus Astorre cum uxore Antiope. Sepeliebat Azzolinus. Half-way through his tale, Dante stopped: 'Seine Fabel lag in ausgeschütteter Fülle vor ihm; aber sein strenger Geist wählte und vereinfachte'. Behind the mask of Dante we glimpse Meyer's rigorous, selective, deliberate method of composition.

Since Meyer had so much in common with Paul Heyse, freedom from *bürgerlich* responsibilities and financial worries, attachment to Italy, devotion to highest artistic ideals (Heyse's *L'Arrabbiata* used to be considered a model *Novelle*), why is Meyer still honoured and Heyse neglected? It is not because of Heyse's mass production – twelve times as many *Novellen* as Meyer – for Heyse's best works are as formally elegant as those of Meyer – but because of the sentimental fragrance of old lace and lavender which lingers in most of Heyse's narratives.

Meyer, nevertheless, stands at the end of a line of development, for his *Novellen*, although they could be imitated, could lead to no further refinement. In his turning-away from contemporary life to history and distanced violence, there is also an element of *fin-de-siècle* aestheticism, reflecting the decay of the *Bürgertum* in which the *Novelle* had developed and flourished.

VII. FADED FICTION

The Victorian Age, if we can apply this phrase to the German literary scene,[43] was prolific in all forms of prose fiction, the characteristic genre of *Bürgertum* and of Poetic Realism. Much was of an ephemeral nature, but some writers, like Paul Heyse and Paul Ernst whom we have already mentioned, once considered leading lights, now loom dimly in the past. We can give only a brief glimpse of some of the once familiar figures.

Louise von François (1817–93), daughter of noble French *émigré* and *petit-bourgeois* Saxon parents, was at home in both worlds and wrote novels and *Novellen* realistically reflecting the world she saw but without penetrating deeply into its problems. Her best-known works are the novels, *Die letzte Reckenburgerin* (1871) and *Frau Erdmuthens Zwillingssöhne* (1873), and the *Novelle: Der Katzenjunker* (1879).

An admirer of François, but a writer of much greater significance, was the Baroness Marie von Ebner-Eschenbach, born Countess Dubsky. Her lifespan coincided exactly with that of Emperor Francis Joseph (1830–1916) and her work reflects the mellow decadent atmosphere of late nineteenth-century Austria. She and Conrad Ferdinand Meyer were twin nominees of the committee for the Schiller prize. Kaiser Wilhelm refused to accept either because they were not 'German'. The decision may have some historical and logical justification with respect to Switzerland, but it shows glaringly the degree to which *kleindeutsch* thinking prevailed in Bismarck's Reich and it must have been galling to descendants of noble families of the Holy Roman Empire. Marie was born at Schloß Zdischlawitz in Moravia, which provides the setting for many of her stories. In 1848 she married Wenzel Freiherr von Ebner-Eschenbach who rose to be a field marshal of the Austrian army, but in characteristic and paradoxical Austrian fashion was more of a scholar than a soldier.

Marie's realistic depictions of aristocrat and peasant milieux are often mellowed by rich humour, as in the tale *Die Freiherren von Gemperlein* (in *Neue Erzählungen*, 1878). *Dorf- und Schloßgeschichten* (1884) contains *Krambambuli*, a story to stir the heart of all dog-lovers. Man's faithful friend is torn between loyalty to past and present masters. In a critical struggle, the dog decides for the former, realizes his mistake, and avoids his master's house, until the last moment when he returns to die with his nose on the threshold.

Baroness von Ebner-Eschenbach's fame spread far. Three of her stories appeared quite early in translations: *Das Gemeindekind* (1887) and *Zwei Comtessen* (1885) were published in England in 1893.

Lotti, die Uhrmacherin (1881) is a gripping story of a woman fading from the prime of life and sacrificing her dearest possession, her 'Uhrensammlung', to save from debts and 'Vielschreiberei' the man who rejected her and married another eighteen years before. Her sacrifice fails to save the man but brings Lotti together with her cousin Gottfried. Through her sacrifice she found happiness at last at the side of a kindred spirit.

Two of her autobiographical writings are of special interest: *Meine Kinderjahre* (1906) and *Meine Erinnerungen an Grillparzer* (1916). Her life at beloved Schloß Zdischlawitz and in Vienna kept her apart from the bourgeois and industrial worlds. But through her Moravian and Czech lineage and country environment, she was quite familiar both with rural life and with current problems in the Habsburg domains. Two of her stories treat the insurrection of Polish peasants in Galicia in 1846: *Der Kreisphysikus* and *Jakob Szela* (1884). The former depicts the transformation of a materialistic selfish doctor into a humane protector of the rebel Dembowski.

That the Ebner-Eschenbachs left no progeny seems symbolic of the nearing end of old Austria and her ancient aristocracy.

Ferdinand von Saar (1833–1906) was in many ways a kindred spirit of Ebner-Eschenbach. Born in Vienna of aristocratic parents, von Saar resigned his commission in the army in 1860, in order to devote his life to literature. His first *Novelle, Innocens, ein Lebensbild* (1866), is reminiscent of Storm's melancholy and nostalgia. Four of his best stories were published under the title *Novellen aus Österreich* (1877). Further collections were *Schicksale* (1888) and *Frauenbilder* (1891). The collective title of three stories, *Herbstreigen* (1897), anticipates Trakl's autumnal mood and suggests Saar's awareness of the sinking Habsburg world. On 24 July 1906 he was driven by intestinal pain to take his own life, repeating Stifter's fate, and at his death as a peer of the realm he was living in rooms rented in the dwelling of a senior letter-carrier. Yet he left an estate of 50,000 gold crowns. His life and death not only mirror Austria but merge aristocrat and bourgeois.

An Austrian Realist of quite a different complexion was Peter Rosegger (1848–1913), who rose from peasant origins and journeyman tailor to become a highly regarded author. His work is rooted in the soil of his native Steiermark, but his peasant stories fall short of Gotthelf's. *Jakob der Letzte* (1888) depicts the losing struggle of the small farmer against the large landowner, but Rosegger's best work is his novel *Der Gottsucher* (1883).

The Viennese Ludwig Anzengruber (1839–89) is best known for his drama, but Fontane gave his narrative prose high rating, perhaps because of the realistic grappling with religious, political, and social problems. His best works of fiction are the novel *Der Sternsteinhof* (1885) and the *Erzählung, Der Schandfleck* (1877).

The novel *Ekkehard* (1862), set in the tenth century, of Viktor von Scheffel (1826–86) is now 'gesunkenes Kulturgut' as are the *Kulturgeschichtliche Novellen* (1856) of Wilhelm Riehl (1823–97) and the novels of Friedrich Spielhagen (1829–1911): e.g., *Problematische Naturen* (1860) and *Sturmflut* (1876). The historical 'Professorenromane' of Felix Dahn (1834–1912) have also faded: *Kampf um Rom* (1876) and *Odins Trost* (1880).

The Mecklenburger Fritz Reuter (1810–74) is distinguished by his humour and his use of *plattdeutsch*, which he raised to a literary level. As *Burschenschaftler* at the University of Jena he was arrested in 1833 and condemned to death in 1836. The sentence was commuted, but he was released only after seven years in prison. His use of dialect is therefore politically motivated by his rebellion against the Mecklenburg feudal aristocracy whose speech he rejected. His novels, in part autobiographical, and full of humour and tolerance (despite his prison-years), brought him wealth and fame: *Ut de Franzosentid* (1859), *Ut mine Festungstid* (1863), and *Ut mine Stromtid* (1862–64).

Gustav Freytag (1816–95), born in Silesia, is more significant and problematic. Until well into the twentieth century, his *magnum opus, Soll und Haben* (1855), was considered to be a major milestone on the path of the *Bildungsroman*. In one respect its significance is undisputed: *Soll und Haben* is the most representative novel of *Bürgertum*. Anton Wohlfahrt develops all the virtues of a man of commerce from elementary book-keeping to managing far-flung business interests. The book gives a vivid, realistic picture of this now vanished way of life. It has also quite a lot of vigorous action, almost suggestive of cowboys and Indians on the American prairies in the same years, but this is where Freytag's novel becomes problematic, for his 'bad Indians' are the Poles and his 'good cowboys' are the Germans in town and country who have a mission to civilize the Poles. This racial prejudice, embodied in the idiom 'eine polnische Wirtschaft', makes the contemporary reader uncomfortable in more than one sense. The *Drang nach Osten* has been reversed and Freytag's once German Silesia is now Polish. Freytag's other novels are of minor import: *Die verlorene Handschrift* (1864) and *Die Ahnen* (1872–80), which attempted in many volumes to depict generations of a German family from the fourth century to 1870!

Nineteenth-century fiction and Poetic Realism took a new turn and ended in a blaze of glory in the work of Theodor Fontane (see below, pp. 155–80).

NOTES

1. K. K. Polheim, ed., *Theorie und Kritik der deutschen Novelle von Wieland bis Musil,* Tübingen, 1970, 119.

2. ibid., 151–3.

3. For a fuller discussion of theory of the *Novelle,* see E. K. Bennett, *A History of the German Novelle,* Cambridge, 1934; 2nd rev. edn., 1961 (first chapter) and Polheim, op. cit.

4. Hermann Augustin, 'Ärztliches zu Adalbert Stifters Tod', *Vierteljahresschrift des Adalbert Stifter-Instituts des Landes Oberösterreich,* IX, 1959, 19–34.

5. Gustav Konrad in B. von Wiese, ed., *Deutsche Dichter des 19. Jahrhunderts,* 372. Fritz Novotny, *Adalbert Stifter als Maler,* Vienna, 1941, contains 107 reproductions of paintings and sketches (incl. 10 colour-plates) by Stifter from 1823 to 1866. See also many reproductions (some in colour) in Alois Großschopf, *Adalbert Stifter: Leben, Werk, Landschaft. Zum hundertsten Todestag des Dichters,* Linz, 1968.

6. Murray – an old Scottish noble name carried to Hungary, according to M. Enzinger, *Gesammelte Aufsätze zu Adalbert Stifter,* Vienna, 1967, 152.

7. Not only the name Stephen but the progressive outlook point to a possible model in Graf Stepan (István) Széchényi, 'der große Ungar' whose liberal, enlightened, but conciliatory championship of Magyar rights was unfortunately replaced by that of Lajos Kossuth as the Revolution of 1848 approached. It was only in 1830 that the Hungarian language gained official status along with Latin and German. Stifter's narrator, the guest in east Hungary, senses the new spirit in the land: 'Es war mir, als hörte ich den Hammer schallen, womit die Zukunft dieses Volkes geschmiedet wird. Jedes in dem Lande zeigt auf kommende Zeiten, alles Vergehende ist müde, alles Werdende feurig'.

8. That Stifter was conscious of his affinity with Goethe is apparent from his remark: 'Ich bin kein Goethe, aber einer aus seiner Verwandtschaft' (letter to Heckenast of 13 May 1854).

9. Letter to his publisher Heckenast cited by Eric A. Blackall, *Adalbert Stifter. A Critical Study,* Cambridge, 1948, 311–12.

10. Roy Pascal, *The German Novel,* Manchester, 1956, 68.

11. op. cit., 317. J. P. Stern in *Re-interpretations, Seven Studies in Nineteenth-century German Literature* (London, 1964, 287) credits W. Rehm for this suggestion (*Nachsommer: zur Deutung von Stifters Dichtung,* Berne, 1951).

12. Stern, op. cit., 289.

13. ibid., 291.

14. *Adalbert Stifter als Dichter der Ehrfurcht,* Zürich, 1952.

15. op. cit., 292–3.

16. Cited by Urban Roedl, *Adalbert Stifter,* Reinbek, 1965, 153.

17. Letter to Johannes Urzidil, 15 June 1963, in *Vierteljahresschrift des Adalbert Stifter-Instituts des Landes Oberösterreich,* XIII (1964), 21.

18. *Die Entstehung des Doktor Faustus. Roman eines Romans,* Amsterdam, 1949, 123–4.

19. Ernst Alker, *Die deutsche Literatur im 19. Jahrhundert,* Stuttgart, 1961, 457.

20. The name 'Heinrich' must be purely coincidental, since Keller in Berlin and Stifter in Linz were writing at the same time. The name may indicate the debt of both to Goethe, alluding to Faust's use of 'Heinrich' through the Gretchen-episode.

21. Thomas Mann seems to have been unaware of two versions. cf. *Die Entstehung des Doktor Faustus,* 161.

22. *Green Henry,* trs. A. M. Holt, London, 1960; review *Times Literary Supplement,* 23 September 1960. The translator is the widow of the late Professor Holt of the University of Toronto.

23. op. cit., 30–51.

24. cf. *Sämtliche Werke*, ed. Jonas Fränkel, Erlenbach-Zürich and Munich, 1926, XVII, 66 (first version) and IV, 13–14 (second version).

25. Josef Hofmiller: 'Der Ur-Heinrich' in *Interpretationen 3: Deutsche Romane von Grimmelshausen bis Musil*, Frankfurt, 1963, 182–9, esp. 185. For the original see Fränkel, ed. cit., XVIII, 85–9.

26. Franz Beyel: *Zum Stil des Grünen Heinrich*, Tübingen, 1914, 40.

27. H. Boeschenstein, *Gottfried Keller: Grundzüge seines Lebens und Werkes*, Berne, 1948, 101. It is a striking reminder of the developed culture of rural Switzerland that *Wallenstein* rather than *Tell* was performed.

28. Goethe's Sonnet 'Natur und Kunst'.

29. op. cit., 100–5.

30. *Gesammelte Briefe*, ed. Carl Helbing, Berne, 1950–54, II, 372.

31. Section headed: Am 3. Dezember.

32. In von Wiese, *Deutsche Dichter des 19. Jahrhunderts*, 540.

33. It is safe to say that if Raabe could have foreseen the horrendous consequences of anti-semitism, he would not have made his villain a Jew. Raabe was not a racist.

34. Barker Fairley, *Wilhelm Raabe. An Introduction to his Novels*. Oxford, 1961; cf. esp. 168–80.

35. Wilhelm Oberdieck, 'Wilhelm Raabes Begegnung mit dem Absurden'. *Jahrbuch der Raabe-Gesellschaft*, 1968, 99.

36. op. cit., esp. 1–18.

37. Raabe's names are often allusive, humorous, meaningful. Schaumann is a 'show man' or the 'man who shows the way', but in view of his historical and archaeological proclivities, his name may also allude to Heinrich Schliemann (1822–90), excavator of Troy and Mycenae. Schliemann was also north German, born in Mecklenburg.

38. Fairley, op. cit., 17.

39. ibid., 16.

40. Th. Fontane, *Sämtliche Werke*, Munich, 1963, XX, 326 f.

41. *Briefe*, ed. Frey, I, Leipzig, 1908, 138.

42. 'Zur Technik der Novelle' in *Der Lotse*, II, 1901–02, quoted in Polheim, *Theorie und Kritik*, 176.

43. cf. Norbert Fuerst, *The Victorian Age of German Literature*, London, 1966.

Chapter 9

LYRIC POETRY FROM POETIC REALISM TO IMPRESSIONISM AND SYMBOLISM

ALMOST EVERY GERMAN major prose-writer has also composed verse. Thomas Mann is a notable exception, if we disregard his 'Gesang vom Kindchen', but even he, with ironic and parodistic intent, concealed verse in his prose, although the narrating monk in *Der Erwählte* proclaims: 'Eines ist gewiß, nämlich, daß ich Prosa schreibe und nicht Verselein, für die ich im ganzen keine übertriebene Achtung hege' (ch. 1).

Thus Stifter and Raabe also wrote a certain amount of poetry, but, although Stifter's verse still appears in Austrian anthologies, neither his nor Raabe's lyrics warrant discussion here. The trinity of Poetic Realism shifts to Keller, Storm, Meyer. But the latter moved towards Symbolism, leaving Keller and Storm to represent the apogee of Poetic Realism in the lyric. Keller and Storm did not have undisputed primacy in their time, however, and a word must be said about the Munich School.

I. THE MUNICH SCHOOL

King Max of Bavaria gathered poets to make his *Residenz* an Athens on the Isar. Emanuel Geibel from Lübeck and Paul Heyse from Berlin were at the centre of this group, who were almost all non-Bavarian. Heinrich Leuthold[1] (1827–79) was Swiss, Graf von Schack from Mecklenburg, Friedrich Bodenstedt from Peine in Hanover, Wilhelm Hertz from Stuttgart, Hermann Lingg from Lindau on Lake Constance.

There was no set programme or manifesto, but they had a club, the Krokodil, and an organ, the *Münchner Dichterbuch*, of which two volumes appeared (1861, 1881). Their common creed was the cult of beauty (*l'art pour l'art*) and antipathy to the political poets. A considerable amount of translation was done; Heyse and Geibel combined to produce a *Spanisches Liederbuch* (1852) and Heyse did an *Italienisches Liederbuch* (1860). Geibel reigned as *Dichterfürst* in this company until he was toppled by the Naturalists, whose leading poet, Arno Holz, had once been Geibel's disciple. Geibel possessed undisputed formal mastery, although critics rejected his work as *Backfischpoesie*.

The Munich poets, less original and less talented, stood aloof from the Poetic Realists (Keller, Storm, Stifter), who supported the ethos of *Bürgertum*. The Munich poets had nothing to say, but said it beautifully in conventional metres.

Despite his bias against relevant social and political themes, Geibel nevertheless fell out with King Ludwig II (who had succeeded King Max in 1864) by writing some verses in favour of German unity. Geibel thereupon rusticated himself and ended his days in his native Lübeck.

II. GOTTFRIED KELLER

Keller's importance as a poet tends to be overshadowed by his fiction. Moreover, the overwhelming majority of his poems antedate his first prose. Between 1843 and 1846 he composed over 300 poems of which not quite half were published in *Gedichte* (1846). In the next three years just over a hundred were written and almost all published in *Neuere Gedichte* (1851). In the following three years barely fifty more were composed for the second edition (1854). Apart from 'occasional' poems, the next thirty years added only forty to the *Gesammelte Gedichte* (1883, 2 vols.). Yet the revision which Keller carried out for subsequent editions was often the essential step in the creation of a great poem. 'Unter Sternen' may serve as an example. It has magnificent opening and closing stanzas:

> Wende dich, du kleiner Stern,
> Erde! wo ich lebe,
> Daß mein Aug, der Sonne fern,
> Sternenwärts sich hebe!
> .   .   .   .
> Schwinge dich, o grünes Rund,
> In die Morgenröte!
> Scheidend rückwärts singt mein Mund
> Jubelnde Gebete!

Between these stanzas the poet, on his nocturnal walk, finds joy and affirmation of life, so that, at the end, he glories in passing from night to day. In the earlier version, however, there was an excrescent additional stanza which made prosaically explicit the poetic images:

> Lieblich diese Sonne lacht
> Und der Tag wird heiter.
> Doch wer nächtlich einsam wacht,
> Kennt noch etwas weiter!

By excising the offending stanza, Keller created a poetic gem, but the instance is instructive because the finally deleted lines illustrate the didactic tendency inherent in Poetic Realism and particularly pronounced in Swiss writers.

After his return from Munich in 1843, Keller was politically active, influenced by the exiled Germans, Freiligrath and Herwegh, then living in Zürich. Some of his most truculent poems of these early years were aimed at the Jesuits, against whom much opposition arose in the canton. On the whole, Keller's radical enthusiasm was of a very patriotic and moderate nature – one might say characteristically Swiss and *bürgerlich*. The poem 'Revolution' begins with a stirring summons:

> 'Es wird schon gehn!' ruft in den Lüften
> Die Lerche, die am frühsten wach;
> 'Es wird schon gehn!' rollt in den Grüften
> Ein unterirdisch Wetter nach.
> 'Es geht!' rauscht es in allen Bäumen
> Und lieblich wie Schalmeienton.
> 'Es geht schon!' hallt es in den Träumen
> Der fieberkranken Nation.

After seven intervening stanzas rich in imagery of political freedom, the final stanza suggests that all political actions must be morally good:

> Doch wenn es nicht von Güte strahlet
> Wie eine hochbeglückte Braut,
> So ist sein Lohn ihm ausgezahlet
> Und seine Freiheit fährt ins Kraut.
> Ein böses Weib, ein gift'ger Drache
> Und böses Volk sind all ein Fluch,
> Und traurig spinnt die beste Sache
> Sich in ihr graues Leichentuch!

Luzius Gessler[2] has subjected all the youthful lyrics to scrutiny through the lens of the early cycle, 'Lebendig Begraben', and finds in conjunction with the recurring tree-image a new interpretation of one of Keller's best-known poems:

Winternacht

Nicht ein Flügelschlag ging durch die Welt,
Still und blendend lag der weiße Schnee.
Nicht ein Wölklein hing am Sternenzelt,
Keine Welle schlug im starren See.

Aus der Tiefe stieg der Seebaum auf,
Bis sein Wipfel in dem Eis gefror;
An den Ästen klomm die Nix herauf,
Schaute durch das grüne Eis empor.

> Auf dem dünnen Glase stand ich da,
> Das die schwarze Tiefe von mir schied;
> Dicht ich unter meinen Füßen sah
> Ihre weiße Schönheit Glied um Glied.

> Mit ersticktem Jammer tastet' sie,
> An der harten Decke her und hin –
> Ich vergeß das dunkle Antlitz nie,
> Immer, immer liegt es mir im Sinn!

This and many other poems of 1846–47 Gessler relates to Keller's unavowed love for Marie Melos. This, in itself, adds only a minor biographical postscript, but Gessler goes on to show the multiple meanings and associations beyond the obvious allusion to the death of nature and its struggle for rebirth. The image of the sprite imprisoned beneath the ice embraces Keller's inhibited love and it also suggests a threat to his poetic world and his creativity, for he is separated from the 'weiße Schönheit', and in his isolation his future prospects appear frozen in hopelessness.

It is true that Keller, the would-be painter, is stronger in the visual than in the musical components, but 'Winternacht' is one poem in which the predominantly pictorial qualities are reinforced to an unusual degree by rhythm and sound. The slow trochees and the sharp front vowels enhance the frozen landscape and suggest the poet's pain.

In 1847 Keller wrote sonnets, ghazals, and *terza rima* poems, but he is not at his best in these confined forms. His importance lies not in formal innovation but in the content of his verse, which bears the stamp of his strong personality. While his rhythms are sometimes rough-hewn (Fontane called them 'fürchterlich'), and while some poems are 'sicklied o'er with the pale cast of thought', his best poems are masterpieces in which emotion, experience, thought, image, and sound merge in a higher synthesis.

Although Keller's poetry is primarily visual in comparison with the musicality of Mörike and Storm, he nevertheless gave the Swiss their national anthem, a poem inspired by early revolutionary aspirations: 'An das Vaterland', already set to music by Wilhelm Baumgartner in 1846. It is difficult to imagine a more appropriate hymn to Switzerland, in its avoidance of all jingoism and its celebration of Swiss landscape, language, and 'Sittlichkeit'. The extra stress in the first line of each stanza gives an added solemnity:

> Als ich arm, doch froh, fremdes Land durchstrich,
> Königsglanz mit deinen Bergen maß,
> Thronenflitter bald ob dir vergaß,
> Wie war da der Bettler stolz auf dich!

The lines reflect a sturdy republican pride and also remind us that Keller's years in Munich strengthened his patriotism.

After hearing Feuerbach lecture in Heidelberg, Keller wrote from Berlin to Wilhelm Baumgartner on 27 March 1851:

Wie trivial erscheint mir gegenwärtig die Meinung, daß mit dem Aufgeben der sogennannten religiösen Ideen alle Poesie und erhöhte Stimmung aus der Welt verschwinde! Im Gegenteil! Die Welt ist mir unendlich schöner und tiefer geworden, das Leben ist wertvoller und intensiver, der Tod ernster, bedenklicher und fordert mich nun erst mit aller Macht auf, meine Aufgabe zu erfüllen und mein Bewußtsein zu reinigen und zu befriedigen, da ich keine Aussicht habe, das Versäumte in irgend einem Winkel der Welt nachzuholen.

Under the first impact of Feuerbach, Keller gave poetic expression to his new *Weltanschauung*:

> Ich hab in kalten Wintertagen,
> In dunkler, hoffnungsarmer Zeit
> Ganz aus dem Sinne dich geschlagen,
> O Trugbild der Unsterblichkeit!
>
> Nun, da der Sommer glüht und glänzet,
> Nun seh ich, daß ich wohlgetan;
> Ich habe neu das Herz umkränzet,
> Im Grabe aber ruht der Wahn.
>
> Ich fahre auf dem klaren Strome,
> Er rinnt mir kühlend durch die Hand;
> Ich schau hinauf zum blauen Dome –
> Und such kein bessres Vaterland.
>
> Nun erst versteh ich, die da blühet,
> O Lilie, deinen stillen Gruß,
> Ich weiß, wie hell die Flamme glühet,
> Daß ich gleich dir vergehen muß!

As in the best of Keller's poems, here thought, experience, imagery, and poetic form coincide. Although it contains a definite thought, it is not simply *Gedankenlyrik*, for it embraces a totality of emotional experience. The stream in stanza three is real, perhaps the Rhine, or the Neckar at Heidelberg, but its meaning expands into the familiar symbol of life. The stream 'running, cooling, through the poet's hand' reaffirms his creed of active participation in life. The last line of the penultimate stanza can be applied to Switzerland, but the widest circle of meaning embraces this life on this earth. Similarly, the lily and the flame of the last stanza have multiple associations: life, death, beauty. The lily as a symbol of beauty and purity (but also with funereal associations) summons to the fullest activity in a life which is fleeting and ends in obliteration.

The 'Waldlieder' of 1845 display a variety of metres. The oak forest is celebrated in stately octosyllabic trochaic couplets, while the firs are depicted in four-line trochaic stanzas of alternating three and four stresses:

> Aber auch den Föhrenwald
> Laß ich mir nicht schelten,
> Wenn mein Jauchzen widerhallt
> In dem sonnerhellten!

The forest is a personal experience of nature for Keller and yet he manages to incorporate in the second last stanza a symbol of the ideal ethical community:

> Wenn ein Stamm im Sturme bricht,
> Halten ihn die Brüder;
> Und er sinkt zur Erde nicht,
> Schwebend hängt er nieder.

'Sommernacht' also combines a picture of nature with an ethical theme, as the young men mow the widow's grain through the night and, as dawn breaks, go off to their own daily tasks.

Keller wrote relatively few ballads and this is surprising in view of his narrative talent. One of the best is 'Der Taugenichts' (1851), which combines Romantic-gypsy motifs with harsh reality as the dreamy boy is scolded, and then soothed in sleep by nature.

Is there any ray of the humour which was so conspicuous in Keller's prose? 'Der Taugenichts' has a touch of whimsical humour. There is some wry humour at his own awkwardness at a Berlin dinner-party in 'Jung gewohnt, alt getan' (1854), but the poem ends on a note of remorse and guilt *vis-à-vis* his mother. Elsewhere in the poetry, a humorous note attempts to cover an awkward moment, as in 'Das Köhlerweib ist trunken' and in the picture of Saint Peter squatting mending his old shoes at Heaven's gate in 'Wie glänzt der helle Mond'. The clumsy sonnet 'Der Schulgenoß' ends in a humorous juxtaposition of the schoolboys, one of whom ends up a 'Schelm', the other a poet! Keller's best poetry lacks the humour which sparkles in his prose.

Although Keller wrote relatively few poems in later years, three deserve mention. At forty-seven he was engaged to a Bernese girl who committed suicide by drowning. This inspired the poem 'Die Entschwundene' (1866). In 1872 Keller composed 'Die kleine Passion' – the title only derived from Dürer's woodcuts. Dürer and Keller are both noted for depiction of minute detail, and Keller's 'Passion', in humorous *Knüttelvers*, describes a fly which took seven days to die in a 'dichterliches Buch':

> Am vierten Tage stand es still
> Gerade auf dem Wörtlein 'will'!
> . . .
> Am siebten endlich siegt der Tod,
> Da war zu Ende seine Not.
> Nun ruht im Buch sein leicht Gebein,
> Mög uns sein Frieden ewig sein!

Minute observation of an insect's death is also combined with wider allusions in Goethe's poem 'Parabolisch'.

Keller's 'Abendlied' (1877) is one of his unforgettable poems, expressing in the decline of life his whole *Weltanschauung*. It may be compared to Goethe's 'Lied des Türmers' (*Faust* II), except that Goethe dwells more on life than death and uses a forward-surging iambic rhythm: 'Zum Sehen geboren/Zum Schauen bestellt'. Keller uses a slow, measured trochaic[3] beat appropriate to his reflective contemplation, which is also enhanced by the extension of the same rhyme through the whole stanza:

> Augen, meine lieben Fensterlein,
> Gebt mir schon so lange holden Schein,
> Lasset freundlich Bild um Bild herein:
> Einmal werdet ihr verdunkelt sein!
>
> Fallen einst die müden Lider zu,
> Löscht ihr aus, dann hat die Seele Ruh;
> Tastend streift sie ab die Wanderschuh,
> Legt sich auch in ihre finstre Truh.
>
> Noch zwei Fünklein sieht sie glimmend stehn,
> Wie zwei Sternlein innerlich zu sehn,
> Bis sie schwanken und dann auch vergehn,
> Wie von eines Falters Flügelwehn.
>
> Doch noch wandl' ich auf dem Abendfeld,
> Nur dem sinkenden Gestirn gesellt;
> Trinkt, o Augen, was die Wimper hält,
> Von dem goldnen Überfluß der Welt!

The first stanza celebrates the sequences of images which life has provided through the 'lieben Fensterlein', but in the fourth line the first stressed 'u' vowel occurs in 'verdunkelt' and this becomes the recurring rhyme of the second stanza, with its homey images of the tired wanderer taking off his shoes and, with a sigh of relief, slipping into 'die finstre Truh' – which suggests both a cosy Swiss wall-bed and the dark confines of the grave. The 'Fünklein' and 'Sternlein' of the third stanza refer back to the 'Fensterlein', but now the tiny sparks are growing dim, ready to be extinguished by the wing of a moth. The last stanza, however, celebrates the triumph of life over death: 'Doch noch wandl' ich auf dem Abendfeld'. Nowhere is Keller's affinity with Goethe clearer than in this 'diesseitig' affirmation of life.

III. THEODOR STORM

Storm's lyrics, like his prose, represent a narrower range of theme and mood. The retrospective nostalgia of his *Erinnerungsnovellen* continues in most of his verse, which also is more regional. Even in his years of exile in Prussia, his favourite poetic milieu continued to be Husum, 'die graue Stadt am Meer':

> Am grauen Strand, am grauen Meer
> Und seitab liegt die Stadt;
> Der Nebel drückt die Dächer schwer,
> Und durch die Stille braust das Meer
> Eintönig um die Stadt.
>
> Es rauscht kein Wald, es schlägt im Mai
> Kein Vogel ohn' Unterlaß;
> Die Wandergans mit hartem Schrei
> Nur fliegt in Herbstesnacht vorbei,
> Am Strande weht das Gras.
>
> Doch hängt mein ganzes Herz an dir,
> Du graue Stadt am Meer;
> Der Jugend Zauber für und für
> Ruht lächelnd doch auf dir, auf dir,
> Du graue Stadt am Meer.

As the visual outlines are blurred by the heavy mist pressing[4] on the roofs, so the musical elements and the nostalgic mood assume first importance.

The appeal to auditory sensation is even more apparent in 'Meeresstrand', which builds up both a mood and a seascape almost entirely on sounds:

> Ans Haff nun fliegt die Möwe,
> Und Dämmrung bricht herein;
> Über die feuchten Watten
> Spiegelt der Abendschein.
>
> Graues Geflügel huschet
> Neben dem Wasser her;
> Wie Träume liegen die Inseln
> Im Nebel auf dem Meer.
>
> Ich höre des gärenden Schlammes
> Geheimnisvollen Ton,
> Einsames Vogelrufen—
> So war es immer schon.
>
> Noch einmal schauert leise
> Und schweiget dann der Wind;
> Vernehmlich werden die Stimmen,
> Die über der Tiefe sind.

Preoccupation with time is a constant theme,[5] for Storm, an atheist, brooded on transience and the relentless march of time which drives to obliteration. Perhaps for this reason, he favours noon when time seems to stand still, as in 'Abseits' (1848):

Es ist so still; die Heide liegt
Im warmen Mittagssonnenstrahle,
Ein rosenroter Schimmer fliegt
Um ihre alten Gräbermale;
Die Kräuter blühn; der Heideduft
Steigt in die blaue Sommerluft.

Laufkäfer hasten durchs Gesträuch
In ihren goldnen Panzerröckchen,
Die Bienen hängen Zweig um Zweig
Sich an der Edelheide Glöckchen,
Die Vögel schwirren aus dem Kraut—
Die Luft ist voller Lerchenlaut.

Ein halbverfallen niedrig Haus
Steht einsam hier und sonnbeschienen;
Der Kätner lehnt zur Tür hinaus,
Behaglich blinzelnd nach den Bienen;
Sein Junge auf dem Stein davor
Schnitzt Pfeifen sich aus Kälberrohr.

Kaum zittert durch die Mittagsruh
Ein Schlag der Dorfuhr, der entfernten;
Dem Alten fällt die Wimper zu,
Er träumt von seinen Honigernten.
– Kein Klang der aufgeregten Zeit
Drang noch in diese Einsamkeit.

The French Storm-biographer, Robert Pitrou,[6] tells us that the 'Kätner' and his thatched cottage really existed:

> ...il s'appelait Heidbur, habitait la lande aux alentours de Schwesing [a village north-east of Husum] et son fils Carsten se souvenait fort bien de l'après-midi (un peu avant 1848) où un quidam de la ville (Stadtminsch) ...avait longuement contemplé son père, lui et leur hutte, sans piper mot. Plus tard en 1850, pendant le siège de Friedrichsstadt il avait, à Husum, revu...le promeneur d'autrefois, et entendu dire que c'était l'avocat Storm.

This vignette is of minor import, but it does tell us something of Storm's silent, brooding disposition and of his realistic mode of composition. Yet the poem far transcends the real situations and sounds (or in this case: silence) which inspired its creation.

The title and the opening lines suggest undisturbed, peaceful noontide stillness, balance, and harmony. The pink heather swathes the tombstones with a warm rosy glow, uniting the peace of death with life. If the first stanza stresses rest and silence, the second suggests bustling activity in nature through sounds of beetles crawling, bees humming, birds whirring, and the lark's piping. The first stanza had dwelt on vegetation, the second on animal life; with the third we are introduced to humans: the cotter half asleep and his young son carving a pipe with which, perhaps, to imitate the song of the lark.

In the final stanza, drowsiness embraces all. The word 'Mittagsruh' gently recalls 'Mittagssonnenstrahle' of stanza one. Not a breath stirs as the striking of the village clock 'zittert' – faintly reaching the ear and intensifying the silence. The old man, now slumbering, dreams of his honey-harvest which the bees produce on their own.

Underlying this peaceful poetic scene are two deep-seated themes: first, Storm's philosophical theme of time and transience; and secondly the reflection of the rebellion and military action not far away – the ill-fated campaign of local volunteers and Prussians against the Danes in the summer of 1848 – and the threat to peace and continuity. It is curious that all other verbs are present – vivid 'historical' presents – except the last 'drang'. Peter Spycher wonders whether this past tense may not subtly suggest that time (distant clock) and the political strife ('aufgeregte Zeit') have already penetrated this idyllic present which therefore already belongs to the past.[7] It may also be noted that the six-line stanzas with AB AB CC rhymes are almost elegiac, thus adding another hint of a backward look at what is gone beyond recall.

'Sommermittag' (1854) presents a similar lazy noon-time scene with the miller and his men peacefully snoring, but the poem ends with a slightly humorous note, as the miller's daughter takes advantage of the prevailing slumber:

> Sie geht und weckt den Müllerburschen,
> Der kaum den schweren Augen traut:
> 'Nun küsse mich, verliebter Junge;
> Doch sauber, sauber, nicht zu laut'.

'Für meine Söhne' illustrates the strong *bürgerlich* moral sensitivity of Storm. Each of the six stanzas stresses one moral virtue. Stanza five emphasizes hard work, but with respect for others:

> Arbeit scheue nicht und Wachen;
> Aber hüte deine Seele
> Vor dem Karrieremachen.

It is poignant, in reading this, to recall the anxieties which the father later suffered through his eldest son's early alcoholic excesses.

Also moving is the grief evoked by the two poems 'Einer Toten' on the death of his sister Helene from puerperal fever following childbirth in 1847 – a motif which forms the turning-point scene in *Der Schimmelreiter*.

Even his 'Heidebilder' and seascapes involve his preoccupation with memory and transience, as in the following late poem of 1875:

> Über die Heide hallet mein Schritt,
> Dumpf aus der Erde wandert es mit.
>
> Herbst ist gekommen, Frühling ist weit –
> Gab es denn einmal selige Zeit?

> Brauende Nebel geisten umher;
> Schwarz ist das Kraut und der Himmel so leer.
>
> Wär ich hier nicht gegangen im Mai!
> Leben und Liebe, – wie flog es vorbei!

In spite of his attachment to Schleswig-Holstein, Storm's prose has little dialect and his poetry almost none. Yet he wrote a poem in low German 'An Klaus Groth', a compatriot whose dialect verse (*Quickborn*, 1852), along with Fritz Reuter's prose, raised *plattdeutsch* once more to a literary level. Storm's friendly admiration of Groth shows that he was not unsympathetic to the effort to rehabilitate *plattdeutsch*:

> Wenn't Abend ward,
> Un still de Welt un still dat Hart;
> Wenn möd up't Knee di liggt de Hand,
> Un ut din Husklock an de Wand. . . .

This survey has attempted to convey the general character of Storm's poetry, with stress on its musicality.[8] It is only fair, however, to end with an exception to the rule, in a poem again inspired by death. By way of introduction to the poem, we may remember that Storm, after the death of his sister Cäcilie, wrote to his wife, Constanze, on 29 October 1863: '. . . Du weißt es ja, ich glaube, daß der Tod das völlige Ende des einzelnen Menschen ist'. And to Mörike he wrote on 3 June 1865: 'Sie wissen ja, daß ich Ihren glücklichen Glauben nicht zu teilen vermag; Einsamkeit und das quälende Rätsel des Todes sind die beiden furchbaren Dinge, mit denen ich jetzt den stillen unablässigen Kampf aufgenommen habe'.

In 1879 Storm witnessed the untimely death of sixteen-year-old Graf Theodor Reventlow, son of his friend the Landrat von Husum, and in the same year published his poem 'Geh nicht hinein'. Fritz Martini has pointed out the complete break with Storm's previous verse. Unrhymed, jerky free rhythms, in a dissolution of syntax and metre, this poem 'will nicht mehr . . . im Dienst des Poetischen stehen, sondern es will Erkenntnis aussagen'.[9] Martini claims that the poem anticipates Expressionism.

IV. CONRAD FERDINAND MEYER

In many respects the opposite of the robust integrated *Bürger*, Keller, the sickly neurotic Meyer had a life of frustration and tragedy quite different from those which befell (but did not overwhelm) Keller. Born in Zürich in 1825 into an affluent patrician family, Meyer was as aristocratic as possible in Switzerland. His father died when he was fifteen and it was decided that he should prepare for a respectable bourgeois occupation. Meyer shut himself in a darkened room with books and went out to walk or swim only at night. Family friends thought he was dead and his mother spoke continuously of 'poor Conrad'. He was brought up bilingual and early decided to be a poet – but in which language? His preference in literature and his prolonged sojourns in Lausanne and Geneva drew him to French. His insecurity was enhanced by religious doubts and in 1852 he became a patient in the asylum of Préfargier near Neuchâtel. It turned out that his illness was not insanity but neurotic introversion and he was soon released. At this time he was reconverted to Calvinism under the influence of Vulliemin. At thirty-six he lost his mother, who took her own life while a mental patient, and he now relied on his admiring sister Betsy. After his mother's death, he had ample means to travel and live as he wished. In Paris he found a Catholicism and a corruption which clashed with his French ideals formed in Calvinist Switzerland. He was well advanced in years before he could grow a moustache. He married at fifty, produced a family and a bourgeois paunch, and became a conversationalist.

Venice, Florence, Rome, and Burckhardt's *Die Kultur der Renaissance in Italien* strengthened his Southern attachment and yet the rise of Bismarck and Prussia made him opt for the German North.

He was almost forty and had nourished his poetic ambitions for over a quarter of a century when his first book appeared, anonymously, *Zwanzig Balladen von einem Schweizer* in 1864 (under his own name as *Balladen* in 1867). The Franco-Prussian War gave the inspiration for his long narrative poem *Huttens letzte Tage* (1871) which brought him fame. There followed twenty productive years in which he was held in high esteem, especially by Storm and Heyse, although Meyer suffered from the feeling that Keller did not give him full approval.

In 1891, at his own request, he re-entered an asylum, but he did not die insane. He spent his last five years, lucid but withdrawn, in his country house at Kilchberg near Zürich, where he died in 1898.

His historically distanced prose was long held superior to his poetry, in part because Goethe and the Romantics had created a lyric tradition based on experience, emotion, subjectivity, song, and spontaneity (or the illusion of it). Meyer was determined to conceal his experiences and emotions, in verse as well as in prose. Yet in both forms his inner life is revealed through symbols. The pursuit of classic forms and artistic perfection gives him some affinity with Platen and the Munich school: 'Genug ist nicht genug!... Genug kann nie und nimmermehr genügen!' (from the poem 'Fülle'). But the tension between inner and outer life in his poetry points forward to the Symbolists of the *fin de siècle*. These qualities may be illustrated by 'Der Marmorknabe', which recounts the excavation of a marble youth in Italy. A young girl and an archaeologist speculate on the identity of the unearthed deity. To the girl, since he has wings and bears a torch, he must be Amor. The scholar, oblivious of the girl, pronounces his verdict:

> Er löscht die Fackel. Sie verloht.
> Dieser schöne Jüngling ist der Tod.

It is not necessary to know anything about Meyer's life and personality in order to appreciate this simple, realistic poem, its images, and obvious symbols which bring together life and death in the same figure whose attributes are viewed differently through the eyes of the young maiden and those of the elderly scholar. But there is a deeper layer of symbolism, for Meyer is also referring to his own lost or 'dead' youth.

The poem 'Der römische Brunnen' has external similarity with Rilke's 'Römische Fontäne'. In Meyer's poem *enjambement* conveys by sound and image the water falling into successive basins, while the first word dramatically depicts the initial rising jet:

> Aufsteigt der Strahl und fallend gießt
> Er voll der Marmorschale Rund,
> Die, sich verschleiernd, überfließt
> In einer zweiten Schale Grund;
> Die zweite gibt, sie wird zu reich,
> Der dritten wallend ihre Flut,
> Und jede nimmt und gibt zugleich
> Und strömt und ruht.

The realistic picture still links Meyer with Poetic Realism. The poem expresses a classic unity of polar attributes: stillness and movement. The eternal flux is contained by eternal laws of being (the 'Schalen'). Both elements are necessary, for without the containing basins, the water would be dissipated and lost; without the constant renewal there would be stagnation. There is also a suggestion of progression in life and in art: receiving and passing on.

This kind of symbolism, however, does not make Meyer a Symbolist poet, for, as Fritz Strich points out,[10] all lyric poetry is symbolic in some degree, but in Classical and Romantic verse the symbols are usually diverse and self-evident from the context or from general usage. Symbolist poems, on the other hand, use *one* symbol in multiple and subtle ways (*vide* Poe, Baudelaire, and Mallarmé). If, as Strich claims, Meyer used water – normally a symbol of life – as a symbol of death through a considerable number of poems, then the poem 'Der römische Brunnen' assumes another more esoteric dimension of symbolic meaning.

According to Strich, Meyer's mother's suicide by drowning led to an identification of mother and water: 'Aus dem mütterlichen

Leben geht alles Leben hervor; das mütterliche Element nimmt es wieder zu sich'.[11]

'Zwei Segel' consistently adheres to the symbol of marriage, without making it explicit, for it is characteristic of Symbolists to take pride in subtlety and artfulness. In this way they overcome ennui and nausea caused by vulgar life and this is essentially Schopenhauer's release from the Will. In opposition to life, death and art are drawn together.

'Im Spätboot' is externally realistic: a late ferry, a tired man who falls asleep during the crossing of the Zürcher See. But the fifth line hints at developing symbolism as the 'black smoke from the funnel weaves overhead'. The 'Karger Schein' of the ship's lantern hardly penetrates the blackness:

· · ·

> Steigt ein Schatten aus und niemand ein . . .
> Schmerz und Lust erleiden sanften Tod.
> Einen Schlummrer trägt das dunkle Boot.

The realistic boatman has assumed the guise of Charon ferrying 'Schatten'.

The same symbolic motif runs through the following poems: 'Die toten Freunde', 'Eingelegte Ruder', 'Lethe', 'Schwüle', 'Schwarzschattende Kastanie'. In the latter poem, the title-line, repeated four times, represents in the upper sphere the dark depths:

· · ·

> Und Kinder schwimmen leuchtend weiß
> Im Gitter deines Blätterwerks,
> Schwarzschattende Kastanie!
> Und dämmern See und Ufer ein
> Und rauscht vorbei das Abendboot,
> · · ·

The children 'gleaming white' swim in the prison ('Gitter') of the black shadowed foliage; this suggests life embraced in death.

A relatively early poem, 'Lethe', which like all his works underwent much revision, has been shown by Henel[12] to be based on a picture by the Swiss painter Charles Gleyre, which Meyer saw in Paris in 1857. The symbolism of water and death is here explicit, but the symbolic connection between Lethe (death) and art is concealed in the voice of the *dead* beloved resounding like a little silver bell: 'Die Stimme ist das einzige, was dem Dichter erhalten bleibt, er hört sie "immerfort". Sie ist die Poesie, und ihre Schönheit, ihr Silber, ist zugleich die Schönheit des Todes'.[13]

The development of Meyer's poetry is clear from a comparison of 'Lethe' with the later poem 'Stapfen', in iambic blank verse concealing symbolic meaning beneath a straightforward narrative, for Henel points out that the beloved is not a person but a symbol of

Meyer's memory of his 'selig-unselige' youth: 'seine "verlorene Jugend" ist die frühverstorbene Geliebte, aber sie ist zugleich die "junggebliebene Tote", deren Stapfen er auf allen Wegen seines Lebens und Dichtens begegnet'.[14]

Meyer renewed the ballad by expanding form and content. Instead of the conventional four-line stanzas of three or four stresses, he used rhymed couplets (*Huttens letzte Tage*), even long trochaic octosyllables in four-line stanzas having a single fourfold rhyme, e.g., in 'Mit zwei Worten', a legend related of Becket's father, Gilbert, whose Saracen wife tracked him down from Palestine to London with only two words of English. The opening stanza illustrates the form:

> Am Gestade Palästinas, auf und nieder, Tag um Tag,
> 'London?' frug die Sarazenin, wo ein Schiff vor Anker lag.
> 'London!' bat sie lang vergebens, nimmer müde, nimmer zag,
> Bis zuletzt an Bord sie brachte eines Bootes Ruderschlag.

Huttens letzte Tage has been variously described as an epic, a narrative poem, a ballad collection, a lyric garland. It has something of all these forms. Meyer toiled at this favourite work, revising, deleting, altering, adding, for each of the nine editions which he saw through the press.[15] It consists of cantos (or separate ballads) presenting episodes or memories in Hutten's life as he nears death. Behind the ambivalent character of Hutten, torn between chivalrous combat and ascetic withdrawal, between Erasmus and Rome on the one hand and Luther and Protestantism on the other, lies the divided personality of Meyer himself. We find reflected not only Meyer's re-established Protestant faith (cf. canto 'Luther') but all the dichotomies of his soul:

> Ich bin kein ausgeklügelt Buch,
> Ich bin ein Mensch mit seinem Widerspruch.

The most striking formal development, however, lies in Meyer's use of iambic blank verse for ballads. In the edition of his *Gedichte* (1882) forty-four of 191 poems are unrhymed. While blank verse had been used occasionally by Mörike and Storm, Meyer moved perceptibly towards Impressionism in the clipped terseness of 'Die Füße im Feuer'. This ballad finds a messenger of the King of France unknowingly taking refuge in the house whose Huguenot mistress he had killed three years before, by holding her feet in the fire in order to make her disclose her husband:

> Drei Jahre sinds ... Auf einer Hugenottenjagd ...
> Ein fein, halsstarrig Weib ..., 'Wo steckt der Junker? Sprich!'
> Sie schweigt. 'Bekenn!' Sie schweigt. 'Gib ihn heraus!' Sie schweigt.
> Ich werde wild. Der Stolz! Ich zerre das Geschöpf ...
> Die nackten Füße pack ich ihr und strecke sie
> Tief mitten in die Glut ... 'Gib ihn heraus!' Sie schweigt ...
> Sie windet sich ...

In the morning the Huguenot host's hair has turned white over-
night. He parts from his unwelcome guest:

> Die Ebne öffnet sich. Im Felde geht ein Pflug.
> Der Reiter lauert aus den Augenwinkeln: 'Herr,
> Ihr seid ein kluger Mann und voll Besonnenheit
> Und wißt, daß ich dem größten König eigen bin.
> Lebt wohl. Auf Nimmerwiedersehn!' Der Andre spricht:
> 'Du sagst's! Dem größten König eigen! Heut ward
> Sein Dienst mir schwer . . . Gemordet hast du teuflisch mir
> Mein Weib! Und lebst! . . . Mein ist die Rache, redet Gott'.

This ending has been often mentioned as evidence of Meyer's strong
Protestant faith, but there is also in the poem evidence of his obsession
with scenes of cruelty and violence, already noted in the *Novellen*.

Meyer's achievement as a poet is a remarkable *tour de force* overcoming obstacles, inhibitions, and destructive neurotic inclinations
– the latter, of course, also closely related to his powerful creative
drive. His poetry still shares many characteristics of Poetic Realism,
but forges links with Symbolism and Impressionism. Meyer was a
poet of transition, not merely in the sense of moving from school to
school but in undergoing constant change and development himself.

V. DETLEV VON LILIENCRON

Detlev Freiherr von Liliencron was born in Kiel in the same year as
Nietzsche (1844) and died in 1909. His baronial family had become
impoverished, largely because his grandfather had married a peasant
girl. He served as a Prussian officer and was wounded in both Austro-
Prussian and Franco-Prussian wars. In 1875 he retired 'Wunden-
und Schulden halber', emigrated to America where he taught
languages and music and even painted walls in New York, before
returning to Germany two years later, to hold minor administrative
posts in his native province. He was nearing forty when his first
volume of verse, *Adjutantenritte*, appeared in 1883.

The yardstick of poetic success is variable. One authority claims
that the success of this book enabled him 'forthwith to dedicate his
life to his writings',[16] while another states that *Adjutantenritte* was a
book 'which shocked and delighted the few who read it (23 copies
were sold in two years!)'.[17] He did give up his administrative post,
but he certainly did not live in affluence on his royalties! Rather he
lived from hand to mouth for literature, at first in Munich, then in
Altona near Hamburg, increasing his income by giving poetry
readings. From 1900 he enjoyed a small pension.

He came to literature through the back door. Unintellectual,
without academic training or aesthetic experience, he expressed

himself directly and forcefully. His temperament illustrates the not uncommon combination in the north German Junker of aristocratic and military pride with an earthy *bonhomie*. He arrived on the literary scene just as Naturalism and Impressionism were about to dominate and his nature fits both. His parody of both the popular and the art ballad is full of Naturalist touches:

> Das war der König Ragnar,
> Der lebte fromm und frei
> Er trug gepichte Hosen
> Wie seine Leichtmatrosen,
> Die rochen nicht nach Rosen,
> Das war ihm einerlei.

Impressionism as a label was carried over from painting (Manet, Degas, Monet, Renoir) and in French literature was represented by Baudelaire, Verlaine, and Mallarmé. Basically it denotes the attempt to re-evoke in the beholder an impression or mood experienced by the artist – hence an obvious link with Storm's 'Stimmungslyrik'. The natural object is only the starting-point for sense-impressions and stirrings in the soul. The aesthetic criterion is intensity of impression or mood. Impressionism is more evident in poetry than in prose, and in Germany overlaps Naturalism, with which it shares many characteristics and against which it also rebels. Liliencron, Dauthendey, and Dehmel rejected Arno Holz's programme of 'konsequenter Naturalismus', which aimed at reproducing a slice of life. The Impressionist poet wanted more: a poetic mood, a symbol, an exotic atmosphere, a heightened awareness, and a deepened inwardness. If Naturalism tended to stress the grim and unpleasant, then Liliencron's 'Tod in Ähren' is both Impressionistic and Naturalistic:

> Im Weizenfeld, in Korn und Mohn,
> Liegt ein Soldat, unaufgefunden,
> Zwei Tage schon, zwei Nächte schon,
> Mit schweren Wunden, unverbunden.
>
> Durstüberquält und fieberwild,
> Im Todeskampf den Kopf erhoben.
> Ein letzter Traum, ein letztes Bild;
> Sein brechend Auge schlägt nach oben.
>
> Die Sense sirrt im Ährenfeld,
> Er sieht sein Dorf im Arbeitsfrieden,
> Ade, Ade, du Heimatwelt –
> Und beugt das Haupt, und ist verschieden.

Impressionism is striking in the laconic terseness, parataxis, suppression of adjectives in favour of nouns.

On the other hand, a stanza from the late long poem *Poggfred* is virtually a Naturalist manifesto:

Ein Dichter ist? Der, der mit leichten Beinen
In Schlamm und Blumen auf der Erde steht.
Dem Veilchenduft und Stallgestank von Schweinen,
Ob 'schön', ob 'häßlich', um die Nase weht,
Der Seidenhemden oder Bauernleinen
Gebraucht, wie's ihm beliebt; Fluch wie Gebet.
Sein Erstes sei: den Boden recht begreifen,
In dem des Menschen Lebenskerne reifen.

Another battle-aftermath combines Impressionist and Naturalist qualities:

In Erinnerung

Wilde Rosen überschlugen
Tiefer Wunden rotes Blut.
Windverwehte Klänge trugen
Siegesmarsch und Siegesflut.

Nacht. Entsetzen überspülte
Dorf und Dach in Lärm und Glut.
'Wasser!' Und die Hand zerwühlte
Gras und Staub in Dursteswut.

Morgen. Gräbergraber. Grüfte.
Manch ein letzter Atemzug.
Weither, witternd, durch die Lüfte
Braust und graust ein Geierflug.

The grief of the bereaved father who learns of the death of his son – 'ein Knabe noch' – in the battle of Kolin (18 June 1757) finds poignant expression in 'Wer weiß wo'. As often, Liliencron concludes with a personal or general reflection on life and death:

Und der gesungen dieses Lied,
Und der es liest, im Leben zieht
Noch frisch und froh.
Doch einst bin ich, und bist auch du,
Verscharrt im Sand, zur ewigen Ruh,
Wer weiß wo.

In other poems, Liliencron expresses the exhilaration of the dashing soldier in pursuit of the enemy ('Kleine Ballade') or of the fair sex ('Viererzug'). His best-known poem, 'Die Musik kommt', uses Impressionist techniques to portray the approach and the passing of a military band leading the parade. But at the end we are left with a questioning of all this 'pomp and circumstance':

Klingling, tschingtsching und Paukenkrach,
Noch aus der Ferne tönt es schwach,
Ganz leise bumbumbumbum tsching;
Zog da ein bunter Schmetterling,
Tschingtsching, bum, um die Ecke?

Liliencron clearly has affinity with the Symbolists. The military parade as a symbol of life ending in death recurs in various guises in a number of poems: implicit in the rider's refrain in 'Zwei Meilen Trab'; in the echo in 'Viererzug'; reflected in clouds, cranes, larks, and maidens in 'Märztag':

> Kurzes Glück schwamm mit den Wolkenmassen;
> Wollt' es halten, mußt es schwimmen lassen.

Although his basic themes of life and death, war and love, are usually set in nature, Liliencron wrote sometimes against the backdrop of the modern industrial city, perhaps inspired by his friend Dehmel. 'In einer großen Stadt' compares the individual in the urban mass to a drop evaporating into nothingness. In this flux from life to death recurs the refrain: 'Der Orgeldreher dreht sein Lied'. His capacity for injecting poetic life into mundane objects and metaphors (commas, freight-carriages, express bills of lading) is illustrated in the poem, 'Auf einem Bahnhof':

> . . .
> Der neue Mond schob wie ein Komma sich
> Just zwischen zwei bepackte Güterwagen.
> . . .
> Um mich war's leer; ein letzter Zug hielt fertig,
> Die letzten Arbeitsmüden zu erwarten.
> Ein Bahnbeamter mit knallroter Mütze
> Schoß mir vorüber mit Eilgutformularen.
> Sonst nichts. Nur oben stand der Jupiter.
> Die blauen Flammen lohten geisterhaft,
> Und aus der Stadt her drang verworrner Ton.

VI. RICHARD DEHMEL

Although younger and of different background and character, Dehmel (1863–1920) was linked with Liliencron in friendship and in poetry. It is tempting to see in this 'Dichterpaar' a parallel – on a lower plane, of course – with Goethe and Schiller. Liliencron is the intuitive (Schiller's 'naiv') confident Goethean man of the world, while Dehmel represents the cerebral (Schiller's 'sentimentalisch') critical intellect. This comparison has only limited validity, however, for the true key to Dehmel's personality and poetry is to be found in the drastic tension between strong sensuality and highly developed intellect. This dichotomy is depicted drastically in the poem 'Bergpsalm', against the background of the storm lashing the forest and the throbbing industrial city with its oppressed proletariat. The poet, with fierce emotion, submits to reason:

> Die Kiefer knarrt und ächzt, mein Mantel knattert:
> Empor aus deinem Rausch! Mitleid, glüh' ab!
> Laß dir die Kraft nicht von Gefühlen beugen!
> Hinab! laß deine Sehnsucht Taten zeugen!
> Empor, Gehirn! Hinab, Herz! Auf! hinab!

The Impressionist side of Dehmel is striking in 'Helle Nacht', which is virtually a translation of Verlaine's 'La lune blanche luit dans les bois', but Dehmel differed from Liliencron in his socialism, which he shared with many Naturalists, and this made him more an urban poet.

Born the son of a forester in the heart of the Spreewald, Dehmel's depiction of nature is limited to this boyhood milieu. The forest usually enters as contrast to the city or as personification of proletarian protest. All his school years were marked by a violent father-son conflict which is reflected in his 'Lied an meinen Sohn', in which the storm-lashed forest symbolizes his battles with his father. The message, 'zornlacht der Sturm', is: 'sei Du! sei Du! (Dehmel was one of the earliest admirers of Nietzsche). In the final stanza, Dehmel admonishes his son *not* to obey paternal authority:

> Und wenn dir einst von Sohnespflicht,
> Mein Sohn, dein alter Vater spricht,
> Gehorch ihm nicht, gehorch ihm nicht;

At school Dehmel suffered a concussion in a fall from the horizontal bar. It has been suggested that this injury was related to his later epileptic seizures (which led to his rejection for military service) and that this is related to the apocalyptic visions conjured up in poems such as 'Anno Domini 1812':

> Düster wie von Blutschnee glimmt die lange Straße,
> wie von Blutfrost perlt es in den Birken,
>
> . . .
>
> 'Grob am Himmel stand die schwarze Wolke,
> fressen wollte sie den heiligen Mond;
>
> . . .
>
> Hohl verschluckt der Mund der Nacht die Laute,
> dumpfhin rauschen die Hufe, die Glocken wimmern,
> auf den kahlen Birken flimmert
> rot der Reif, der mondbetaute.
> Den Kaiser schauert.

Erotic problems played a major role in his life and verse. They were problems because of the extremes within him. The more debonair Liliencron was twice divorced and thrice married, without demonic tensions becoming apparent.

There were three Jewish women who played a central part (in addition to other women in secondary roles). At university in Berlin, when his father had cut off his funds, Dehmel moved in with his friend Franz Oppenheimer, whose sister he married three years later, over the strenuous opposition of her parents. Marriage meant redemption and this is the title given his first volume of poems, *Erlösungen* (1891). Julius Bab has pointed out how the most striking poem of this collection, 'Stromüber', anticipates the threat to his marriage as the poet sees through his wife's face in the boat the face of another.[18] In fact Käthe, who lived as one of the family rather than as nursemaid, exercised a sensuous attraction which became irresistible when Frau Dehmel took her child to the sea and left Käthe at home in Berlin. This marriage-crisis was overcome, although the suicide of Käthe two years later left its mark on the poet. But almost at once another crisis arose in his desperate love for the Jewish poetess Hedwig Lachmann. Her marriage to another brought Dehmel to the verge of suicide and induced tortured dreams and hallucinations, reflected in poems such as 'Ohnmacht', in which the impure rhymes and harsh transitions from iambic to trochaic beat produce the effect of a soul driven to frenzy. In 1901 he divorced Paula Oppenheimer and married the third Jewess in his life, Ida Auerbach, whose love inspired another cycle of poems including 'Manche Nacht'.

Meanwhile his second volume, *Aber die Liebe*, had appeared in 1893. It contains the poem 'Bastard', whose ending has been described as a life-manifesto:

> Und sollst in dein Lüsten
> Nach Seele dürsten wie nach Blut,
> Und sollst dich mühn von Herz zu Herz
> Aus dumpfer Sucht zu lichter Glut.

Dehmel denied that these lines were programmatic and claimed they were inspired by Rembrandt's 'Rape of Persephone'.

The book, however, contained a cycle of twenty poems, 'Die Verwandlungen der Venus', with titles such as 'Venus Primitiva', 'Venus Homo', 'Venus Domestica', 'Venus Adultera', 'Venus Perversa', and 'Venus Sapiens'. The latter depicts the love of David and Jonathan. Dehmel denied that this contained any homosexual allusion and claimed he used the figures as a symbol of the triumph of *Geist* in his marriage conflict. But the bourgeois public was scandalized and Dehmel faced obscenity charges in Munich, where the volume had been published, and was acquitted.

The other side of his personality, the cerebral intellect, can be seen in the service of socialism, and his 'Arbeiterpoesie' may be regarded as his most distinctive contribution. Paradoxically, the revolutionary student 'promovierte' with a dissertation proving that fire insurance should be exclusively in the hands of the state, and then took a position in a privately owned insurance company. The symbols suggesting the inevitable victory of the proletarian revolution need no elucidation in 'Bergarbeiterlied' or in 'Erntelied'. The latter is of special interest because it was probably modelled on Liliencron's 'Mühle in der Ferne', which invokes the mill as symbol of fate and death. Dehmel uses the same object as a symbol of the Marxist inexorable progress of proletarian victory:

Erntelied

Es steht ein goldnes Garbenfeld,
das geht bis an den Rand der Welt.
Mahle, Mühle, mahle!

Es stockt der Wind im weiten Land,
viel Mühlen stehn am Himmelstrand.
Mahle, Mühle, mahle!

Es kommt ein dunkles Abendrot,
viel arme Leute schrein nach Brot.
Mahle, Mühle, mahle!

Es halt die Nacht den Sturm im Schoß,
und morgen geht die Arbeit los.
Mahle, Mühle, mahle!

Es fegt der Sturm die Felder rein,
es wird kein Mensch mehr Hunger schrein.
Mahle, Mühle, mahle!

Another famous revolutionary poem, 'Der Arbeitsmann', contains the lines:

Und uns fehlt nur eine Kleinigkeit,
Um so frei zu sein, wie die Vögel sind:
Nur Zeit.

It is still an excellent poem, but as with so many other aspects of Marxist ideology, progress and technology have so shortened the work-week that this point is no longer relevant.

It seems paradoxical that Dehmel should have become such a firm friend and admirer of Baron Liliencron and that, as a socialist, despite his exemption, he should have volunteered for the army in 1914. But it is in character that he volunteered as a private and that he served to the end.

VII. RÉSUMÉ

Out of Poetic Realism there arose in the 1880s and 1890s a multiplicity of currents and counter-currents: Symbolism, Impressionism, Naturalism, Aestheticism (Oscar Wilde, Stefan George), neo-Romanticism (represented by Prinz Emil zu Schönaich-Carolath and the first poems of Hermann Hesse: *Romantische Lieder*, 1898). The latter trend was not only a reaction against the crass excesses of Naturalism, but an intensification of a movement which had never died in Germany, where Romantic verse forms and themes had continued through the century. The breakdown into overlapping and contradictory 'schools' points already to the eclecticism which, except for the Expressionist interlude, was to prove to be the rule for the twentieth century.

We have focused on the major figures and the main developments. In the case of Dehmel we have emphasized his 'Arbeiterpoesie', sacrificing some of the Impressionism which he shares with Liliencron. This emphasis has been deliberate, for even at the risk of oversimplification, it seemed better to avoid obscuring the major issues by introducing a host of more or less secondary poets and trends. For the same reason we have refrained from mentioning the voluminous prose writings of Liliencron and Dehmel.

The strength of Liliencron's poetry stands out in comparison with the exotic perfumed synaesthesia of other Impressionists, such as Max Dauthendey (1867–1918), whose first volume, *Ultraviolet* (1893), contains the poem:

Rosenduft

Weinrot brennen Gewitterwinde,
Purpurblau der Seerand.
Hyacinthentief die ferne Küste.

Ein Regenbogen, veilchenschwül,
Schmilzt durch weichrauchblaue Abendwölken.

Im Taudunkel lacht
Eine heiße Nachtigall.

The Impressionist penchant for new word-coinage, which was used trenchantly and judiciously by Liliencron, becomes in Dauthendey's hands the playful decorative device of an aesthete.

Depending on one's perspective, Liliencron and Dehmel may be regarded as marking the end of an epoch or as the harbingers of the twentieth century. As central figures in an age of transition, they are, of course, both the last of the old and the first of the new age. As we have seen, links with twentieth-century Expressionism go back through Liliencron at least to Storm. And Dehmel's 'Großstadt-poesie' and 'Armeleutepoesie' prefigure developments in such diverse poets as Rilke and Brecht in the following century.

NOTES

1. Leuthold may have been the most gifted of the group and he was certainly the most problematic. He was filled with an ambivalent *Haß-Liebe* towards his native Switzerland and her *Bürgertum*. He was far more conscious of form than Geibel and sought contacts with the French Parnassiens (Gautier, de Lisle). He died insane.

2. *Lebendig Begraben. Studien zur Lyrik des jungen Gottfried Keller*, Berne, 1964, esp. 108–10. In his book, *Gottfried Keller: Life and Works* (London, 1968), J. M. Lindsay seems unfamiliar with Gessler's re-evaluation of this cycle which Lindsay totally rejects, finding it '. . . in poor taste, an unsavoury exercise in the macabre, which cannot possibly have appealed to many readers. The whole conception of the cycle reflects a primitive, childish fear of the poet, and several lines reach a level of tastelessness and sheer ugliness which can seldom have been surpassed' (106).

3. S. S. Prawer, *German Lyric Poetry*, London, 1952, 175, reads the stresses of the first line differently: Aúgen, meine liében Fensterlein. While this is no doubt possible, regular trochaic stresses seem to fit better both the stanzaic pattern and the poetic intent.

4. Storm first wrote 'deckt', later substituting the much more effective (although realistically impossible) 'drückt'.

5. cf. A. Menhennet, 'The Time-Element in Storm's Later Novellen', *GLL*, XX (1966), 43–52; also W. Brecht, 'Storm und die Geschichte', *DVLG*, III (1925), 444–62.

6. *La Vie et l'Oeuvre de Theodor Storm*, Paris, 1920, 110.

7. In von Wiese, *Die deutsche Lyrik*, II, 191 ff.

8. Walter Silz, 'Theodor Storm: Three Poems', *GR*, XLII (1967), 292–300 stresses 'the auditory, musical quality of verse'.

9. Fritz Martini, 'Ein Gedicht Theodor Storms: "Geh nicht hinein" '. *Schriften der Theodor-Storm-Gesellschaft*, no. 6 (1957), 9–37.

10. Fritz Strich, ' "Das Spätboot" von C. F. Meyer' in *Die Kunst der Interpretation,* Zürich, 1955, 239–73.

11. ibid., 248.

12. Heinrich Henel, 'Conrad Ferdinand Meyer: *Lethe*' in von Wiese, *Die deutsche Lyrik*, II, 217–29. See also the same author's *The Poetry of Conrad Ferdinand Meyer*, Madison, 1954, 106–7 *et passim*.

13. Henel in von Wiese, op. cit., 226.

14. ibid., 238.

15. cf. R. B. Roulston, *Conrad Ferdinand Meyer: 'Huttens letzte Tage'*, Baltimore, 1933; also historisch-kritische Ausgabe, Berne, 1970.

16. A. Closs, *The Genius of the German Lyric*, 2nd edn., London, 1962, 309.

17. J. Bithell, *Modern German Literature 1880–1938*, London, 1939, 117.

18. Julius Bab, *Richard Dehmel*, Leipzig, 1926, 86–8.

Chapter 10

THEODORE FONTANE
AND THE SOCIAL NOVEL

I. PREPARATORY YEARS

FONTANE was born in 1819 in Neuruppin, near the site of the Prussian victory over the Swedes at Fehrbellin (1675), and he died in Berlin in 1898. The novels which won world fame[1] were all written in the last two decades, and the best of them in the last decade of his life. If Fontane had died short of sixty, he would be known in history as a minor poet and balladeer, as a journalist and war-correspondent, author of books of travel and regional history. Yet the first sixty years provided a necessary preparation for his late masterpieces which mirror the society of Berlin and Brandenburg.

Theodor was the descendant of French Huguenots welcomed by the elector of Brandenburg after the revocation of the Edict of Nantes (1685). His father, Louis Henri, born in 1797, took part as a volunteer in the campaign of 1813 against Napoleon. Father and son both became apothecaries and both married within the Huguenot community of Berlin. The father was a man interested in almost everything except his profession. He directed the earlier education of his eldest son, Theodor, and many idiosyncratic paternal traits are discernible in the *Apotheker*, Gieshübler, in *Effi Briest*, just as the Baltic port, Kessin, of this novel reflects Swinemünde, whither the family had moved with Micawber-like hopes of better prospects.

From 1833 Theodor lived in Berlin with an uncle who introduced his young nephew to café-life and witty conversation. His family background and this early acquaintance with urbane society strengthened his penchant for *causerie* which was to become the structural backbone of his novels. He served his *Lehrjahre* as pharmacist in Burg, Dresden, Leipzig, and briefly also in his father's latest establishment in Letschin.

His professional status enabled him to fulfil his obligatory military service as a 'one-year volunteer' officer-candidate in the Kaiser Franz Grenadier Guard Regiment in Berlin. An indulgent commanding officer granted him leave to visit England with a friend who footed the bill. Since 1843 he had been a member of the literary club 'Tunnel über der Spree' where his ballads had won acclaim.

With the expiration of his contract with the Bethany Hospital in Berlin in 1849, he resolved to abandon his pharmaceutical career and to live henceforth by his pen.

Meanwhile Fontane had experienced the Revolution of 1848 in Berlin. His attitude to these events reflects the two poles of his nature: *Ordnungssinn* and *Freiheitsliebe*. In retrospect he made light of his theatrical pose on the barricades with a stage-prop musket for which there were no bullets. Conscious of his ridiculous situation he refrained from further participation. Yet in spite of his conservative 'Tunnel'-friends, mostly barons, officers, *Assessoren*, the correspondence with his aristocratic friend Bernhard von Lepel shows Fontane's awareness of the approaching storm as early as 1846 and his fundamental sympathy with the rising liberal-democratic tide. His semi-outsider position as an anglophile descendant of French Huguenots reinforced his rejection of singleminded decisions and one-party stands in favour of objective multiple perspectives. This tendency to qualify and to see both sides developed in the later novels into what has been called the 'Fontane-Konzessionsstil'.[2] Near the end of his life Fontane was asked to answer in a guest-book the question: 'Lieben Sie das Ideale oder das Reale?' Fontane replied: 'Die Diagonale'. This transverse perspective illuminates his attitudes to *Ordnung* and *Freiheit*, to the nineteenth-century polar forces of conservatism and revolution.

Shaken by the Danish victory at Idstedt (1850), Fontane was already in Hamburg *en route* to volunteer for military service in Schleswig, when he was overtaken by a message from a 'Tunnel'-friend, offering a post in the 'Literary Bureau of the Ministry of the Interior'. Fontane accepted the position and forthwith married his Huguenot fianceé Emilie Rouanet. The job vanished in a departmental reorganization within two months and this evoked the first of many marital quarrels, since Emilie could never reconcile herself to the economic insecurity of a writer.

In 1852 and 1854 Fontane went to England as correspondent for a Berlin paper. The last sojourn filled nearly four years.[3] In 1855 he briefly visited Paris, but the brilliant capital of the Second Empire failed to eclipse the attraction of London. The essays and articles of this period were subsequently published in three volumes: *Ein Sommer in London* (1854); *Jenseits des Tweed*; and *Aus England-Studien und Briefe über Londoner Theater, Kunst und Presse* (both 1860).

In 1859 Fontane took the English desk of the conservative *Kreuzzeitung*. This appointment left him much free time to embark upon a project conceived a year earlier in Scotland: a regional description and history of the Mark Brandenburg. This occupied him intensively for the next decade and intermittently thereafter, for the *Wander-*

ungen durch die Mark Brandenburg came to an end only in 1889 with *Fünf Schlösser*. This labour too may be regarded as a prolegomenon to the novels portraying Junker families.

The *Wanderungen* were interrupted by Bismarck's three wars in which Fontane served as correspondent for his paper. Captured by the French, Fontane was saved from execution as a spy only by the last-moment intervention of Bismarck acting through the United States ambassador in Paris. The three war-books are weighted with statistics and operation orders, but the volume relating his own experiences is more lively: *Kriegsgefangen. Erlebtes 1870.*

The 'diagonal' position of Fontane in politics is reflected in his switch from the conservative *Kreuzzeitung* to the liberal *Vossiche Zeitung* in 1870. He resigned the latter post in 1876 to become First Secretary of the Royal Academy. His decision to ask to be relieved of this position, which had seemed to offer security but which had thrust him between feuding cliques, provoked the most serious domestic storm. But Fontane was already at work on his first novel, *Vor dem Sturm*, which was published in 1878 when the author was nearing sixty. This diffuse historical novel in four volumes grew naturally out of the *Wanderungen*, but is also influenced by the obvious models of Sir Walter Scott and Willibald Alexis.

II. THE POET

Although he was more prolific in verse in earlier years, when his 'Tunnel'-ballads won acclaim, Fontane continued to write both lyrics and ballads through most of his life.

In his *Stimmungslyrik* he appears to emulate Storm, without quite attaining the level of the best of the latter's work. The poem 'Glück' may illustrate this:

> Sonntagsruhe, Dorfesstille,
> Kind und Knecht und Magd sind aus,
> Unterm Herde nur die Grille
> Musizieret durch das Haus.

The mood of Sunday-rest and village-peace is slightly marred by a Rococo touch in the verb 'musizieret' – and it is quite possible that Fontane did this deliberately, to introduce an element of wit or movement. 'Mittag' illustrates a similar mood:

> Am Waldessaume träumt die Föhre,
> Am Himmel weiße Wölkchen nur;
> Es ist so still, daß ich sie höre,
> Die tiefe Stille der Natur.

> Rings Sonnenschein auf Wies' und Wegen,
> Die Wipfel stumm, kein Lüftchen wach,
> Und doch, es klingt, als ström' ein Regen
> Leis tönend auf das Blätterdach.

Of greater interest to the student of Fontane are some of the late poems which may be broadly described as 'philosophical' and which reveal both the *joie de vivre* and the spirit of resignation which infuse his novels. 'Was mir gefällt' shows the capacity to find pleasure in trivial, mundane, daily events:

> Du fragst: ob mir in dieser Welt
> Überhaupt noch was gefällt?
> Du fragst es und lächelst spöttisch dabei.
> Lieber Freund, mir gefällt noch allerlei:
> Jedes Frühjahr das erste Tiergartengrün,
> Oder wenn in Werder die Kirschen blühn,
> Zu Pfingsten Kalmus und Birkenreiser,
> Der alte Moltke, der alte Kaiser,
> Und dann zu Pferd, eine Stunde später,
> Mit dem gelben Streifen der 'Halberstädter';
> Kuckucksrufen, im Wald ein Reh,
> Ein Spaziergang durch die Läster-Allee,
> Paraden, der Schapersche Goethekopf
> Und ein Backfisch mit einem Mozartzopf.

In the following verses the poet hovers between gay participation in life and ironical renunciation:

> Ein Chinese ('s sind schon an 200 Jahr)
> In Frankreich auf einem Hofball war.
> Und die einen frugen ihn: ob er das kenne?
> Und die andern frugen ihn: wie man es nenne?
> 'Wir nennen es tanzen', sprach er mit Lachen,
> 'Aber wir lassen es *andere* machen'.
>
> Und dieses Wort, seit langer Frist,
> Mir immer in Erinnerung ist.
> Ich seh' das Rennen, ich seh' das Jagen,
> Und wenn mich die Menschen umdrängen und fragen:
> 'Was tust du nicht mit? Warum stehst du beiseit?'
> So sag' ich: 'Alles hat seine Zeit.
> Auch die Jagd nach dem Glück. All derlei Sachen,
> Ich lasse sie längst durch andere machen'.[4]

Resignation and a serene readiness for death, reminiscent of Dubslav Stechlin, may be glimpsed in 'Leben':

> Leben; wohl dem, dem es spendet
> Freude, Kinder, täglich Brot,
> Doch das Beste, was es sendet,
> Ist das Wissen, das es sendet,
> Ist der Ausgang, ist der Tod.[5]

The best of Fontane's ballads still find a place in most anthologies.

It has been astutely observed that Fontane needed a foreign spark to ignite his brightest flame, for his ballads on Prussian themes – even the best of them such as 'Prinz Louis Ferdinand' – fall behind those inspired by English, Scottish, or Nordic themes and models: 'Archibald Douglas', 'Gorm Grymme'. The earlier ballads were inspired by Percy's *Reliques* and Sir Walter Scott, but Fontane later used the ballad form for recording contemporaneous events, such as the disastrous accident marring an imposing feat of modern technology in 'Die Brück am Tay' and the passive quiet heroism of an inland sailor on Lake Erie in 'John Maynard'. The application of ancient means and measures to realistic current events has a piquant effect.

III. THE NOVELS AND *Novellen*

As with Raabe, it remains largely an academic question whether we classify certain of the shorter works of prose fiction as tales, novels, or *Novellen*, for the genius of both authors lay in areas other than *Novellenform*. Nevertheless, there is consensus that at least three are contributions to the *Novelle: Grete Minde* (1880), *Ellernklipp* (1881), and *Schach von Wuthenow*[6] (1883). All three have historical backgrounds.

Grete Minde is set in and around the Tangermünde of about 1615 and demonstrates the affinity of *Novelle* and drama, for it moves with the inexorable impact of a *Schicksalstragödie*. The turning-point or climax comes with the flight of Grete, who is denied both affection and justice by her brother and sister-in-law, well-to-do burghers, who withhold the legacy rightfully belonging to Grete. In the runaway lovers, Grete and Valtin, drifting downstream, we are reminded of Keller's *Romeo und Julia auf dem Dorfe*, and their life with the strolling players evokes Storm's *Pole Poppenspäler*. But in the holocaust which consumes the entire community because of the denial of justice we are even more vividly reminded of Kleist's *Michael Kohlhaas*.

Although historical in its setting on the eve of the collapse of Frederician Prussia at Jena in 1806, *Schach von Wuthenow* is sufficiently close to Fontane's own time to share the qualities of his characteristic novels of contemporary society. It is a story of vanity and individual weakness in the face of society, for Schach's code of honour compels him to marry the pock-marked Victoire. He commits suicide when ridiculed on account of the physical blemishes of his bride. This is an extreme reaction indeed, but it is intended to symbolize the brittleness of a Prussia which has failed to progress during a whole generation since the death of Frederick the Great.

Moreover, there are complicating factors: Schach is dimly but in-
sufficiently conscious of the inner strength and beauty of the outwardly disfigured Victoire and he is also deeply in love with her
mother! It is possible that Fontane intended this also to allude to the
introversion of Prussian society.

Of the sixteen works of prose fiction which followed *Vor dem
Sturm* in the last eighteen years of Fontane's life, some fall short of
greatness, yet all are highly readable and all reflect in some degree
the remarkable genius of their creator. In such a prolific output it is
not surprising that some works are derivative, such as *Stine*, which
picks up the theme of *Irrungen, Wirrungen* and plays it out in a
tragic vein, for Graf von Haldern is even weaker than Botho and,
faced with Stine's rejection of a marriage which would defy social
convention, commits suicide. It is also true that Fontane is not at
his best in settings far from Berlin and the Mark, for example *Graf
Petöfy*, set in Vienna and Hungary. Nevertheless, the magnitude of
Fontane's achievement is astonishing, especially in view of his diverse
activities: literary and dramatic critic (he earned the gratitude of
the Naturalists for his enthusiastic reception of Hauptmann's *Die
Weber*); chronicler (still finishing the *Wanderungen* in 1888); poet
still turning out verses; autobiographer (*Meine Kinderjahre, Von
Zwanzig bis Dreißig*); and above all indefatigable letter-writer. (The
Briefe an Georg Friedländer, published only in 1954, cast new and
indispensable light on his last works and on his social and political
opinions.)

The typical Fontane-novel focuses on society and social problems
and is closer to the French, English, and Russian nineteenth-century
tradition than to the German *Bildungsroman*. Although this puts
Fontane in the mainstream of European fiction, it is only his genius
which keeps him afloat. To identify the special qualities of his genius
is an elusive task which many have undertaken. It is elusive especially
in the deceptive lightness of tone: the easy flow of table-talk and
bantering, witty *causerie* which is a central structural feature of his
best works. The variations of which this is capable are astonishing
when we recall the *Tischgespräche* in the humble cottage of Frau
Nimptsch where Botho, for the amusement of Lene and the others,
gives a brilliant parody of table-talk in high society. The lightness of
tone is deceptive because the conversations contain numerous symbolic or leitmotival allusions.

Fontane's work is characterized also by an ironic, non-committed
attitude – in part an attribute of age, but an attitude which, one
feels, Fontane must always have possessed in some degree. There are
always at least two sides to everything. This becomes the virtual
theme and structure of *Unwiederbringlich* (1892), so that, despite
Graf Holk's adulterous escapade in Copenhagen, his wife is also not

free of guilt for the situation leading to the divorce, and her inability to recover former happiness when the pair are remarried leads to her suicide at the end. The capacity for seeing both sides, good and bad, means that Fontane is far from being an apologist for the Junkers as a class, for his protagonists represent a wide range of ethical values. Nor is Fontane simply conservative, as we shall see especially in his last novel, *Der Stechlin* (1898).

Despite consensus on his greatness and his rightful place in European literature, Fontane has not been without critics of individual works – his 'Krittikker', as Wrschowitz (*Der Stechlin*) would say. Ernst Alker admits only one novel, *Effi Briest*, to the status of 'Dichtung' without reservation.[7] One wonders whether some German critics are not misled by Fontane's light tone to the false assumption that his work lacks weight. Yet Fontane has also been criticized for overburdening his novels with symbols and for making the symbols too obvious, such as the Chinese 'outsider' in *Effi Briest*. But, as we shall see, this symbolic figure is used with great finesse and complexity through the whole novel.

Fontane, with his urbane scepticism, stands in absolute contrast to Nietzsche, at least in the latter's tendentious Zarathustra-phase. It is therefore not surprising that Fontane has been accused of weakness in failing to take a stand.[8] Possibly too much emphasis has been placed on his French Huguenot ancestry and concomitant Calvinist predestination.[9] Although he had only a drop of Prussian blood (one grandparent) and although his parents used French a good deal in the home, Fontane nevertheless felt himself essentially Prussian and, in fact, was deeply concerned with what he thought in the 1890s to be Prussia's parlous state and uncertain future. French was still to some extent the language of high society, as it had been in the time of Frederick the Great, and the use of French phrases and *Fremdwörter* is not necessarily a sign of French background or influence. The French element was significant, however, in giving Fontane an awareness of difference, something of the outsider's perspective.

The French elements are so obvious that they tend to obscure the other foreign influence: England. This extends far beyond the ballads and travel-books. Fontane was not a francophile but an anglophile. There are reflections of this in almost every novel: in Graf Barby (*Der Stechlin*), moulded by his prolonged stay as diplomat in London; Graf Holk, who after his divorce takes refuge in England (*Unwiederbringlich*); Mr Armstrong and his amusingly forthright opinions on Prussian landgrabbing in 1866 (*Irrungen, Wirrungen*). Beyond such specific examples, it could be claimed that Fontane's ultimate stand is essentially British: in the face of adversities and awareness of an antiquated and decadent social and political order, keep a stiff upper lip. Wüllersdorf says as much near the end of *Effi Briest*, after Innstetten has ruined his life by his duel and divorce, inspired by allegiance to a hollow code of honour, and when his decoration and promotion inspire nihilistic thoughts:

> In der Bresche stehen und aushalten, bis man fällt, das ist das beste. Vorher aber im kleinen und kleinsten so viel herausschlagen wie möglich und ein Auge haben dafür, wie die Veilchen blühen. . . . Oder auch wohl nach Potsdam fahren und in die Friedrichskirche gehen, wo Kaiser Friedrich liegt . . . Und wenn Sie da stehen, dann überlegen Sie sich das Leben von *dem*. . . .[10]

This stoic acceptance and the capacity for rising above the blows of fate can be seen in Botho von Rienäcker, who, although he lacks the strength to break with convention and society, has the quiet British determination to bear his fate and make the best of it.

Fontane has been accused of neglecting the urban industrial proletariat – Döblin's *Berlin Alexanderplatz* shows a totally different aspect of the same city only two or three decades later – and it is claimed that Fontane was biased against the rising bourgeois capitalist entrepreneurs. It is true that his cast is usually drawn from the high and the low, from the Junkers and the servants, but he shows constant sympathy for the latter (e.g., Lene, Stine, Engelke, Agnes, Roswitha, Hedwig, Elfriede, Frau Schmolke), and it is true that the bourgeois characters are often caricatured (Wrschowitz and Cujacius in *Der Stechlin* and Gideon Franke in *Irrungen, Wirrungen*), or satirized as in *Frau Jenny Treibel*, which is the one major novel – perhaps ranking fourth or fifth in the canon – dealing exclusively with the bourgeois milieu. The money-conscious 'bourgeoise', Frau Treibel, ambitious wife of a *nouveau riche* dye-manufacturer, foils the will of her weak son, Leopold, to marry Corinna, daughter of Jenny's former beau, Professor Schmidt. The latter embodies the typical Fontane qualities of sympathetic but detached observation and ironic resignation. At the end he and his daughter come to regard 'diese Treibelei als einen Irrtum, als einen Schritt vom Wege'. Corinna enters a far more suitable match with her cousin, Marcell Wedderkopp, a young archaeologist and *Gymnasialoberlehrer*.

The one novel which could oust *Frau Jenny Treibel* from fourth place is *Unwiederbringlich* (1892), which Demetz claims has been neglected by German critics because of its 'Distanzierung nach Norddeutschland und Dänemark'.[11] Demetz goes on to note the praise of Swiss critics such as Max Rychner and Conrad Ferdinand Meyer, who observed in it 'feine Psychologie, feste Umrisse, höchst lebenswahre Charaktere und über alles doch ein gewisser poetischer Hauch'. In Demetz's opinion,

Unwiederbringlich bleibt das makelloseste *Kunstwerk* Fontanes:– ohne Schlacke und Sentimentalität; kühl, gefaßt, kontrolliert; ein Buch ganz aus Elfenbein; der einzige deutsche Roman der Epoche, der den Wettstreit selbst mit Turgenjew oder gar Trollope und William Dean Howells nicht zu scheuen hat.[12]

Despite Demetz's brilliant analysis of the novel's structure and psychology, most critics still give top honours to the trio: *Irrungen, Wirrungen, Effi Briest,* and *Der Stechlin.*

iv. *Irrungen, Wirrungen* (1888)

With the passage of time all of Fontane's novels of contemporary society have acquired some of the attributes of the historical novel, as an age now past unfolds in all its detail and colour. At first glance the theme of *Irrungen, Wirrungen* may seem irrelevant and as antiquated as the Prussian Junkers with their class prejudices and conventions. But the problem has a basic and universal aspect applicable to any epoch. Botho faces the choice between true but *déclassé* love on the one hand and duty to family, class, and tradition on the other. Divested of its particular attributes, the theme raises pertinent questions: can an individual hold out against all the social and moral pressures, in order to grasp happiness? Or will not individual happiness elude his grasp in any event? Is it better to sever all ties with the past, with one's family, profession, and moral code, in order to follow the dictates of the heart in Romantic isolation from the world? Or is it the lesser of two evils to renounce the claim to personal happiness?

It may also be claimed that the theme lies not so much in Botho's agonizing choice between conflicting loyalties, as in the attitudes of the protagonists and of the narrator, so that the atmosphere of resignation, of melancholy, irony, and scepticism, the lingering echoes and after-effects become thematic rather than merely formal elements. If such is the case, this novel fulfils the claim of Henry James that 'in proportion as the work is successful the idea permeates and penetrates it, informs and animates it, so that every word and every punctuation-point contribute to the expression'.[13]

The Eden-like garden in which we meet the lovers in the opening pages is dominated by the sham 'Schloß'-façade of Dörr's market-garden-dwelling, and the setting June sun casts ominous shadows. Again it is a fateful omen that Frau Dörr introduces the lovers to their happiness, just after raising the veil on her own 'dark' past with her 'Graf mit seine fuffzig auf'm Puckel'. There is, of course, marked contrast between the idyllic love of Lene and Botho and Frau Dörr's past liaison. Yet the latter's affair and her present dull, crotchety husband prepare for the advent of Gideon Franke, after Lene's romance is shattered by the impact of reality.

The structural principle of contrast is allied with that of balance and the latter is suggestive of the theme of *Ordnung*. The novel, for example, falls naturally into two contrasting halves: the first embraces the garden-world of the Dörrs and the ever-glowing hearth of Frau Nimptsch. Into this sheltered world of the lovers there enter only echoes of the wider social sphere. The second half deals with Botho's *mariage de convenance* with Countess Käthe[14] and the upper-class milieu which reflects broader political and social problems. Each half contains thirteen chapters.

The climax or turning-point comes in the episode at Hankels Ablage and the three chapters devoted to this employ multiple contrasts. The first two chapters mark the climactic bliss of the lovers in their retreat into which the outside world impinges, in the third chapter, with the arrival of Botho's fellow officers and their *demi-monde* 'Damen'. But even the euphoria of the first part of their sojourn is countered by hints of the untenable situation: the knowing embarrassment of the innkeeper, the naïve indiscretions of his wife, Botho's stammering efforts to avoid designating Lene's status, and the contrasting pictures in the bedroom. 'Washington Crossing the Delaware' and 'The Last Hour at Trafalgar' remind Lene of the abyss separating her world from Botho's, since she cannot decipher the English titles. They also point symbolically to the impending decision and tragic ending of their relationship, for Prussia expects Botho to do his duty. The remaining picture, 'Si jeunesse savait', also evokes multiple allusions, but primarily it offends Lene's 'delicate sensuality' because of its 'lustfulness'. When Botho asks Lene which boat they should take, 'die Forelle' or 'die Hoffnung', Lene replies: 'Natürlich die Forelle. Was sollen wir mit der Hoffnung?' (ch. 11).

Fontane's irony varies from the comical and obvious, as in Frau Dörr's conversations and in the allusions to Schiller's *Jungfrau von Orleans*, to more subtle situations. The dilemma of young Rexin ironically turns the tables, obliging Botho now to defend *Ordnung*, *Pflicht*, *Junkertum*, and *Familie* against the claims of true love. Käthe seems oblivious of the irony of her reports on the Hanoverian reactions to Prussianization. But there may be a more subtle ironic double-level of interpretation of her own character. Behind her superficial chatter she may be concealing with conscious irony her own deeper knowledge of Botho and his past. When she finds the ashes in the fireplace, she says: 'Liebesbriefe, zu komisch' (ch. 26). And when, in the last lines of the novel, Käthe reads with amusement – 'es ist doch zu komisch' – the queer names in the marriage announcement, Botho rejoins: 'Was hast du nur gegen Gideon,

Käthe? Gideon ist besser als Botho'. This final irony probes on the deepest level the whole social problem.

Of the poetic devices employed by Fontane, the leitmotiv has attracted most attention and exerted a fascination on Thomas Mann, who elaborated this technique with the greatest virtuosity. It is characteristic of Fontane and his place in Poetic Realism that most of the leitmotival allusions are embedded in simple colloquial figures of speech, or settings and actions rooted in every-day reality. The mention of the strawberry-kiss by 'Queen Isabeau' re-evokes with vivid contrast that between Botho and Lene.

In a letter of 14 July 1887 to Emil Dominik, Fontane wrote of the thousand finesses which he had imparted to this favourite work. The multiple associations of the leitmotiv *Binden* is one of the most skilful. During the luncheon in Hiller's restaurant (ch. 7), Baron Osten is glad to have the conversation diverted from Bismarck and high politics to local situations. He tells Botho: 'Du bist doch so gut wie gebunden' and reminds his nephew of the bride's qualities: 'Eine Flachsblondine zum Küssen....' Then we come to the happiest day at Hankels Ablage (ch. 11) and the 'Binden' of the bouquet with a strand of Lene's hair: 'Nun bist du gebunden'. Years later, when his wife is at the spa, Botho reflects: '... warum bestand ich darauf? Ja, es gibt solche rätselhaften Kräfte, solche Sympathien aus Himmel oder Hölle, und nun bin ich gebunden und kann nicht los'. He tries to free himself from these memories by burning Lene's love-letters. As the flames die away, he says: 'Ob ich nun frei bin?.. Will ich's denn? Ich will es *nicht*. Alles Asche. Und *doch* gebunden' (end of ch. 22). This last recurrence of the leitmotiv spans in a flash the whole range of contrasting associations from the *Bindung* to class, family, and betrothed to the opposing tie of true love. The *Binden*-motif also illustrates the interlocking of leitmotivs, for its last occurrence also re-evokes the ever-glowing hearth of Frau Nimptsch, which symbolized the warmth of the relationship between Botho and Lene in the first half of the novel – and which was missing and had to be replaced by a makeshift arrangement in Frau Nimptsch's new dwelling. Now we are aware that Botho has just returned from placing everlastings on her grave (thereby connecting with another leitmotiv: duty, honour, *Ordnung*). In this last scene we are conscious, moreover, of the fact that the fire in Botho's hearth lacks the life-giving warmth associated with Lene and her circle. We wonder whether this marriage is to remain childless and thus symbolic of an aristocracy without a future. On this point Fontane gives no conclusive answer. On the one hand Käthe flippantly remarks that Botho's brother can provide the neces-sary heir, but on the other hand Käthe has just returned from a spa whose waters are noted for effectiveness in curing sterility in female patients, and there may be a hint of a deeper relationship in the mood of the couple after Käthe's return, the immolation of Lene's letters, and in the domesticity of the closing breakfast scene.

Botho is a weak and passive hero, but perhaps for that reason gains our sympathy in almost the same degree as Lene. Both lives are affected permanently and both adjust as well as possible, accepting the conventional standards.

That the lovers, Botho and Lene, are 'elective affinities' is symbolized above all in their joint allegiance to *Ordnung*, to what is fitting, proper, and honourable. This theme is first associated with Lene through Frau Dörr's comments:

> Und wenn ich mir nu der Lene ihren Baron ansehe, denn schämt es mir immer noch, wenn ich denke, wie meiner war. Un nu gar erst die Lene selber. Jott, ein Engel is sie woll grade auch nich, aber *propper und fleißig* un *kann alles und is für Ordnung und fürs Reelle.* (ch. 1)

Later Botho asks Lene about Frau Dörr's past affair and Lene replies: 'Sie spricht davon wie von einem unbequemen Dienst, den sie *getreulich* und *ehrlich* erfüllt, hat, bloß aus *Pflichtgefühl*' (ch. 5). At Hankels Ablage Botho admires the 'ordentlichen Arbeitstaktschlag' at the boat-works. The motif assumes a contrasting ironic air when 'Queen Isabeau' tells Lene she is going to give up this *demi-monde* life, buy a pub, and marry a widower: 'Denn das muß ich Ihnen sagen, ich bin für *Ordnung* und *Anständigkeit* und die Kinder *orntlich* erziehen, und ob es seine sind oder meine, is janz egal....' (ch. 13).

On the return from Hankels Ablage, Botho is confronted by his mother's letter and the necessity of a decision. He reflects that to him the best things in life are 'Einfachheit, Wahrheit, Natürlichkeit. Das alles hat Lene; damit hat sie mir's angetan, da liegt der Zauber, aus dem mich zu lösen mir jetzt so schwerfällt' (ch. 14). Riding into the fields, he watches the workmen taking their midday meal:

> Arbeit und täglich Brot und Ordnung.... Denn Ordnung ist viel und mitunter alles. Und nun frag' ich mich. War *mein* Leben in der 'Ordnung'? Nein. Ordnung ist Ehe....
>
> Ja, meine liebe Lene, du bist auch fur Arbeit und Ordnung und siehst es ein und machst es mir nicht schwer ... aber schwer ist es doch ... für dich und mich. (ch. 14)

When Gideon Franke seeks of Botho a character-reference for his bride, Lene, Botho sums up '... sie hat das Herz auf dem rechten Fleck und ein starkes Gefühl für Pflicht und Recht und Ordnung'. To this Franke adds, after his homily on the commandments:

> Ja, Herr Baron, auf die Proppertät kommt es an und auf die Honnettität kommt es an und auf die Reellität.... Auf die Wahrheit kommt es an, und auf die Zuverlässigkeit kommt es an, und auf die Ehrlichkeit. (ch. 20)

We have already noted the ironic implications of Botho's advice to his young friend, Rexin, not to break with 'Stand und Herkommen und Sitte'. It is ironic, too, that Käthe, returning from the spa, seems to be herself a convert to similar virtues and the simple life: 'Ach, Botho, welcher Schatz ist doch ein unschuldiges Herz. Ich habe mir fest vorgenommen, mir ein reines Herz zu bewahren' (ch. 25). When the reunited couple chat after breakfast on their balcony overlooking the Zoo, we recall the Nimptsch cottage – introduced in the second line of the novel: 'schräg gegenüber dem "Zoologischen" ' – and inwardly we contrast the earlier conversations between Botho and Lene with Käthe's gossip about the spa visitors.

The leitmotival complex embracing *Arbeit, Ordnung, Ehrlichkeit, Natürlichkeit, Einfachkeit* is not used to extol the Junkers as a class. It has been astutely observed that these are middle-class virtues and that Botho's attraction to them betrays a tendency away from his own class. Among the Junkers it is only he and his old uncle who embody these virtues. Botho's cynical fellow officers represent the younger generation of the aristocracy. In *Stine*, the tragic complement of the *Irrungen, Wirrungen*-theme, Fontane expresses his disillusionment with Prussian *Junkertum* more directly through the words of Graf von Haldern:

> Ich bin nicht so verrottet wie du glaubst . . . ich habe von der göttlichen Weltordnung nicht die Vorstellung, daß sie sich mit dem Staatskalender und der Rangliste vollkommen deckt. Ja, ich will dir noch mehr sagen: ich habe Stunden, in denen ich ziemlich fest davon überzeugt bin, daß sie sich *nicht* damit überdeckt. Und es werden, und vielleicht in nicht allzuferner Zukunft, die Regulierungszeiten kommen . . . und vielleicht auch wieder die Adam- und Evazeiten. (ch. 12)

With these words Fontane conjured up an intuitive prophecy of the revolutionary and anarchistic trends of the twentieth century. His fiction is enhanced by these insights and by the ambivalent depiction of types and classes, but his greatness as a novelist rests upon the creation of vivid individuals – *schuldig-unschuldig* – and upon the formal artistry and subtlety of character-presentation and novel-structure.

v. *Effi Briest* (1895)

Despite the title's indication of Effi's central position, sympathy for her endearing, if superficial, character and tragic death is balanced by sympathy for Innstetten – 'ein Mann von Charakter, ein Mann von Prinzipien . . . auch ein Mann von Grundsätzen . . . und das ist, glaub ich, noch etwas mehr', as Effi describes him at the end of chapter 4. It is quite possible to be enthralled by the vivid, witty characterization and by the vicissitudes of the protagonists. But the novel possesses another dimension expressed by Innstetten near the end: 'Man ist nicht bloß ein einzelner Mensch, man gehört einem Ganzen an, und auf das Ganze haben wir beständig Rücksicht zu nehmen, wir sind durchaus abhängig von ihm' (ch. 27). The strands of individual characterization and symbolic meaning are woven into a number of subtle leitmotival complexes.

Effi passes from girlish games on her father's country estate into matrimony with Baron Innstetten – a former beau of her mother – because it is expected of her and because she is eager for novelty and change of scene. She misses warmth and spontaneity in her older ambitious husband (but she shares his ambition) and is drawn into a clandestine affair with Major Crampas, despite the fact that she sees through him. Her relief at the news of the move to Berlin leads her almost to give her secret away. The Berlin years are full of happiness and contentment – until, when Effi is away at the spa, Innstetten inadvertently discovers Effi's love-letters from Crampas. Thus Fontane has placed the Junker code on a razor's edge. Is the 'man of principle' obliged to fight a duel over an affair buried nearly seven years in the past?

> Es *muß* eine Verjährung geben, Verjährung ist das einzig Vernünftige. . . . Ich bin jetzt fünfundvierzig. Wenn ich die Briefe fünfundzwanzig Jahre später gefunden hätte, so wär ich siebzig. Dann hätte Wüllersdorf gesagt: 'Innstetten, seien Sie kein Narr'. . . . Aber wo fängt es an? Wo liegt die Grenze? Zehn Jahre verlangen noch ein Duell, und da heißt es Ehre, und nach elf Jahren oder vielleicht schon bei zehneinhalb heißt es Unsinn. Die Grenze, die Grenze. Wo ist sie? War sie da? War sie schon überschritten? Wenn ich mir seinen letzten Blick vergegenwärtige . . . so hieß der Blick: 'Innstetten, Prinzipienreiterei. . . . (ch. 29)

Ironically, by revealing the past stain on his honour to his friend Wüllersdorf, Innstetten has committed himself to the duel commanded by the Junker code, for it is now no longer a private matter for his conscience. He is as much a victim of the society he represents as is Effi, and he knows that the step he is taking will ruin his life, despite his subsequent reinstatement and his ultimate decoration and promotion which induce only nihilistic reflections: 'je mehr man mich auszeichnet, je mehr fühle ich, daß dies alles nichts ist. Mein Leben is verpfuscht' (ch. 35).

Years after the divorce, when Effi has successfully pleaded with the Minister's wife for permission to see her daughter, the granting of the request is reported with the words: 'Ihr Herr Gemahl. . . . ein Mann, der nicht nach Stimmungen und Laune, sondern nach Grundsätzen handelt' (ch. 32).

But what is one to do when the bottom falls out of one's life and one realizes that the social and political system which one upholds is a hollow sham? Innstetten toys with the idea of losing himself in darkest Africa 'unter lauter pechschwarze Kerle, die von Kultur und Ehre nichts wissen. Diese Glücklichen! Denn gerade *das*, dieser ganze Krimskram ist doch an allem schuld' (ch.35). From these morbid and nihilistic temptations, he is brought back by Wüllersdorf to recognition of his own 'principles' – that it is better to 'stand in the breach until one falls'. There can be little doubt that this is Fontane's own attitude. Like his protagonist, Innstetten, aware of the hollow and brittle façade of Prussian society, Fontane tended to favour the upholders of *Ordnung*, because the alternative of anarchy seemed the greater evil. Even if the Junker code of honour is a meaningless idolatry, it is better to submit as long as it is valid enough to offer 'Hilfskonstruktionen' without which life is impossible. In the words of Wüllersdorf: '... unser Ehrenkultus ist ein Götzendienst, aber wir müssen uns ihm unterwerfen, so lange der Götze gilt' (end ch. 27).

This leitmotiv of sacrifice to a bloodthirsty idol thus, at the end, clearly embraces Innstetten and the whole Junker world. Earlier allusions had pointed only to Effi as the sacrificial victim, beginning with the ominous man-eating shark in the Kessin house, and continuing in the allusions of Crampas to Heine's 'Vitzliputzli' and 'Spanische Atriden'. When Effi is only too conscious of her guilt, the couple go for a summer holiday to the island of Rügen in the Baltic. Not only does Effi learn that a village on the island bears the name Crampas, but they visit the altar of the pagan 'Hertadienst' and are shown the groove in the stone for carrying away the blood of the victim. The goddess Herta recalls the opening scenes of childish games with Herta and Berta Jahnke and the name points forward to the coming sacrifice, for Herta, in Teutonic mythology, was the goddess of fertility, who, according to Tacitus, was worshipped with orgies and mysterious nocturnal rites. Innstetten goodnaturedly gives in to Effi's request to depart at once for Copenhagen: 'Ich will dich mit Rügen nicht quälen'[15] (ch. 24).

The sacrifice-motif is at many points linked with adultery. Even as Effi is preparing her trousseau, the estate-manager, Pink, has seduced the gardener's wife. Reluctantly Effi's father has had to let him go: '... übrigens ungern. Es ist sehr fatal, daß solche Geschichten fast immer in die Erntezeit fallen. Und Pink war sonst ein ungewöhnlich tüchtiger Mann ...' (ch. 4).

Later Effi is fascinated with the *artiste*, die Tripelli, and her frank avowal of her liaison with a Russian prince. The variation in the motif here lies in the fact that die Tripelli, *qua artiste*, is an outsider and therefore beyond the reach of the *Götzendienst*.

Roswitha, herself an outsider as a Roman Catholic, enters the story and Effi's life at the critical point in her relationship with

Crampas, and there is no doubt that Effi's heart is won by Roswitha's pitiful story of her girlhood seduction and subsequent expulsion by her outraged father brandishing red-hot pokers.[16] It is highly ironic, however, that Effi, on returning from a rendezvous on the beach with Crampas, thinks she has caught Roswitha flirting with coachman Kruse, and rebukes her. In fact, Kruse is busy polishing the harness, despite the drizzle, for, he says, 'alles muß seine Ordnung haben'.[17] It is possible that Kruse's mentally deranged wife, sitting day after day in her rocking-chair, petting a black hen, has been the sacrificial victim of a *Schritt vom Wege* on the part of her husband, and this would account for his sympathetic and penitential deference towards her.

In his otherwise perceptive comparison of *Effi Briest* with *Madame Bovary* and *Anna Karenina*, J. P. Stern finds the 'imagery of a mysterious Chinaman' to be 'the only blemish in the novel ... a piece of bric-à-brac left over by poetic realism'.[18] It is difficult to accept this adverse judgement, for the Chinaman represents far more than a symbolic prefiguration of Effi's fate as an 'outsider'. The multiple strands of the Chinaman-ghost-motif form a central structural and thematic link. T. E. Carter[19] has demonstrated how this complex leitmotiv is associated both with Innstetten's ambition and his control over Effi's 'Erziehung'. Crampas explains to Effi:

> Also Innstetten, meine gnädige Frau, hat außer seinem brennenden Verlangen, es koste, was es wolle, ja, wenn es sein muß unter Heranziehung eines Spuks, seine Karriere zu machen, noch eine zweite Passion: er operiert nämlich immer erzieherisch, ist der geborene Pädagog ... (end ch. 16).

Effi finds this 'grausam' and there is a delicious element of irony in the fact that Innstetten's 'pedagogic' motive to keep his wife in bounds has the opposite effect and motivates her 'Schritt vom Wege'.[20] More important, however, the Chinaman comes increasingly to symbolize her sense of guilt. Allusions to the Chinaman, the shark, and the crocodile in the Kessin house run through the novel accumulating multiple symbolic associations. Even the move to Berlin does not obliterate Effi's guilt, for Johanna has brought the imprint of the Chinaman from the back of a chair.

It is illuminating to analyze the network of motifs embracing flight, swinging, gliding (Flucht, Schaukel, Schlitten).[21] At the beginning, this motif emphasizes Effi's prominent trait of youthful vivacity and desire to soar above the earth: 'rasch, rasch, ich fliege aus' (ch. 2). Her behaviour is in striking contrast to the conventional reserve of the other girls. A few lines further we read: 'sie flog ... hin'. Her pleasure in quick movement in the air, especially with a strong wind, reveals how her nature unfolds freely and unrestrained in the breeze – as it does later when she rides in the nor'wester with Crampas. In her childhood games, climbing, swinging, teeter-totter predominate. Her father has promised to erect a 'Mastbaum' near the 'Schaukel' so that Effi may soar aloft like a midshipman. Only the German word 'Schaukel' provides the necessary link, for it means a swing on ropes and a see-saw, and it recurs even in such compounds as 'Schaukelstuhl'.

Shortly before the marriage, her mother tries to pry out of Effi her real feelings towards Innstetten and Effi replies:

> Er hat keine Ahnung davon, daß ich mir nichts aus Schmuck mache. Ich klettere lieber und schaukle mich lieber, und am liebsten immer in der Furcht, daß es irgendwo reißen oder brechen und ich niederstürzen könnte. Den Kopf wird es ja nicht gleich kosten. (end ch. 4)

Mother Briest sees only the problem of social propriety: 'Du hättest ... doch wohl Kunstreiterin werden müssen. Immer am Trapez, immer Tochter der Luft'[22] (ch. 1).

Effi's 'Schaukel' as described in the opening chapter has associations of decay and danger: 'die Pfosten der Balkenlage schon etwas schief stehend'. We take leave of Effi finally in her grave by the arbour beside this 'Schaukel'. On a brief visit to Hohen-Cremmen, now the wife of a high official, Effi is still enthralled by the 'Schaukel':

> Am liebsten aber hätte sie wie früher auf dem durch die Luft fliegenden Schaukelbrett gestanden und in dem Gefühle: 'jetzt stürze ich', etwas eigentümlich Prickelndes, einen Schauer süßer Gefahr empfunden. (ch. 15)

Once more, at the end, Effi mounts the swing, sick, lonely, outcast from the world, returning from the walk in the garden with Pastor Niemeyer:

> Sie flog durch die Luft, und bloß mit einer Hand sich haltend, riß sie mit der andern ein kleines Seidentuch von Brust und Hals und schwenkte es wie in Glück und Übermut. (ch. 34)

The little word 'wie' brings out the stark contrast in this re-evocation of all the accumulated associations of this leitmotiv. She tries to recapture the thrill, but it is only 'wie Glück' – happiness remembered but no longer present. She goes on to say to Pastor Niemeyer: 'Ich hab' es nur noch einmal versuchen wollen ... mir war, als flög ich in den Himmel'. To her question whether she might be admitted, the pastor replies: 'Ja, Effi, du wirst'.

The 'Schaukel'-motif merges into the leitmotiv of gliding or sliding through space. Innstetten tries to cheer up his wife by talk of the sleighbells and white robes of winter, thus betraying his lack of understanding of Effi's nature, for she discloses that her interests lie elsewhere: 'Es ist ja himmlisch, so hinzufliegen, und ich fühle ordentlich, wie mir so frei wird und wie alle Angst von mir abfällt' (ch. 10). Strange words for a bride! Later, returning from a Christmas party with the country gentry, Effi scorns protective devices: 'Ich kann die Schutzleder nicht leiden; sie haben so was Prosaisches. Und dann, wenn ich hinausflöge, mir wär es recht, am liebsten gleich in die Brandung' (ch. 19). We are thus prepared for the next and decisive recurrence of this motif: when they have to change sleighs and Effi finds herself alone with Crampas, following the others 'im Flug' with Crampas declaring his passion. While Innstetten characteristically takes a safe detour, Crampas takes Effi straight through the dangerous 'Schloon'.[23]

The development of the 'Flucht-Schlitten-Schaukel' complex of symbolic motifs has led up to this point. Effi succumbs in a moment of ecstasy to the sensation of free soaring flight beyond conscious responsibility. In a sense the identification of her personality with this motif is also an apology for her transgression.

The symmetry of the novel is reflected in the two servants: the loyal but stern Johanna who sides with Innstetten and the faithful, warm Roswitha, herself an earlier victim, who finds her way back to Effi. When Roswitha writes to Innstetten to ask for the dog Rollo, Wüllersdorf comments on her: 'Ja – die ist über uns' (ch. 35). In view of the symbolic, representative nature of the characters, this can be taken as a clear hint from Fontane that the proletariat possessed elements destined to oust the ruling Junkers. Fontane's letters to Friedländer in the last years of his life offer more direct evidence of Fontane's disillusionment with the Prussian state and the Junker class.

What constitutes real nobility for Fontane emerges from the first conversation of Effi with Apotheker Gieshübler, whose first name, Alonzo, Effi correctly divines, is derived from his mother, daughter of a Spanish consul in Kessin. Gieshübler is an 'outsider' both through his exotic maternal ancestry and through his physical deformity, and in part his devotion to Effi derives from his awareness of 'outsider' affinities in Effi which threaten her existence. When Gieshübler explains that he is the fourth of his line in the family of Kessin apothecaries, 'und wenn es einen Apothekeradel gäbe...', Effi completes the statement: 'so würden Sie ihn beanspruchen dürfen'. Effi would take that for granted, because such things are most easily conceded by the oldest families. She is a descendant of the Briest who captured Rathenow on the eve of Fehrbellin, but

> mein Vater, da reichen keine hundert Male, daß er zu mir gesagt hat: 'Effi ... *hier* sitzt es, bloß hier, und als Froben das Pferd tauschte, da war er von Adel, und als Luther sagte: "hier stehe ich", da war er erst recht von Adel'. (ch. 8)

In this novel Fontane's brilliant use of witty, apparently casual, but allusive conversation is seen at its best. There is hardly a remark

which is not both realistically natural and at the same time redo-
lent with symbolic or leitmotival allusions to the thematic texture.
Two examples must suffice. When Innstetten returns with news of
their impending move to Berlin (ch. 21), he observes that everything
is as it was on the day of their arrival in Kessin, 'nur der Haifisch
... verhält sich etwas ruhiger'. He finds Effi has changed (for the
better!): 'Du hattest so was von einem verwöhnten Kind, mit einem
Male siehst du aus wie eine Frau' (ch. 21). Innstetten depicts their
future lives as *Ministerialrat und -rätin* in Berlin, concluding
'... in einem halben Jahr wirst du kaum noch wissen, daß du hier
in Kessin gewesen bist und nichts gehabt hast als Gieshübler und
die Dünen und die Plantage'. Effi is so conscious of her guilt on
the dunes (ch. 17) that she almost gives herself away with relief at
the prospect of escape to Berlin: 'Gott sei Dank'.

When Effi and Crampas are picnicking on the dunes, Effi plays
hostess: 'Es tut mir leid, Major, Ihnen diese Brötchen in einem
Korbdeckel präsentieren zu müssen...' Crampas interrupts: 'Ein
Korbdeckel ist kein Korb' (ch. 17). Every reader will get the
immediate point since 'einen Korb geben' is a standard idiom for
'jilting', but an esoteric allusion greets the philologist who knows the
origin of the phrase, for according to Grimm, in the Middle Ages
ladies were supposed to have hauled their lovers up the castle walls
in a basket. If the member of the gentle sex wished to be rid of the
importunate male, she would let the basket fall from a height which
might lead to fatal results for the adventurous wooer. Thus there is
a buried allusion to Crampas's fate.

Innstetten's second in the duel, Buddenbrooks, provided Thomas
Mann with the name that made him famous. Indeed the table-
talk in the Buddenbrook house reminds us of Fontane's brilliant
and allusive style, just as the conversations of Tony and young
Morten on the Baltic dunes have more than a merely environmental
similarity with the talks between Effi and Crampas. 'Honig' and
'auf den Steinen sitzen' become important leitmotivs in Mann's
novel.

Although Fontane was usually content as narrator to retreat
behind his characters and to let the action develop through
causerie, and although his correspondence with Spielhagen acknow-
ledges the superiority of this realistic-naturalistic technique, yet he
was no slave to this convention. In chapter 32 we read: ' "Schicken
Sie mir doch einfach Roswitha..." hatte Rummschüttel gesagt.
Ja, war denn Roswitha bei Effi? War sie statt in der Keith- in der
Königrätzerstraße? Gewiß war sie's, und zwar sehr lange schon...'
Pascal is quite right to point to the subtle artistry of this author-
intrusion.[24] It prefigures similar tricks of shift of perspective through
author-intrusion in Thomas Mann, especially in *Der Zauberberg*.[25]

vi. *Der Stechlin* (1898)

Against the critics who see this novel marred by structural diffuse-
ness and *causerie* for the sake of *causerie*,[26] it may be claimed that
it was Fontane's aim to draw a balance-sheet of Prussian society
at the end of the century. If this is so, then the opposite criticism,
that of Lukács, may be valid: that Fontane drew too narrow a
circle, neglecting the 'fourth estate'. Fontane could have broadened
his social panorama by letting us see not merely the symbolic red
roofs of the Globsow factory-workers.[27] But perhaps it was wise on
Fontane's part to refrain from attempting to characterize a part of
society alien to him. Perhaps he believed that the revolutionary
threat was sufficiently adumbrated by the symbols, especially the
red cockerel ready to rise from Stechlin lake, the red stockings
which rile the 'petrefact' Domina Adelheid, and the red roofs – as
well as the red stripe added to Prussia's flag by Bismarck.

The hilarious tone of the conversation between Frau Imme and
Hedwig should not blind us to the very real complaints of servants
whose 'Schlafgelegenheit' in better dwellings might still be a
'Hängeboden' or a 'Badestube' used for everything but bathing.
Hedwig tells us there is a 'Polizeiverbot' and she thinks 'Hänge-
boden' are forbidden in the new dwellings:

> Ach, Frau Imme, die Polizei is doch ein rechter Segen. Wenn wir die
> Polizei nich hätten – und sie sind auch immer so artig gegen einen – so
> hätten wir gar nichts. Mein Onkel Hartwig, wenn ich ihm so erzähle, daß
> man nicht schlafen kann, der sagt immer: 'Kenn ich, kenn ich; der Bour-
> geois tut nichts fur die Menschheit. Und wer nichts für die Menschheit
> tut, der muß abgeschafft werden'. (ch. 14)

Behind the light chatty tone, there are ironic allusions here to
Fontane's theme of *Ordnung* (police), criticism of bourgeois society,
and awareness of revolutionary forces waiting in the wings.

Far from being episodic, padded with irrelevant *causeries* and a
huge cast of peripheral Dickensian caricatures unconnected with
what little plot there is, most critics have increasingly come to
share Thomas Mann's opinion that *Der Stechlin* surpasses in artistry
even *Effi Briest*,[28] even if the structure is additive rather than
dialectical, as Demetz claims.[29]

Before passing judgement on its formal merits or shortcomings,
one needs to discern the theme which is certainly not subsumed in
the external action: a Junker dies and a young couple marry.
There has been much discussion as to whether or not it is a
political novel (as Fontane once designated it himself). It is, of
course both political and supra-political. The by-election in Rheins-
berg and a multitude of references to local and worldwide events

provide a foreground of immediate political and social action. But Fontane, at the end of his life, was more deeply worried by the future trends not only of Prussian society but of western Europe. This is the basic theme, and it may be that the quasi-metaphysical and even religious or mythical dimensions of this theme are too weighty for the protagonists and their situations, but one can only admire the skill, subtlety, and serene irony with which Fontane created his multiple layers of symbols and myths.

Even the title is elusive with multiple allusions, for 'Stechlin' is the name of the lake, the forest, the village, the 'Schloß', as well as of the principal character, Dubslav. The concluding words, in a letter from Melusine: 'es ist nicht nötig, daß die Stechline weiterleben, aber es lebe *der Stechlin*' carry multiple associations, but primarily refer to the 'Stechlinsee' whose remarkable symbolic qualities expand as leitmotivs, after being introduced in the opening paragraph:

> Zwischen flachen, nur an einer einzigen Stelle steil und kaiartig steigenden Ufern liegt er da, rundum von alten Buchen eingefaßt, deren Zweige von ihrer eigenen Schwere nach unten gezogen, den See mit ihrer Spitze berühren. Hie und da wächst ein weniges von Schilf und Binsen auf, aber kein Kahn zieht seine Furchen, kein Vogel singt, und nur selten, daß ein Habicht drüben hinfliegt und seinen Schatten auf die Wasserfläche wirft. Alles still hier. Und doch, von Zeit zu Zeit wird es eben an dieser Stelle lebendig. Das ist, wenn es weit draußen in der Welt, sei's auf Island, sei's auf Java, zu rollen und zu grollen beginnt oder gar der Aschenregen der hawaiischen Vulkane bis weit in die Südsee hinausgetrieben wird. Dann regt sich's auch *hier* und ein Wasserstrahl springt auf und sinkt wieder in die Tiefe. Das wissen alle, die den Stechlin umwohnen, und wenn sie davon sprechen, so setzen sie wohl hinzu: 'Das mit dem Wasserstrahl, das ist nur das Kleine, das beinah Alltägliche; wenn's aber draußen was Großes gibt, wie vor hundert Jahren in Lissabon, dann brodelt's hier nicht bloß und sprudelt und strudelt, dann steigt statt des Wasserstrahls ein roter Hahn auf und kräht laut in die Lande hinein'.

This passage begins with an apparently realistic, if ominous, description of nature, but it develops into the realm of myth open to symbolic multiple allusions.[30] The political revolutionary connotations need no comment, but the relationship of the principal persons to the Stechlinsee is a symbolic measure of their openness, their possession of 'Eigentlichkeit' and 'Herz'. Dubslav, Woldemar, Lorenzen, Armgard, and Melusine stand in intimate relationship to the symbolic lake. 'Die Aufgesteiften', the 'petrefact' aristocrats such as Dubslav's sister Adelheid, der Edle Herr von Alten-Briesach (the pride [!] of the local gentry), the Prinzessin with her sham renunciation of the aristocracy, the hypocritical or 'unecht' bourgeois *nouveaux riches* (Gundermanns), all these are cut off from contact with the mythical lake and are therefore a danger and a liability to future social and political development.

One begins to wonder whether *any* detail is episodic or gratuitous, when one realizes the pointed allusions of the story of the Siamese princess (which Demetz considered an inorganic excrescence)[31] and the circumstances in which it is told, namely to a circle of conservative mummies (unregenerate outdated Junkers) or hypocrites (bourgeois *nouveaux riches*). How skilfully Fontane weaves into the preliminary dialogue a reminder to these narrow snobs that 'they have a king in Siam too'! The Siamese princess, abducted, raped, recovered, could be cured of fatal brooding over her lost virginity only by a mythical ritual purification: bathing in the blood of sacrificed animals administered by high priests. The blood makes symbolic contact with the red symbol of revolution. But the immediate frame of the Siamese story concerned the function of the duel which had its origin as a restorative ritual, but which has become a mere mechanical act without meaning or cathartic effect in contemporary society. There is thus evoked a symbolic suggestion that there can be no regeneration without a revolutionary bloodbath, and simultaneously the counter-suggestion that a mythical-religious act may avert violence. It is also possible that an act of faith is all that is needed to restore virtue, for Dubslav later alludes to this story when, in conversation with his 'petrefact' sister Adelheid, he declares of Armgard, who is now married to his son: 'wer keusch ist, bleibt keusch' (ch. 39).

No final answers are given, but various possible solutions are explored, largely through symbolic allusions. And Dubslav von Stechlin is himself a symbol. With humorous irony he hints at his representative status on the plane of the Kaiser or Bismarck. For Bismarck too lives in retirement in a 'Kate' and moreover has no Stechlinsee: 'Nu, den hat er schon ganz gewiß nicht. So was kommt überhaupt bloß selten vor' (ch. 1). Dubslav and those of his circle who share intuitive communion with the chthonic, mythical lake are genuine and possess openness. These qualities hold an element of optimism for the future, even though Dubslav cannot suppress his scepticism at Lorenzen's utopian plans for social improvement and land-resettlement.

Just as the whole future is problematic, so is the elder daughter of Graf Barby, Melusine, whose first marriage has failed. Although we are led to believe that it was not her fault, yet Melusine, like the Siamese princess, is 'schuldig-unschuldig'. It is therefore by no means inconsequential which of the two countesses Woldemar chooses. Melusine has, next to Dubslav, the closest contact with the lake, and just as the chthonic forces symbolized in the lake are ambivalent, so is Melusine, for nature possesses the potential for evil as well as good. The Melusine-symbol is described by Cirlot:

When a great disaster was about to befall she would give voice to a scream thrice repeated. ... When she marries, all her children have some physical abnormality. ... Melusine seems to be the archetype of intuitive genius, in so far as intuition is prophetic, constructive and wondrous, and yet at the same time is infirm and malign.[32]

Hence when Dubslav offers to have the frozen lake chopped free for Melusine, so that the red cockerel, 'wenn er nur sonst Lust hat', might appear for her, she quickly declines: 'Die Natur hat jetzt den See überdeckt; da werd ich mich also hüten, irgendwas ändern zu wollen. Ich würde glauben, eine Hand führe heraus und packte mich' (ch. 28).

Her sister, Armgard, is revealed as the helpmate for Woldemar, when she is asked whether she would rather be Mary Stuart or Elizabeth of England. Instead she chooses Elizabeth of Thuringia, a saintly figure whose life was devoted to the service of others. Woldemar finds that her name reminds him of William Tell's wife, and every reader of Schiller's drama knows the solid qualities evoked by this reference.

The assumption has often been made that Dubslav is Fontane's *alter ego*. No doubt he is the mouthpiece and double of Fontane more than any other character, but this identification should not be carried too far. It is characteristic of Fontane and his favourite figures to combine paradoxically both strength and flexibility – 'Herz' and 'Eigentlichkeit' on the one hand and on the other readiness to change and accept contrary views. Old General Poggenpuhl astonished his nephew and niece by his open-mindedness *vis-à-vis* the Junker officer turned actor (*Die Poggenpuhls*, 1896). In Dubslav von Stechlin this paradoxical combination is carried to such an extreme that one may assume that Fontane was consciously parodying himself and his paradoxical position.[33] To his visitors Dubslav dogmatically remarks: 'Alle Lehrer sind nämlich verrückt'. A few lines later, however, he states: 'Er [*Krippenstapel*] ist eigentlich ein Prachtexemplar, jedenfalls ein vorzüglicher Lehrer'. Then follows: 'Aber verrückt ist er doch' (ch. 5). That Fontane was conscious of this trait also seems likely from the symbolic and leitmotival role of Dubslav's 'Museum', which consists of a collection of weathervanes!

In one sense the theme may be said to be the dying of Dubslav, for as a symbolic and representative figure his demise marks the end of an epoch. Moreover, he is early aware of his symptoms of hydropsy and approaching cardiac failure. Dubslav prefers the German medical term 'Wassersucht' (which may contain a veiled allusion to the naval ambitions of William II, a policy pilloried by Fontane in his correspondence with Friedländer). The causes of the malady can mostly 'be traced back to gross variations in the physiological mechanisms that normally maintain a constant water balance in the cells, tissues and blood'.[34] Fontane, the former chemist, knew what he was about when providing an appropriate fatal illness for his symbolic representative of society and the state! Dubslav knows that the prescribed digitalis (Fingerhut) serves only temporarily to strengthen the heart and postpone the end. It is entirely in keeping with the symbolic-mythical-religious plane of the novel that he prefers the local herb-woman to his substitute physician, the social democrat Moscheles.

Dr Wrschowitz and Professor Cujacius are probably the most peripheral as well as the most caricatured figures, and yet their discussions are not mere humorous diversions from the basic theme. In the inimitable words of the outsider Pole, Wrschowitz:

> Frondeur ist Krittikk, und wo Guttes sein will, muß sein Krittikk. Deutsche Kunst viel Krittikk. Erst muß sein Kunst, gewiß, gewiß, aber gleich danach muß sein Krittikk. Krittikk ist wie große Revolution. Kopf ab aus Prinzipp. Kunst muß haben ein Prinzipp. Und wo Prinzipp is, is Kopf ab.
>
> (ch. 13)

The allusions to the revolutionary theme are obvious, but more subtle is the parodistic reference to the basic theme of the novel as criticism of the *status quo*.

The dialectical principle is by no means neglected in the structure. Dubslav is the antithesis of his bigoted sister Adelheid, as Pastor Lorenzen is the opposite of his ecclesiastical superior Koseleger. Fontane has, however, both dialectical and diagonal cross-references. If Dubslav is the withdrawn, retired, country gentleman, while Graf Barby is the cosmopolitan man of the world, having married a Swiss (and therefore out of his nation as well as his class) and having spent many years in the diplomatic service in London, Woldemar, nevertheless, quickly senses the spiritual kinship of Barby and his father. They have both come to similar conclusions about the state of the world, the one from within, the other as a result of his wide contacts with the outside world.

If we look for works comparable to *Der Stechlin*, we think first of Thomas Mann, whose *Buddenbrooks* was begun in the year *Der Stechlin* appeared, and whose theme of decadence and death is conveyed with similar conversational, symbolic, and leitmotival techniques. Of all Mann's works it is perhaps *Der Zauberberg* which most resembles Fontane's last novel[35] because of its symbolism, its critical metaphysical and psychological probing.[36]

Fontane is a Janus-like figure – a late representative of nineteenth-century Poetic Realism but, especially in his last finished work, pointing forwards to newer trends and techniques. Thomas Mann claimed that just as *Effi Briest* was the novel which from a social and moral viewpoint extended far beyond Fontane's epoch, so it is *Der*

Stechlin 'der dies in artistischer Beziehung tut, der Wirkungen kennt, Kunstreize spielen läßt, die weit über allen bürgerlichen Realismus hinaus liegen'.[37]

The art of Fontane represents the apogee of the nineteenth century and of 'bürgerlicher Realismus', but at the same time transcends the age and points forward to the twentieth century.

NOTES

1. It has long been customary to rank Fontane's masterpieces with those of Flaubert, Tolstoy, Dickens, Thackeray, and Meredith. For one of the later comparative studies see Stern, op. cit. Yet Brian Rowley pointed to the anomaly that in 1961 none of Fontane's novels had appeared in English ('Theodor Fontane: A German Novelist in the European Tradition?', *GLL*, XV [1961], 71–88). Rowley answers his title question in the affirmative, and the translations for which he called, began to appear in the late 1960s: *Beyond Recall* (*Unwiederbringlich*), trs. Douglas Parmée, London, 1964/ Oxford World's Classics no. 602/; *Effi Briest*, trs. Douglas Parmée, London, 1967/Penguin Classics L 190/; *A Suitable Match* (*Irrungen, Wirrungen*), trs. Sandra Morris, London, 1968.

2. cf., e.g., Max Rychner, 'Theodor Fontane: Der Stechlin' in *Interpretationen 3: Deutsche Romane von Grimmelshausen bis Musil*, ed. Jost Schillemeit, Frankfurt, 1966, 227 *et passim*; also Heiko Strech, *Theodor Fontane. Die Synthese von Alt und Neu. 'Der Stechlin' als Summe des Gesamtwerks*, Berlin, 1970, 38 f. *et passim*.

3. cf. D. Barlow, 'Fontane's English Journeys', *GLL*, VI (1953), 169–77.

4. 'Aber wir lassen es andere machen' (1888), *Sämtliche Werke*, ed. Keitel, Munich, 1964, VI, 353.

5. Whether line 4 should read 'daß es endet' or 'das es sendet' is still disputed. Thomas Mann, among others, insisted on our reading.

6. Interpreted by von Wiese, *Die deutsche Novelle*, II.

7. op. cit., 498.

8. This is essentially Georg Lukács's criticism in accusing Fontane of not portraying adequately the fourth estate. Cf. *Deutsche Realisten des 19. Jahrhunderts*, Berlin, 1956.

9. cf. e.g., Strech, op. cit, esp. 105–17.

10. The Emperor Frederick was mortally stricken with cancer of the throat when he succeeded William I, 9 March 1888. He died 15 June of the same year. The capacity for deriving pleasure from the simple things of life reflects Fontane himself – cf. the poem quoted above, 158.

11. Peter Demetz, *Formen des Realismus: Theodor Fontane*, Munich, 1964.

12. ibid., 166.

13. 'The Art of Fiction' in *The Portable Henry James*, ed. M. D. Zabal, New York, 1951, 411.

14. Her title is not specified, but mention of 'charming countesses' leads one to assume that Botho is marrying upwards within the Junker class.

15. A typical Fontane *double entendre* for 'rügen' (verb) and 'die Rüge' (noun) mean 'censure, blame'.

16. The name Roswitha has the quality of a hidden cipher, for Hrotsvitha (*c.* 935–1001) was a Saxon poetess who early entered the Benedictine convent of Gandersheim. She wrote Latin plays in which she did not shrink from earthy dialogues and spicy situations. *Abraham* depicts the conversion of a woman of loose morals.

17. In her apparently casual answer to Kruse's remark, Roswitha alludes to the strange story of the Chinaman which she has heard from Frau Kruse. This is a striking example of the interlocking and expanding of motifs.

18. op. cit., 319.

19. 'A Leitmotif in Fontane's *Effi Briest*', GLL, X (1956–57), 38–42.

20. The title of the play put on in the winter by the Kessin dramatic society with Crampas as director and Effi in the title role.

21. Some of the aspects of *Fliegen-Schaukeln* are treated by Mary E. Gilbert: 'Fontane's *Effi Briest*', *Der Deutschunterricht*, XI (1959) Heft 4, 63–75, but the main thrust of her excellent article is to examine the real episode that underlies the novel and to show how Fontane changed the characters and circumstances with unsurpassed 'Formgefühl'.

22. 'Kunstreiterin' points forward to Effi's fascination with the outsider Künstlerin die Tripelli.

23. Gilbert, op. cit., 73, perceptively suggests that the 'Schloon' is the symbolic landscape of Effi's soul: 'eine sandige Brachlandschaft, in die unversehens das Element hineinschleicht, nicht offen, sondern unterirdisch, den Sand in einen trügerischen Morast verwandelnd'.

24. op. cit., 211.

25. cf., e.g., opening section 'vingt et un' in chapter 7: 'So verging eine Zeit, – es waren Wochen, wohl drei bis vier, von uns aus geschätzt, da wir uns auf Hans Castorps Urteil und messenden Sinn unmöglich verlassen könne'; or the passage at the end of Castorp's first three weeks in the sanatorium: 'Hier steht eine Erscheinung bevor, über die der Erzähler sich selbst zu wundern gut tut, damit nicht der Leser auf eigene Hand sich allzusehr darüber wundere'.

26. Demetz, op. cit., 183; H-C. Sasse, *Theodor Fontane. An Introduction to the Novels and Novellen*, Oxford, 1968, 157–62; Pascal, op. cit., 206.

27. Glass-workers as representatives of the new industrial proletariat remind the reader of *Irrungen, Wirrungen* of the saying: 'Glück und Glas, wie leicht bricht das!'

28. 'Anzeige eines Fontane-Buches', *Berliner Tageblatt*, 1914, reprinted in *Rede und Antwort*, 1922.

29. op. cit., 183.

30. cf. Vincent J. Günther, *Das Symbol im erzählerischen Werk Fontanes*, Bonn, 1967, esp. 96, where he goes so far as to postulate a deliberate 'Verfremdungstechnik' in this description.

31. op. cit., 185.

32. J. E. Cirlot, *A Dictionary of Symbols*, New York, 1962, 197.

33. cf. Stretch, op cit., 38–45.

34. *Encyclopaedia Britannica*: Edema, dropsy, hydrops.

35. *Der Stechlin* is meant and not the unfinished *Mathilde Möhring*, which was published posthumously in 1908.

36. Siegfried Holznagel goes so far as to compare the academic debaters Wrschowitz and Cujacius with Naphta and Settembrini (cf. Günther, op. cit., 118), but Fontane's pair are more Dickensian distorted caricatures symbolizing the decadence surrounding the principal protagonist.

37. *Gesammelte Werke*, X [*Reden und Aufsätze*], Oldenburg, 1960, 582.

Chapter 11

RETROSPECT AND OUTLOOK

LOOKING BACK at the nineteenth century as a whole, we can discern a number of general characteristics. It is the last period which exhibits normative trends or 'schools'[1] and of these it is Poetic Realism which reflects the dominant image of the age. Poetic Realism was the literary reflection of the relatively stable social and political structure of the increasingly prosperous middle class or *Bürgertum*. The Marxist may say, of course, not without some justification, that this literature was created by and for a relatively small segment of the population. But we have yet to see a culture based on the masses and not on an élite. In any case the image of the dominant middle class of the nineteenth century was long accepted by society as a whole and was challenged only by exceptional 'outsiders' such as Karl Marx, Heine, and Nietzsche.

The situation is complex, however, and even those authors most committed to upholding the moral, intellectual, or social values of this society are sometimes most interesting precisely when they are critical of the *status quo* and when they are advocating at least reform (if not revolution). Keller, Raabe, Stifter, and even Storm occasionally act as seismographs registering protest and dissatisfaction.

We have tried also to show how the nineteenth century may be seen as standing under the aegis either of reaction or of revolution, conservatism or liberalism, tradition or change, acceptance or rejection of the rules and models of Classicism.[2] These reactionary or revolutionary forces are, of course, rarely available in pure chemical isolation, and one of the fascinating aspects of this literature is the analysis of the ratio of these twin ingredients in the make-up of individual authors and works. Even basically conservative writers, such as Grillparzer, Stifter, and Schopenhauer, contain many catalytic prophetic and revolutionary insights.

Every age has to reinterpret the past and our study has necessarily involved a measure of re-evaluation. We have observed how some reputations have faded almost into oblivion. Looking back, we cannot help but attach vital significance to *avant-garde* precursors of developments in the twentieth century. The dramas of Brecht, Grass, Peter Weiss, Handke clearly have their antecedents in Büchner and

Grabbe. The ballads of Brecht with their amalgam of folk-song and political points are foreshadowed in the verse of Heine. And Nietzsche is the archetype of the Socratic sceptical questioner of all traditional authority and convention. It is not likely that once famous and now eclipsed writers like Geibel, Heyse, and Freytag will ever recover their former stature. The earlier eulogistic rating of such authors now seems ill-founded and probably prompted by the innate conservatism of *Bürgertum* and concomitant complacency with excess sentiment and stress on purity of form. It has not been our aim to rehabilitate such authors as these, who seem justly relegated to the periphery of literary history, but rather to make a case for renewed interest in 'conservative' writers who may have suffered unduly from over-emphasis on the relevance of the 'revolutionary' current.

Gotthelf, Keller, Stifter, Grillparzer, and Hebbel should be among those to benefit from reassessment. Grillparzer and Hebbel are moreover both problematic and ambivalent in their relationship to the twin forces of the century. The philosophical background of Hebbel's tragedies implies the necessity and inevitability of change. He is basically fascinated by the ambivalent and tragic situation of the individual caught between stasis and mutation. Keller, Stifter, and Storm are 'conservative' writers whose best works deserve a permanent place in literary history. Moreover, there is a problematic element in all three, and toward the end of their lives they became increasingly pessimistic, as they saw the virtues of *Bürgertum* undermined and questioned. Nestroy focused upon the weaknesses of the society of his time through the cynical comic probing of manners, morals, and politics in the Austria to which he was, at heart, so warmly attached.

Lyric poetry is more an individual matter. Yet in the struggle of nineteenth-century poets to find new forms, means, and themes, we have a gentler reflection of the same antithetical forces at work. We have seen how Heine, Droste-Hülshoff, Lenau, and C. F. Meyer in various ways transcended their time and pointed forward to the next century. But some of the greatest poetry of the period came from the pens of more 'conservative' poets, such as Mörike, Platen, Storm, and Keller. At the end of the century Liliencron and Dehmel presented the antithetical trends personified and intertwined in a complex relationship.

We dealt with Fontane at length, partly because in retrospect his stature as a literary artist looms larger with time, and partly because in style and content his work points forward in so many ways to the twentieth century. Moreover, Fontane was the most representative writer of his century, engaged in every kind of literary pursuit,[3] a writer whose works both represent and at the same time transcend

Poetic Realism. His novels also illustrate the forces of conservatism and liberalism interconnected with infinite subtlety. Fontane's novels are now an invaluable source of insight for the historian[4] as well as the literary critic and general reader. After two World Wars and a succession of social, economic, and political revolutions in the Western world, the views of Fontane, the 'gentle critic', have renewed relevance. Even the typical twentieth-century dilemma of C. P. Snow's 'Two Cultures' – the disparate trends of technological and scientific progress on the one hand and on the other existential isolation, *Angst*, despair, and social disintegration – we find prefigured in germinal form in Fontane's nineteenth century: an age of the most rapid industrial, technological, and scientific development and at the same time moving towards dehumanization, scepticism, loss of religious faith and of social stability.

There is no need to restate the obvious truth: that any age must have its roots in the preceding era. But the connections of our own century with the preceding one seem particularly close and relevant. Looking forward to the twentieth century from our nineteenth-century vantage-point, we can see how the polar forces of reaction and revolution continued to operate. Thomas Mann's conservative, nostalgic, ironic portrayal of decadent *Bürgertum* is countered by his brother Heinrich's revolutionary castigation of the same Wilhelmian era.[5] The one movement or 'school' which, at least briefly, swept most writers into its orbit, Expressionism, contained within itself widely disparate components: optimism and pessimism, revolutionary ardour and passive despair. And the most conspicuous stylistic feature of Expressionism, the use of disjointed, unrelated images, points forward to the subsequent breakdown into isolated, eclectic, disparate literary manifestations, mirroring the fractured image of man in the contemporary world.

As we look back at the nineteenth century from the anarchic or chaotic world of today, we seem to see a relatively orderly political, social, and literary epoch, in which everything falls neatly into place. This may evoke a nostalgic longing or disparaging scorn. But we have tried to show that such a simplistic view of the nineteenth century is not true or that it is at least a vast oversimplification. We have endeavoured to indicate something of the complexities, something of the underground and *avant-garde* forces running counter to prevailing tendencies. The ignominious defeat of liberal political aspirations in 1848 had catastrophic results for the long-term political future of Germany. But by a sort of Hegelian dialectical process, literary giants emerged from the buried clash of antinomies on which was erected the conservative structure of the seemingly invincible but hollow empire of Bismarck. In the long run, the literary or artistic image of a nation may be stronger and truer than its ephemeral political embodiment. The image of Fontane waxes while that of Bismarck wanes.

NOTES

1. Naturalism and Expressionism only briefly prevailed in the twentieth century, which soon developed a heterogeneity of styles reflecting social and political disequilibrium.

2. cf. Michael Hamburger, *Reason and Energy. Studies in German Literature*, London and New York, 1957, and *Contraries*, New York, 1970. The latter is mainly a reprint of the 1957 volume with three added chapters, including one each on Nietzsche and Thomas Mann.

3. While he did not himself write plays, Fontane was one of the most active and astute dramatic critics of the age.

4. cf., e.g., Joachim Remak, *The Gentle Critic: Theodor Fontane and German Politics 1848–1898*, Syracuse, 1964.

5. cf. the novel trilogy *Das Kaiserreich*, especially vol. I, *Der Untertan*, written 1912–14, published 1917–18.

BIBLIOGRAPHY

I. HISTORICAL BACKGROUND:
POLITICAL, SOCIAL, CULTURAL

Bithell, Jethro: *Germany, a Companion to German Studies*, rev. edn. by M. Pasley, London, 1972.

Bramstedt, E. K.: *Aristocracy and the Middle Classes in Germany. Social Types in German Literature 1830–1890*, London, 1964. (Original edition under the name E. Kohn-Bramstedt, 1937.)

Burckhardt, Jakob C.: *Force and Freedom: an Interpretation of History* (trs. of *Weltgeschichtliche Betrachtungen*), 2nd edn., New York, 1955.

Craig, Gordon A.: *The Politics of the Prussian Army, 1640–1945*, Oxford, 1955.

Crankshaw, Edward: *The Habsburgs*, London, 1971.

Dahrendorf, Ralf: *Society and Democracy in Germany*, London, 1968.

Dorpalen, Andreas: *Heinrich von Treitschke*, New Haven, Conn., 1957.

Engels, Friedrich: *Revolution and Counter-Revolution*, ed. L. Krieger, Chicago, 1967.

Eyck, Erich: *Bismarck and the German Empire*, London, 1950.

Eyck, Frank: *The Frankfurt Parliament 1848–1849*, London, 1968.

Flenley, Ralph and Spencer, Robert: *Modern German History*, 4th rev. edn., London, 1968.

Friedjung, Heinrich: *The Struggle for Supremacy in Germany, 1859–1866*, trs. and abridged by A. J. P. Taylor and W. E. McElwee, London, 1935.

Hamerow, Theodore S.: *Restoration, Revolution, Reaction: Economics and Politics in Germany 1815–1871*, Princeton, 1958.

——: *The Social Foundations of German Unification*, Princeton, 1969.

Henderson, W. O.: *The Zollverein*, 2nd edn., London, 1959.

Holborn, Hajo: *A History of Modern Germany*, vol. II *1648–1840*, New York, 1964; vol. III *1840–1945*, New York, 1969.

Howard, Michael: *The Franco-Prussian War*, London, 1962.

Kohn, Hans: *The Habsburg Empire, 1804–1918*, Princeton, 1961.

Krieger, Leonard: *The German Idea of Freedom*, Boston, 1957.

Langer, W. L.: *The Revolutions of 1848*, New York, 1971.

Legge, James Granville: *Rhyme and Revolution in Germany: a Study in German History, Life, Literature and Character 1813–1850*, London, 1918.

Macartney, Carlile Aylmer: *The Habsburg Empire, 1790–1918*, London, 1968.

Mann, Golo: *The History of Germany since 1789*, trs. Marion Jackson, London, 1968.

Meinecke, Friedrich: *The German Catastrophe: Reflections and Recollections*, trs. Sidney B. Fay, Cambridge, Mass., 1950.

Pflanze, Otto: *Bismarck and the Development of Germany*, vol. I *The Period of Unification*, Princeton, 1963.

Pinson, Koppel S.: *Modern Germany: its History and Civilization*, 2nd edn., New York, 1966.

Ramm, Agatha: *Germany 1789–1919: a Political History*, London, 1967.

Ritter, Gerhard: *The German Problem: Basic Questions of German Political Life, Past and Present*, trs. Sigurd Burckhardt, Columbus, Ohio, 1965.

——: *The Sword and the Scepter: the Problem of Militarism in Germany*, vol. I *The Prussian Tradition 1740–1890*, trs. Heinz Norden, Coral Gables, Florida, 1969.

Sagarra, Eda: *Tradition and Revolution: German Literature and Society 1830–1890*, London, 1971.

Steefel, L. D.: *Bismarck, the Hohenzollern Candidacy and the Origins of the Franco-Prussian War*, Cambridge, Mass., 1962.

Stolper, Gustav: *The German Economy, 1870 to the Present*, trs. Toni Stolper, New York, 1967.

Taylor, A. J. P.: *The Course of German History*, rev. edn., London, 1961.

——: *The Habsburg Monarchy, 1809–1918*, London, 1948.

Walker, Mack: *Germany and the Emigration, 1816–1885*, Cambridge, Mass., 1964.

Windell, G. G.: *The Catholics and German Unity, 1866–1871*, Minneapolis, 1954.

II. PERIODS, MOVEMENTS, GENRES

Alker, Ernst: *Die deutsche Literatur im 19. Jahrhundert*, Stuttgart, 1961.

Bauer, Roger: *La réalité royaume de Dieu. Études sur l'originalité du théâtre viennois dans la première moitié du XIXe siècle*, Munich, 1965.

Bennett, E. K.: *A History of the German Novelle*, 2nd rev. edn., Cambridge, 1961.

Bithell, Jethro: *Modern German Literature 1880–1938*, London, 1939.

Boeschenstein, Hermann: *German Literature of the Nineteenth Century*, London, 1969.

Brinkmann, Richard: *Wirklichkeit und Illusion: Studien über Gehalt und Grenzen des Begriffs Realismus für die erzählende Dichtung des neunzehnten Jahrhunderts*, 2nd edn., Tübingen, 1960.

Butler, E. M.: *The Saint-Simonian Religion in Germany*, Cambridge, 1926.

Castle, Eduard: *Dichter und Dichtung aus Österreich. Ausgewählte Aufsätze*, Vienna, 1951.

Closs, A. (ed.): *Reality and Creative Vision in German Lyrical Poetry*, London, 1963.

——: *The Genius of the German Lyric*, 2nd rev. edn., London, 1962.

David, Claude: *Zwischen Romantik und Symbolismus, 1820–1885*, Gütersloh, 1966.

Friesen, Gerhard K.: *The German Panoramic Novel of the 19th Century*, Berne and Frankfurt, 1971.

Fuerst, Norbert, *The Victorian Age of German Literature*, London, 1966.

Gregor, Joseph: *Das österreichische Theater*, Vienna, 1948.

Grimm, Reinhold (ed.): *Deutsche Romantheorien: Beiträge zu einer historischen Poetik des Romans in Deutschland*, Frankfurt, 1968.

Günther, Werner: *Dichter der neueren Schweiz*, Berne and Munich, vol. I, 1963; vol. II, 1968.

Guthke, Karl S.: *Geschichte und Poetik der deutschen Tragikomödie*, Göttingen, 1961.

——: *Die Mythologie der entgötterten Welt. Ein literarisches Thema von der Aufklärung bis zur Gegenwart*, Göttingen, 1971. (Ch. 4 deals with Grabbe, Büchner, Heine, Nietzsche.)

——: *Wege zur Literatur. Studien zur deutschen Dichtungs- und Geistesgeschichte*, Berne and Munich, 1967.

Hamburger, Michael: *Reason and Energy in German Literature*, London and New York, 1957, repr. revised and enlarged under title *Contraries*, New York, 1970. (Essays on Büchner, Heine, Nietzsche.)

Hermand, Jost (ed.): *Der deutsche Vormärz: Texte und Dokumente*, Stuttgart, 1967.

——: *Von Mainz nach Weimar 1793–1919. Studien zur deutschen Literatur*, Stuttgart, 1969.

——, and Windfuhr, Manfred (ed.): *Zur Literatur der Restaurationsepoche 1815–1848*, Stuttgart, 1970.

Höllerer, Walter: *Zwischen Klassik und Moderne: Lachen und Weinen in der Dichtung einer Übergangszeit*, Stuttgart, 1958.

188 THE NINETEENTH CENTURY

Himmel, Hellmuth: *Geschichte der deutschen Novelle*, Berne and Munich, 1963. [Sammlung Dalp no. 94]

Killy, Walther: *Wirklichkeit und Kunstcharakter. Neun Romane des 19. Jahrhunderts*, Munich, 1963.

Klein, Johannes: *Geschichte der deutschen Lyrik*, Wiesbaden, 1957.

——: *Geschichte der deutschen Novelle*, 2nd edn., Wiesbaden, 1954.

Koch, Franz: *Idee und Wirklichkeit: Deutsche Dichtung zwischen Romantik und Naturalismus*, Düsseldorf, 1956.

Kunz, Josef: *Die deutsche Novelle im 19. Jahrhundert*, Berlin, 1970.

Lukács, Georg: *Deutsche Realisten des 19. Jahrhunderts*, Berlin, 1956.

Malmede, Hans Hermann: *Wege zur Novelle: Theorie und Interpretation der Gattung Novelle in der deutschen Literaturwissenschaft*, Stuttgart, 1966.

Mann, Otto: *Geschichte des deutschen Dramas*, Stuttgart, 1963.

Martini, Fritz: *Deutsche Literatur im bürgerlichen Realismus, 1848–1898*, Stuttgart, 1964.

Mayer, Hans: *Von Lessing bis Thomas Mann. Wandlungen der bürgerlichen Literatur in Deutschland*, Pfullingen, 1959.

Mews, Siegfried (ed.): *Studies in German Literature of the Nineteenth and Twentieth Centuries* (Festschrift for Frederic E. Coenen), Chapel Hill, 1970.

Natan, Alex (ed.): *German Men of Letters*, London, 1961–: vol. I: Droste-Hülshoff, Grillparzer, Hebbel, Storm, Keller, C. F. Meyer, Fontane; vol. II: Nietzsche; vol. V: Mörike, Lenau, Stifter, Gotthelf, Platen, Nestroy.

Pascal, Roy: *The German Novel*, Manchester, 1956.

Polheim, K. K.: *Theorie und Kritik der deutschen Novelle von Wieland bis Musil*, Tübingen, 1970.

Prawer, S. S.: *German Lyric Poetry*, London, 1952.

Ritchie, J. M. (ed.): *Periods in German Literature*, London, 1966.

Rommel, Otto: *Die Alt-Wiener Volkskomödie*, Vienna, 1952.

Sagave, Pierre Paul: *Recherches sur le roman social en Allemagne*, Aix-en-Provence, 1960.

Schmidt, Adalbert: *Dichtung und Dichter Österreichs im 19. und 20. Jahrhundert*, vol. I, Salzburg and Stuttgart, 1964.

Sengle, Friedrich: *Biedermeierzeit*, vol. I, Stuttgart, 1971.

Silz, Walter: *Realism and Reality. Studies in the German Novelle of Poetic Realism*, Chapel Hill, 1954.

Staiger, Emil: *Meisterwerke deutscher Sprache aus dem 19. Jahrhundert*, Zürich, 1948.

——: *Die Kunst der Interpretation*, Zürich, 1955.

Stern, J. P.: *Re-interpretations: Seven Studies in Nineteenth-century German Literature*, London, 1964. (Grillparzer, Büchner, Schopenhauer, Heine, Stifter, Fontane)

——: *Idylls and Realities: Studies in Nineteenth-century German Literature*, London, 1971.

von Wiese, Benno (ed.): *Die deutsche Novelle von Goethe bis Kafka*, 2 vols., Düsseldorf, 1962.

—— (ed.): *Die deutsche Lyrik*, 2 vols., Düsseldorf, 1956.

—— (ed.): *Deutsche Dichter des 19. Jahrhunderts*, Berlin, 1969.

——: *Das deutsche Drama*, 2 vols., Düsseldorf, 1958.

——: *Von Lessing bis Grabbe. Studien zur deutschen Klassik und Romantik*, Düsseldorf, 1968.

——: *Die deutsche Tragödie von Lessing bis Hebbel*, Hamburg, 1964.

III. SPECIFIC AUTHORS

Alexis

Thomas, Lionel: *Willibald Alexis. A German Writer of the Nineteenth Century*, Oxford, 1964.

Anzengruber

Kleinberg, Alfred: *Ludwig Anzengruber. Ein Lebensbild*, Stuttgart and Berlin, 1921.

Knight, A. H. J.: 'Prolegomena to the Study of Ludwig Anzengruber' in *German Studies Presented to Walter Horace Bruford*, London, 1962.

Büchner

Benn, M. B.: 'Anti-Pygmalion: An Apologia for Georg Büchner's Aesthetics', *MLR*, LXIV (1969), 597–604.

Cowan, Roy C.: 'Grabbe's *Don Juan und Faust* and Büchner's *Dantons Tod*. Epicureanism and Weltschmerz', *PMLA*, LXXXII (1967), 342–51.

——: Introduction and notes in edition of *Dantons Tod*, Waltham (Mass.), Toronto, London, 1969.

Hamburger, Michael: see Section II.

Höllerer, Walter: '*Dantons Tod*' in *Das deutsche Drama*, vol. II (see Section II).

Jacobs, Margaret: Introduction and notes in edition of *Dantons Tod and Woyzeck*, 3rd rev. edn., Manchester, 1971.

Lindenberger, Herbert: *Georg Büchner*, Carbondale, Illinois, 1964.

Knight, A. H. J.: *Georg Büchner*, Oxford, 1951.

Martens, Wolfgang (ed.): *Georg Büchner*, Darmstadt, 1965 (an anthology containing some of the best critical articles prior to

1964 by Viëtor, Landau, Gundolf, Pongs, Lukács, Hans Mayer, Kurt May, Claude David, Martens, Mautner).

Mayer, H.: *Georg Büchner und seine Zeit*, Wiesbaden, 1946.

Peacock, Ronald: 'A Note on Georg Büchner's Plays', *GLL*, X (1957), 189–97.

Stern, J. P. 'A World of Suffering: Georg Büchner' in *Re-interpretations* (see Section II).

Viëtor, Karl: *Georg Büchner: Politik, Dichtung, Wissenschaft*, Berne, 1959.

Dehmel

Bab, Julius: *Richard Dehmel*, Leipzig, 1926.

Fritz, Horst: *Literarischer Jugendstil und Expressionismus: Zur Kunsttheorie, Dichtung und Wirkung Richard Dehmels*, Stuttgart, 1969.

Hirschenauer, Rupert: 'Anno Domini 1812' in *Wege zum Gedicht*, vol. II, Munich, 1968.

Droste-Hülshoff

Berglar, Peter: *Annette von Droste-Hülshoff in Selbstzeugnissen und Bilddokumenten*, Reinbek [Rowohlt-Monographie], 1967.

Chick, Edson: 'Voices in Discord: Some Observations on *Die Judenbuche*', *GQ*, XLII (1969), 142–57.

Favier, Georges: 'La Tour d'Annette von Droste', *ÉG*, XXII (1967), 146–72.

Feise, Ernst: '*Die Judenbuche* von Annette von Droste-Hülshoff', *Monatshefte*, XXXV (1943), 401–15.

Gausewitz, Walter: 'Gattungstradition und Neugestaltung: Annette von Droste-Hülshoffs *Die Judenbuche*', *Monatshefte*, XL (1948), 314 f.

Hallamore, Joyce: 'The Reflected Self in Annette von Droste's Work: a Challenge to Self-Discovery', *Monatshefte*, LXI (1969), 59–74.

Henel, Heinrich: 'Annette von Droste-Hülshoff. Erzählstil und Wirklichkeit' in *Festschrift für Bernhard Blume. Aufsätze zur deutschen und europäischen Literatur*, Göttingen, 1967, 146–72.

Heselhaus, Clemens: *Annette von Droste-Hülshoff: Werk und Leben*, Düsseldorf, 1971.

——: 'Eine Drostesche Metapher für die Dichterexistenz', *Jahrbuch der Droste-Gesellschaft*, IV (1962), 11–17.

Mare, Margaret Laura: *Annette von Droste-Hülshoff*, Lincoln (Nebraska) and London, 1965.

McGlathery, James M.: 'Fear of Perdition in Droste-Hülshoff's

Judenbuche', in *Lebendige Form*, ed. J. L. Sammons and E. Schürer, Munich, 1970, 229–44.

Rölleke, Heinz: 'Erzähltes Mysterium: Studie zur *Judenbuche* der Annette von Droste-Hülshoff', *DVLG*, XLII (1968), 399–426.

Silz, Walter: *Realism and Reality*, Chapel Hill, 1954, 36–51.

Staiger, Emil: *Annette von Droste-Hülshoff*, 2nd ed., Frauenfeld, 1962.

Ebner-Eschenbach

Fussenegger, Gertrud: *Marie von Ebner-Eschenbach oder Der gute Mensch von Zdisslawitz: Ein Vortrag*, Munich, 1967.

O'Connor, E. M.: *Marie von Ebner-Eschenbach*, London, 1928.

Fontane

Attwood, Kenneth: *Fontane und das Preußentum*, Berlin, 1970.

Barlow, D.: 'Fontane's English Journeys', *GLL*, VI (1953), 169–77.

——: 'Symbolism in Fontane's *Der Stechlin*', *GLL*, XII (1958–59), 282–6.

Bonwit, Marianne: 'Effi Briest und ihre Vorgängerinnen, Emma Bovary und Nora Helmer', *Monatshefte*, XL (1948), 445 ff.

Carter, T. E.: 'A Leitmotif in Fontane's *Effi Briest*', *GLL*, X (1956–1957), 38–42.

Demetz, Peter: *Formen des Realismus: Theodor Fontane*, Munich, 1964.

Downs, B. W.: 'Meredith and Fontane', *GLL*, II (1937–38), 201–9.

Faucher, Eugène: 'Fontane et Darwin', *ÉG*, XXV (1970), 7–24, 141–54.

——: 'Le langage chiffré dans *Irrungen, Wirrungen*', *ÉG*, XXIV (1969), 210–22.

Fricke, H.: *Theodor Fontane. Chronik seines Lebens*, Berlin, 1960.

Fuerst, Norbert: 'Fontane's Entanglements' and 'The Berlin Bourgeois' in *The Victorian Age of German Literature*, London, 1966.

Gausewitz, Walter: 'Theodor Fontane – heiteres Darüberstehen?', *Monatshefte*, XLV (1953), 202–8.

Gilbert, Mary E.: 'Fontane's *Effi Briest*', *Der Deutschunterricht*, XI (1959), 4, 63–75.

Günther, Vincent J.: *Das Symbol im erzählerischen Werk Fontanes*, Bonn, 1967.

Mann, Thomas: 'The Old Fontane' in *Essays of Three Decades* (London, 1947): translation of 'Der alte Fontane' in *Adel des Geistes*, Stockholm, 1947; 'Anzeige eines Fontanebuches' (Wandrey) in *Rede und Antwort*, Berlin, 1922.

Müller-Seidel, Walter: 'Fontane: *Der Stechlin*' in *Der deutsche*

Roman vom Barock bis zur Gegenwart, ed. B. v. Wiese, Düsseldorf, 1963.

Nürnberger, Helmuth: *Der frühe Fontane – Politik – Poesie – Geschichte*, Hamburg, 1969.

——: *Theodor Fontane in Selbstzeugnissen und Bilddokumenten*, Reinbek [Rowohlt Monographie], 1968.

Ohl, Hubert: *Bild und Wirklichkeit. Studien zur Romankunst Raabes und Fontanes*, Heidelberg, 1968.

Park, R.: 'Fontane's *Unheroic Heroes*', *GR*, XIV (1939), 232–44.

Remak, Joachim: *The Gentle Critic: Theodor Fontane and German Politics 1848–1898*, Syracuse, 1964.

Reuter, Hans-Heinrich: *Theodor Fontane*, Munich, 1969.

Roch, Herbert: *Fontane, Berlin und das 19. Jahrhundert*, Berlin, 1962.

Rowley, Brian A.: 'Theodor Fontane: A German Novelist in the European Tradition?', *GLL*, XV (1961), 71–88.

Rychner, Max: 'Theodor Fontane: *Der Stechlin*' in *Interpretationen 3: Deutsche Romane von Grimmelshausen bis Musil*, ed. Jost Schillemeit, Frankfurt, 1966.

Sasse, H-C.: *Theodor Fontane. An Introduction to the Novels and Novellen*, Oxford, 1968.

Schillemeit, Jost: *Theodor Fontane, Geist und Kunst seines Alterswerkes*, Zürich, 1961.

Stern, J. P.: 'Realism and Tolerance: Theodor Fontane' in *Reinterpretations: Seven Studies in Nineteenth Century German Literature*, London, 1964.

Strech, Heiko: *Theodor Fontane. Die Synthese von Alt und Neu. 'Der Stechlin' als Summe des Gesamtwerks*, Berlin, 1970.

Vincenz, Guido: *Fontanes Welt. Eine Interpretation des Stechlin*, Zürich, 1966.

Wandrey, C.: *Theodor Fontane*, Berlin, 1919.

Gotthelf

Gallati, Ernst: *Jeremias Gotthelfs Gesellschaftskritik*, Berne and Frankfurt, 1971.

Günther, Werner: *Jeremias Gotthelf. Wesen und Werk*, 2nd edn., Berlin, 1954.

——: *Neue Gotthelf-Studien*, Berne, 1958.

Muschg, Walter: *Jeremias Gotthelf. Eine Einführung in seine Werke* [Dalp-Taschenbücher, 303], Berne, 1954.

Waidson, H. M.: *Jeremias Gotthelf. An Introduction to the Swiss Novelist*, Oxford, 1953.

——: 'Jeremias Gotthelf's Reception in Britain and America', *MLR*, XLIII (1948), 223–38.

Grabbe

Bergmann, Alfred: *Christian Dietrich Grabbe. Chronik seines Lebens*, Detmold, 1954.

——: *Grabbe in Berichten seiner Zeitgenossen*, Stuttgart, 1968.

Cowan, Roy C.: see item 1 under *Büchner*.

——: 'Satan and the Satanic in Grabbe's Dramas', *GR*, XXXIX (1964), 120–36.

——: Introduction and notes in edition of *Scherz, Satire, Ironie und tiefere Bedeutung*, Waltham (Mass.), Toronto, London, 1969.

——: 'Grabbe's *Napoleon*, Büchner's *Dantons Tod* and the Masses', *Symposium*, XXI (1967), 316–23.

Hegele, Wolfgang: *Grabbes Dramenform*, Munich, 1970.

Hornsey, A. W.: *Idea and Reality in the Dramas of Christian Dietrich Grabbe*, Oxford, 1966.

Janke, Rudolf: 'Grabbe und Büchner. Eine psychological-literarische Betrachtung mit besonderer Berücksichtigung des *Napoleon* und *Dantons Tod*', *Germanisch-romanische Monatsschrift*, XV (1927), 274–86.

Mayer, Hans: 'Grabbe und die tiefere Bedeutung', *Akzente* (1965), Heft 1, 79–95.

Nicholls, Roger A.: 'Qualities of the Comic in Grabbe's *Scherz, Satire, Ironie und tiefere Bedeutung*', *GR*, XLI (1966), 89–102.

——: *The Dramas of Christian Dietrich Grabbe*, The Hague, 1969.

Sieburg, Friedrich: *Christian Dietrich Grabbe: Napoleon oder die hundert Tage*, Frankfurt and Berlin, 1963 [*Dichtung und Wirklichkeit*, vol. IV].

Grillparzer

Baumann, G.: *Franz Grillparzer. Sein Werk und das österreichische Wesen*, Freiburg and Vienna, 1954.

Kleinschmidt, Gert: *Illusion und Untergang: die Liebe im Drama Franz Grillparzers*, Lahr, 1967.

Müller, Joachim: *Franz Grillparzer* [Sammlung Metzler no. 31], Stuttgart, 1966.

Nadler, Josef: *Franz Grillparzer*, Vaduz, 1948.

Naumann, Walter: *Grillparzer: das dichterische Werk*, 2nd rev. edn., Stuttgart, 1967.

Seidler, Herbert: *Studien zu Grillparzer und Stifter*, Vienna, 1970.

Wells, George Albert: *The Plays of Grillparzer*, Oxford, 1969.

Yates, Douglas: *Franz Grillparzer: a Critical Biography*, Oxford, 1946.

Yates, W. E.: *Grillparzer: a Critical Introduction*, Cambridge, 1972.

Gutzkow

Hasubek, P.: 'Karl Gutzkow und seine Zeit', *ÉG*, XXV (1970), 75 ff.

Hebbel

Campbell, T. M.: *The Life and Works of Friedrich Hebbel*, Boston, 1919.
Flygt, Sten G.: *Friedrich Hebbel*, New York [TWAS 56], 1968.
——: *Friedrich Hebbel's Conception of Movement in the Absolute and in History*, Chapel Hill, 1952.
Frisch, Helga: *Symbolik und Tragik in Hebbels Dramen*, Bonn, 1961.
Henel, Heinrich: 'Realismus und Tragik in Hebbels Dramen', *PMLA*, LIII (1938), 502–18.
Kreuzer, Helmut (ed.): *Hebbel in neuer Sicht*, Stuttgart, 1963.
Naumann, Walter: 'Hebbels *Gyges und sein Ring*', *Monatshefte*, XLIII (1951), 253–70.
Purdie, Edna: *Friedrich Hebbel. A Study of his Life and Work*, London, 1932.
Simmen, Jean-Pierre: *Theorie und Praxis Friedrich Hebbels: Studien zu 'Gyges und sein Ring' und 'Herodes und Mariamne'*, Berne and Munich, 1969.
Wolf, Hans M. and Marcuse, Ludwig: 'Noch einmal: Hebbel und Hegel', *Monatshefte*, XL (1948), 157–60.

Heine

Arnold, Matthew: 'Heinrich Heine' in *Essays in Criticism*, London, 1865.
Borries, Mechthild: *Ein Angriff auf Heinrich Heine. Kritische Betrachtungen zu Karl Kraus*, Stuttgart, 1971.
Brinitzer, Carl: *Heinrich Heine: Roman seines Lebens*, Hamburg, 1960.
Butler, Eliza Marian: *Heinrich Heine*, London, 1956.
Fairley, Barker: *Heinrich Heine, an Interpretation*, Oxford, 1954.
Feise, Ernst: 'Heinrich Heine, Political Poet and Publicist', *Monatshefte*, XL (1948), 211 ff.
Field, G. W.: Introduction and notes in *Heine: A Verse Selection*, London, 1965.
Galley, Eberhard: *Heinrich Heine*, 2nd edn., Stuttgart, 1967.
Hamburger, Michael: see Section II.
Hofrichter, Laura: *Heinrich Heine*, trs. Barker Fairley, Oxford, 1963.

Kaufmann, Hans: *Heinrich Heine: geistige Entwicklung und künstlerisches Werk*, Berlin, 1967.

Liptzin, S.: *The English Legend of Heinrich Heine*, New York, 1954.

Marcuse, Ludwig: *Heinrich Heine in Selbstzeugnissen und Bilddokumenten*, Reinbek [Rowohlt Monographie], 1966.

Prawer, Siegbert Salomon: *Heine. The Tragic Satirist. A Study of the Later Poetry, 1827–1856*, Cambridge, 1961.

——: *Heinrich Heine: Buch der Lieder*, London [Studies in German Literature, no. 1], 1960.

Rose, William: *Heinrich Heine. Two Studies of his Thought and Feeling*, Oxford, 1956.

Sammons, Jeffrey L.: *Heinrich Heine, the Elusive Poet*, New Haven and London, 1969.

Spann, Meno: *Heine*, Cambridge [Studies in Modern European Literature and Thought], 1966.

Storz, Gerhard: *Heinrich Heines lyrische Dichtung*, Stuttgart, 1971.

Untermeyer, Louis: *Heinrich Heine*, London, 1938.

Vallentin, Antonina: *Poet in Exile: the Life of Heinrich Heine*, trs. Harrison Brown, London, 1934 (repr. 1956).

Windfuhr, Manfred: *Heinrich Heine: Revolution und Reflexion*, Stuttgart, 1969.

Immermann

Windfuhr, Manfred: *Immermanns erzählendes Werk. Zur Situation des Romans in der Restaurationszeit*, Giessen, 1957.

Keller

Beyel, Franz: *Zum Stil des Grünen Heinrich*, Tübingen, 1914.

Böckmann, Paul: 'Deutsche Lyrik im 19. Jahrhundert' in *Formkräfte der deutschen Dichtung vom Barock bis zur Gegenwart*, 1963 (interpretation of 'Abendlied').

Boeschenstein, Hermann: *Gottfried Keller: Grundzüge seines Lebens und Werkes*, Berne, 1948 (repr. 1964).

——: *Gottfried Keller*, Stuttgart [Sammlung Metzler 84], 1969.

Cowan, Roy C.: 'The Symbolic Function of Red and White in G. K.s Poetry', *KFLQ*, XII (1956), 155–67.

Fife, Hildegard Wichert: 'Keller's Dark Fiddler in the 19th Century Symbolism of Evil', *GLL*, LXI (1963), 117–27.

Fuerst, Norbert: 'The Conclusion of Keller's *Grüner Heinrich*', *MLN*, XLV (1940), 285–9.

——: 'The Structure of *L'éducation sentimentale* and *Der grüne Heinrich*', *PMLA*, LVI (1941), 249–60.

Gessler, Luzius: *Lebendig Begraben. Studien zur Lyrik des jungen Gottfried Keller*, Berne, 1964.

Hofmiller, Josef: 'Der Ur-Heinrich' in *Interpretationen 3: Deutsche Romane von Grimmelshausen bis Musil*, Frankfurt, 1963, 182–9.

Lindsay, J. M.: *Gottfried Keller: Life and Works*, London, 1968.

McCormick, E. Allen: 'The Idylls in Keller's *Romeo und Julia*. A Study in Ambivalence', *GQ*, XXXV (1962), 265–79.

Phelps, Reginald H.: 'Keller's Technique of Composition in *Romeo und Julia auf dem Dorfe*', *GR*, XXIV (1949), 34–51.

Preisendanz, Wolfgang: 'Gottfried Keller' in *Humor als dichterische Einbildungskraft. Studien zur Erzählkunst des poetischen Realismus*, Munich, 1963, 143–213.

——: *Der grüne Heinrich* in *Der d. Roman*, ed. B. v. Wiese, vol. II, Düsseldorf, 1963, 76–127.

Remak, Henry H. H.: 'Vinegar and Water: Allegory and Symbolism in the German Novelle between Keller and Bergengruen', in *Literary Symbolism. A Symposium*, ed. Helmut Rehder, Austin and London, 1965, 33–62.

Ritchie, James M.: 'The Place of *Martin Salander* in G. K.'s Evolution as a Prose Writer', *MLR*, LII (1957), 214–22.

Rowley, Brian: *Keller: Kleider machen Leute*, London, 1960.

Silz, Walter: 'Motivation in Keller's *Romeo und Julia*', *GQ*, VIII (1935), 1–11.

——: *Realism and Reality*, Chapel Hill, 1954 (pp. 79–93 on *Romeo und Julia*).

Strich, Fritz: 'G.K.'s Gedicht "Die kleine Passion"', *Neue Schweizer Rundschau*, XX (1952–53), 176–82.

Walzel, Oskar: 'G.K.'s Humor', *Germanisch-romanische Monatsschrift*, XVIII (1930), 188–98.

Lenau

Ivask, Ivar: 'Nikolaus Lenau: Vorläufer der Moderne oder Nachzügler des Barock?', *Wort in der Zeit*, X (1964), 35–41.

Neumann, Gerhard: 'Das "Vergänglich Bild": Untersuchungen zu Lenaus lyrischem Verfahren', *Zeitschrift für deutsche Philologie*, LXXXVI (1967), 485–509.

Schmidt, Hugo: 'Religious Issues and Images in Lenau's Works', *GR*, XXXIX (1964), 163–82.

——: *Nikolaus Lenau*, New York [TWAS 135], 1971.

Liliencron

Boetius, Henning: 'Liliencron heute', *Neue Deutsche Hefte*, III (1967), 125–34.

Brunner, Constantin: 'Liliencron et ses immortels poèmes', *Mercure de France*, CCCLII (1964), 141–4.

Ludwig

Boeschenstein, H.: 'Zum Aufbau von Otto Ludwigs *Zwischen Himmel und Erde*', *Monatshefte*, XXXIV (1942), 343–56.
Lillyman, W. J.: *Otto Ludwig's 'Zwischen Himmel und Erde': A Study of its Artistic Structure*, The Hague, 1967.
——: 'The Function of the Leitmotifs in Otto Ludwig's *Zwischen Himmel und Erde*', *Monatshefte*, LVII (1965), 60–8.
McClain, William H.: *Between Real and Ideal. The Course of Otto Ludwig's Development as a Narrative Writer*, Chapel Hill, 1963.
Weigand, H. J.: 'Zu Otto Ludwigs *Zwischen Himmel und Erde*' in *Fährten und Funde: Aufsätze zur deutschen Literatur*, ed. A. Leslie Wilson, Berne and Munich, 1967.
Wetzel, H.: 'Otto Ludwig *Zwischen Himmel und Erde:* Eine Säkularisierung der christlichen Heilslehre', *Orbis Litterarum*, XXVII (1972), 102–21.

Meyer

Brückner, Hans-Dieter: *Heldengestaltung im Prosawerk Conrad Ferdinand Meyers*, Berne, 1970.
Crichton, Mary: 'Zur Funktion der Gnade-Episode in C. F. Meyers *Der Heilige*' in *Lebendige Form*, ed. Sammons and Schürer, Munich, 1970, 245–58.
Faesi, Robert: *Conrad Ferdinand Meyer*, Frauenfeld, 1925 (repr. 1948).
Fehr, Karl: *Conrad Ferdinand Meyer*, Stuttgart [Sammlung Metzler], 1971.
Henel, Heinrich: *The Poetry of Conrad Ferdinand Meyer*, Madison, Wisconsin, 1954.
Hertling, Günter H.: 'Zur Funktion und Bedeutung der Traumerinnerung bei C. F. Meyer', *ÉG*, XXV (1970), 155ff.
Strich, Fritz: *Die Kunst der Interpretation*, Zürich, 1955. ('"Das Spätboot" von C. F. Meyer', 239–73.)
Williams, W. D.: *The Stories of C. F. Meyer*, Oxford, 1962.
Zach, Alfred: *Conrad Ferdinand Meyer: Dichtkunst als Befreiung aus Lebenshemmnissen*, Frauenfeld and Stuttgart, 1973.

Mörike

Appelbaum, Ilse: 'Zu Mörikes Gedicht "Auf eine Lampe"', *MLN*, LXVIII (1953), 328–33.

Farrell, R. B.: *Mörike: Mozart auf der Reise nach Prag*, London, 1960.

Immerwahr, Raymond: 'Apocalyptic Trumpets: The Inception of *Mozart auf der Reise nach Prag*', *PMLA*, LXX (1955), 390–407.

——: 'The Loves of Maler Nolten', *Rice University Studies*, LVII (1971), 73–87.

Mare, Margaret: *Eduard Mörike: His Life and Work*, London, 1957.

Maync, Harry: *Eduard Mörike*, Stuttgart and Berlin, 1913.

Polheim, K. K.: 'Der Künstlerische Aufbau von Mörikes Mozartnovelle', *Euphorion*, XLVIII (1954), 41–70.

Sammons, Jeffrey L.: 'Fate and Psychology: Another Look at Mörike's *Maler Nolten*', in *Lebendige Form*, ed. Sammons and Schürer, Munich, 1970, 211–28.

Slessarev, Helga: *Eduard Mörike*, New York [TWAS 72], 1970.

Steinmetz, Horst: *Eduard Mörikes Erzählungen*, Stuttgart, 1969.

Storz, Gerhard: *Eduard Mörike*, Stuttgart, 1967.

Unger, Helga: *Mörike-Kommentar zu sämtlichen Werken*, Munich, 1970.

von Wiese, Benno: *Eduard Mörike*, Stuttgart, 1950.

Nestroy

Basil, Otto: *Johann Nestroy in Selbstzeugnissen und Bilddokumenten*, Reinbek [Rowohlt Monographie], 1967.

Brill, Siegfried: *Die Komödie der Sprache. Untersuchungen zum Werke Nestroys* [Erlanger Beiträge Bd. 28], Nürnberg, 1967.

Hein, Jürgen: 'Nestroyforschung (1901–1966)', *Wirkendes Wort*, XVIII (1968), 232–45.

Hillach, Ansgar: *Die Dramatisierung des komischen Dialogs. Figur und Rolle bei Nestroy*, Munich, 1967.

Kuhn, Christoph: *Witz und Weltanschauung in Nestroys Auftrittsmonologen*, Zürich, 1966.

Preisendanz, Wolfgang: 'Nestroys komisches Theater', in *Das deutsche Lustspiel*, ed. Hans Steffen, Göttingen, 1969.

Weigel, Hans: Johann Nestroy [Friedrichs Dramatiker der Weltliteratur, Bd. 27], Velber bei Hannover, 1967.

Nietzsche

Danto, Arthur Coleman: *Nietzsche as Philosopher*, New York, 1965.

Barzun, Jacques: *Nietzsche contra Wagner – Darwin, Marx, Wagner; Critique of a Heritage*, New York, 1941 (repr. 1958).

Camus, Albert: 'Nietzsche et le nihilisme' in *Les temps modernes*, 1951 (repr. *L'homme révolté*, Paris, 1951).

Fairley, Barker: *Nietzsche and the Poetic Impulse*, Manchester, 1935.

Frenzel, Ivo: *Friedrich Nietzsche*, Reinbek [Rowolt Monographie], 1966.

Gide, André: 'Nietzsche' in *Morceaux choisis*, Paris, 1935, 171–84.

Heller, Eric: *The Disinherited Mind: Essays in Modern German Literature and Thought*, 3rd edn., London, 1971. (Essays on Burckhardt and Nietzsche, Nietzsche and Goethe, Rilke and Nietzsche.)

Jaspers, Karl: *Nietzsche: an Introduction to the Understanding of his Philosophical Activity*, trs. C. F. Wallraff and F. J. Schmitz, Tucson, Arizona, 1965.

Jung, Carl Gustav: 'Nietzsches Geburt der Tragödie' in *Psychologische Typen*, Zürich, 1920, 183–96.

Kaufmann, Walter: *Nietzsche: Philosopher, Psychologist, Antichrist*, Princeton, 1950; 3rd rev. and enlarged edn., New York, 1968.

——: *Basic Writings of Nietzsche*. Trs. and ed. with commentaries, New York, 1968.

Mann, Heinrich: 'Nietzsche', *Maß und Wert*, Zürich, 1939.

——: Introduction to *The Living Thought of Nietzsche Presented by Heinrich Mann*, New York, London, Toronto [the Living Thoughts Library], 1939.

Mann, Thomas: 'Nietzsches Philosophie im Lichte unserer Erfahrung', *Die neue Rundschau*, 1947, 359–89 (repr. *Neue Studien*, Stockholm, 1948, 105–59).

Santayana, George: *Egotism in German Philosophy*, New York, 1916.

Schlechta, Karl: *Der Fall Nietzsche: Aufsätze und Vorträge*, 2nd enlarged edn., Munich, 1959.

Schweitzer, Albert: 'Schopenhauer und Nietzsche', in *Kultur und Ethik. Kulturphilosophie*, Munich, 1923.

Thatcher, David S.: *Nietzsche in England, 1890–1914: the Growth of a Reputation*, Toronto, 1970.

Wilcox, John T.: *Truth and Value in Nietzsche. A Study of his Metaethics and Epistemology*, Ann Arbor, 1974.

Platen

David, Claude: 'Sur le lyrisme de Platen', *Formenwandel. Festschrift zum 65. Geburtstag von Paul Böckmann*, Hamburg, 1964, 383–92.

Kluncker, Karlhans: 'Der Dichter und die Dichtung im Werk des Grafen August von Platen', *Castrum Peregrini*, XC (1970), 49–83.

Platen: see section II *under* Alex Natan, vol. V.

Raabe

Bange, P.: 'Stopfkuchen. Le solipsisme de l'original et l'humour', ÉG, XXIV (1969), 1–15.

Brill, E. V. K.: Introduction and notes in edition of Unruhige Gäste, Oxford, 1964.

David, Claude: 'Über Raabes Stopfkuchen' in Lebendige Form, ed. Sammons and Schürer, Munich, 1970, 259–76.

Fairley, Barker: Wilhelm Raabe. An Introduction to his Novels, Oxford, 1961.

——: 'The Modernity of Wilhelm Raabe' in German Studies Presented to L. A. Willoughby, Oxford, 1952, 66 ff.

Fehse, Wilhelm: Wilhelm Raabe. Sein Leben und seine Werke, Brunswick, 1937.

Goetz, Marketa: 'The Short Stories: A Possible Clue to Wilhelm Raabe', GR, XXXVII (1962), 52 ff.

Goetz-Stankiewicz, Marketa: 'The Tailor and the Sweeper. A New Look at Wilhelm Raabe' in Essays on German Literature in Honour of G. J. Hallamore, Toronto, 1968, 152 ff.

——: 'Die böse Maske Moses Freudensteins', Jahrbuch der Raabe-Gesellschaft, 1969, 7–32.

Hanson, William P.: 'Some Basic Themes in Raabe', GLL, XXI (1968), 2–30.

Helmers, Hermann: 'Das Groteske bei Wilhelm Raabe', Die Sammlung, XV (1960), 199 ff.

—— (ed.): Raabe in neuer Sicht, Stuttgart, 1968.

——: Wilhelm Raabe, Stuttgart [Sammlung Metzler], 1968.

Martini, Fritz: 'Wilhelm Raabe und das 19. Jahrhundert', Zeitschrift für deutsche Bildung, LVIII (1933–34), 326 ff.

Mayer, Gerhart: Die geistige Entwicklung Wilhelm Raabes, Göttingen, 1960.

Oberdieck, Wilhelm: 'Wilhelm Raabes Begegnung mit dem Absurden', Jahrbuch der Raabe-Gesellschaft, 1968.

Ohl, Hubert: see under Fontane.

Pongs, Hermann: Wilhelm Raabe, Leben und Werk, Heidelberg, 1958.

Raimund

Michalski, John: Ferdinand Raimund, New York [TWAS 39], 1968.

Prohaska, D.: Raimund and Vienna. A Critical Study of Raimund's Plays in their Viennese Setting, Cambridge [Anglica Germanica], 1970.

Rommel, Otto: Ferdinand Raimund und die Vollendung des Alt-Wiener Zauberstückes, Vienna, 1947.

Schopenhauer

Abendroth, Walter: *Arthur Schopenhauer in Selbstzeugnissen und Bilddokumenten*, Reinbek [Rowohlt Monographie], 1967.

Gardiner, Patrick: *Schopenhauer*, Harmondsworth [Penguin], 1963.

Knox, Israel: *The Aesthetic Theories of Kant, Hegel, and Schopenhauer*, New York, 1936.

Mann, Thomas: *Schopenhauer*, Stockholm, 1938 (trs. *Essays of Three Decades*, London, n.d., and *Essays*, New York [Vintage Books], 1957).

Stifter

Baudet, J. L.: 'La structure reconstituée. Remarques sur la composition de *Der Nachsommer*', *ÉG*, XXVI (1971), 46 ff.

Blackall, Eric A.: *Adalbert Stifter. A Critical Study*, Cambridge, 1948.

Enzinger, M.: *Gesammelte Aufsätze zu Adalbert Stifter*, Vienna, 1967.

Großschopf, Alois: *Adalbert Stifter: Leben, Werk, Landschaft. Zum hundertsten Todestag des Dichters*, Linz, 1968.

Kaiser, Michael: *Adalbert Stifter: eine literaturpsychologische Untersuchung seiner Erzählungen*, Bonn, 1971.

Novotny, Fritz: *Adalbert Stifter als Maler*, Vienna, 1941.

Rehm, W.: *Nachsommer: zur Deutung von Stifters Dichtung*, Berne, 1951.

Roedl, Urban: *Adalbert Stifter in Selbstzeugnissen und Bilddokumenten*, Reinbek [Rowohlt Monographie], 1965.

Seidler, Herbert: see under *Grillparzer*.

Staiger, Emil: *Adalbert Stifter als Dichter der Ehrfurcht*, Zürich, 1952 (repr. 1967).

Stern, J. P.: see Section II.

Stiehm, Lothar: *Adalbert Stifter. Studien und Interpretationen. Gedenkschrift zum 100. Todestage*, Heidelberg, 1968.

Storm

Artiss, David S.: 'Bird Motif and Myth in Theodor Storm's *Der Schimmelreiter*', *Seminar*, IV (1968), 1–16.

Bernd, Clifford: *Theodor Storm's Craft of Fiction*, Chapel Hill, 1966.

Blankenagel, J. C.: 'Tragic Guilt in Storm's *Schimmelreiter*', *GQ*, XXV (1952), 170–81.

Brecht, W.: 'Storm und die Geschichte', *DVLG*, III (1925), 444–62.

Ellis, J. M.: 'Narration in Storm's *Der Schimmelreiter*', *GR*, XLIV (1969), 21–30.

Goldammer, Peter: *Theodor Storm. Eine Einführung in Leben und Werk*, Leipzig, 1968.

Hermand, Jost: 'Hauke Haien – Kritik oder Ideal des gründerzeitlichen Übermenschen', *Wirkendes Wort*, XV (1965), 43–52; repr. in same author's *Von Mainz nach Weimar 1793–1919*, 250–268 (see Section II).

Menhennet, A.: 'The Time-Element in Storm's Later Novellen', *GLL*, XX (1966), 43–52.

Pitrou, Robert: *La vie et l'oeuvre de Theodor Storm*, Paris, 1920

Schuster, Ingrid: *Theodor Storm. Die zeitkritische Dimension seiner Novellen*, Bonn, 1971.

Silz, Walter: 'Theodor Storm: Three Poems', *GR*, XLII (1967), 292–300.

Stuckert, Franz: *Theodor Storm. Der Dichter in seinem Werk*, Tübingen, 1966.

Vinçon, Hartmut: *Theodor Storm*, Reinbek [Rowohlt Monographie], 1972.

Wittmann, Lothar: 'Theodor Storm: *Der Schimmelreiter*', *Deutsche Novellen des 19. Jahrhunderts, Interpretationen zu Storm und Keller*, Frankfurt/M, 1961, 50–92.

Wagner

Barzun, Jacques: *Darwin, Marx, Wagner: Critique of a Heritage*, New York, 1941 (repr. 1958).

Blissett, William: 'Thomas Mann: The Last Wagnerite', *GR*, XXXV (1960), 50–76.

Mann, Thomas: Essays in *Adel des Geistes*, Frankfurt, 1959 (trs. *Essays of Three Decades*, London, n.d.).

——: *Wagner und unsere Zeit*, Frankfurt, 1963.

Mayer, Hans: *Richard Wagner in Selbstzeugnissen und Bilddokumenten*, Reinbek [Rowohlt Monographie], 2nd edn., 1970.

Raphael, Robert: *Richard Wagner*, New York [TWAS 77], 1969.

Reich, John J.: 'The Rebirth of Tragedy: Wagner and the Greeks', *Mosaic*, I (1968), 18–34.

Shaw, George Bernard: *The Perfect Wagnerite; a Commentary on the Niblung's Ring*, London, 1929.

Stein, Jack M.: *Richard Wagner and the Synthesis of the Arts*, Detroit, 1960.

INDEX

Titles are listed under author's name. Page numbers in bold type indicate the more important references.